Adventure Guide to

Oklahoma

Lynne M. Sullivan

HUNTER

HUNTER PUBLISHING, INC.
130 Campus Drive, Edison NJ 08818
(732) 225 1900, (800) 255 0343, fax (732) 417 0482

1220 Nicholson Rd., Newmarket, Ontario,
Canada L3Y 7V1, (800) 399 6858

The Boundary, Wheatley Road, Garsington
Oxford, OX44 9EJ England
01865-361122; fax 01865-361133

ISBN 1-55650-843-3

©1999 Lynne M. Sullivan

Maps by Kim André, © 1999 Hunter Publishing, Inc.
Cover photo: Steve Vidler *(Leo de Wys)*

For complete information about the hundreds of other travel guides
offered by Hunter Publishing, visit our Web site at:
www.hunterpublishing.com

4 3 2 1

Contents

INTRODUCTION   2
    How to Use This Book   3
    Getting There   6
    Getting Around   7
    Getting Started   8
    Adventures   11
    Climate   18
    Get a Pass   20
    Who Ya Gonna Call??   20

OKLAHOMA CITY   25
  History   26
  Touring   27
  Adventures   37
  Where to Stay   39
    Hotels   39
    Chain Hotels   40
    Bed & Breakfasts/Small Inns   40
  Where to Eat   41
  Where to Shop   44
  Touring Nearby Towns   45

TULSA   59
  Touring   59
  Adventures   64
  Where to Shop   66
  Where to Stay   67
    Hotels   67
    Chain Hotels   67
    Bed & Breakfasts   68
  Where to Eat   69
  Touring Nearby Areas   69

NORTHEAST OKLAHOMA   73
  Touring   73
    Hunting the Uncommon   86
  Adventures   89
    On Foot   89
    On Wheels   95
    On Horseback   101
    On Water   102

Where to Stay   111
    Hotels, Resorts & B&Bs   111
    Camping   117
Where to Eat   117
Where to Shop   120
Powwows, Festivals, Arts & Crafts Fairs   123

SOUTHEAST OKLAHOMA   127
  Touring   129
  Adventures   141
    On Foot   141
    On Wheels   157
    On Horseback   161
    On Water   165
  Where to Stay   177
    B&Bs, Lodges & Cabins   177
    Spas   182
    Camping   182
  Where to Eat   183
  Where to Shop   186
  Powwows, Festivals, Arts & Crafts Fairs   187

SOUTHWEST OKLAHOMA   189
  Touring   189
  Adventures   203
    On Foot   203
    On Wheels   214
    On Horseback   218
    On Water   219
  Where to Stay   223
    Hotels & Inns   224
    Campgrounds   226
  Where to Eat   226
  Where to Shop   229
  Powwows, Festivals, Arts & Crafts Fairs   231

NORTHWEST OKLAHOMA   233
  Touring   233
  Adventures   238
    On Foot   238
    On Wheels   249
    On Horseback   253
    On Water   254
  Where to Stay   257
    Hotels, Inns & Ranches   257
    Guest Ranches & Cattle Drives   259
    Camping   260

Where to Eat 260
Where to Shop 262
Powwows, Festivals, Arts & Crafts Fairs 263

■ Maps

Oklahoma 1
Oklahoma City 25
Tulsa 59
Northeast Oklahoma 74
Northeast Oklahoma Adventures 90
Southeast Oklahoma 128
Ouachita National Forest 130
Southeast Oklahoma Adventures 142
Southwest Oklahoma 190
Southwest Oklahoma Adventures 204
Wichita Mountains Wildlife Refuge 206
Northwest Oklahoma Adventures 234

Oklahoma

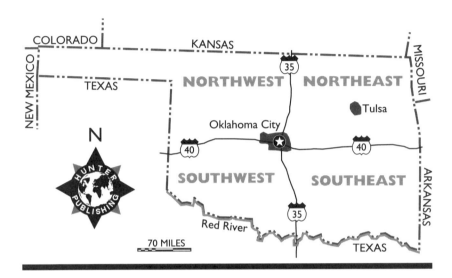

Introduction

The opportunity for adventure in Oklahoma is enormous. The two major urban areas, Oklahoma City and Tulsa, offer explorers a vast variety of museums, parks, gardens, and outdoor activities. When you get out into the countryside, snoop around the small towns, and visit the resorts, state parks, and wilderness areas, you truly experience the best of the state.

Other than mammoth Texas, there isn't a state in North America with more natural and cultural diversity. **Oklahoma City** is the capital and geographic center of the state. Northeast of this midpoint is **"green country,"** a potpourri of mountains, rivers, state parks, and tallgrass prairie. To the southeast is **"Kiamichi country,"** with dense pine forests, tree-rimmed lakes, and misty mountain streams. **"Southwest territory"** offers dramatic landscapes dominated by the Wichita Mountains, which lure artists and writers as well as avid outdoorsmen. The **"high plains"** stretch northwest into the Panhandle, sprinkled with slow-paced towns and geologic mysteries that occur nowhere else in the world.

More Native Americans live in Oklahoma than in any other state. Some of the 39 tribes headquartered here are truly native and lived in the area before Columbus discovered America. Others arrived in the 1830s when the US government established Indian Territory as a convenient dumping ground for native tribes who were hindering white settlement in other states.

The Five Civilized Tribes who established protected capitals here during the 19th century are the Choctaw and Chickasaw from Mississippi, the Seminole from Florida, the Creek from Alabama, and the Cherokee from Carolina, Tennessee, and Georgia. The Cherokee move in 1838 was a four-month struggle that became known as "The Trail of Tears."

Many adventures in this book relate to the Native American people because they have given Oklahoma a distinct personality and authentic character. Numerous place names are Indian words – "Oklahoma" is Choctaw for "red men" – and every region holds events to celebrate Indian customs. If this part of history interests you, use this book to seek out the best powwows, historical re-enactments, and native exhibits.

Expect to be surprised if your idea of Oklahoma comes from reading John Steinbeck's *The Grapes of Wrath*. Steinbeck never set foot on Oklahoma soil, and the image he created of an entire state of "Okies" fleeing from a "desolate, arid dust bowl" was simply fiction. Only a small portion of western Oklahoma experienced the devastating wind-driven drought and destruction that ravaged parts of middle America during the 1920s and 1930s – and even those parts have healed quite nicely.

You won't find singing cowboys dressed up in gaudy outfits like the characters in Rogers and Hammerstein's musical, *Oklahoma!,* either. The true state is something between these two extremes – an extraordinary mix of nature, history, and culture. Big cities and all-but-deserted small towns. Breathtakingly beautiful mountains and miles of tedious flatland. World-class art collections and the World Championship Cow Chip Throw. Some images will always define Oklahoma: Cowboys and Indians; Will Rogers and Troy Aikman; oil tycoons and prohibition-era gangsters; illegal "Sooners" and land-run "Boomers"; Garth Brooks and Belle Starr; Woody Guthrie and Jim Thorpe; dirty-faced rescue workers and the entire University of Oklahoma football team.

This book will help you discover the real Oklahoma. A wide range of activities has been chosen to appeal to most every taste and skill level. There are suggestions for the avid sportsperson seeking the ultimate challenge as well as information on ventures safe enough for families with young children.

If you're a curious armchair traveler, this book describes the state's best-known attractions so that you almost experience them yourself.

If you're looking for solid details on where, when, and how to hike, bike, float, fish, climb, ride, explore, and enjoy Oklahoma's bounty, you'll find them on the following pages.

OK Facts & Stats

- Oklahoma covers 69,919 square miles on the American Great Plains.
- It is bordered by Missouri and Arkansas to the east, Texas to the south and west, New Mexico across the narrow western edge of the panhandle, and Colorado and Kansas to the north.
- Just over 3,000,000 people live in the state – about 70% of them in Oklahoma City and Tulsa, the largest cities.
- Approximately 250,000 Native Americans live in Oklahoma.
- The state capital is Oklahoma City.
- It became the 46th state on November 16, 1907.
- The highest point is Black Mesa at 4,973 feet.
- Nicknamed the Sooner State, Oklahoma's motto is *Labor Omnia Vincit* (Labor Conquers All Things).
- The state bird is the scissor-tailed flycatcher.
- The official state flower is mistletoe, and the state tree is the redbud.

How to Use This Book

Two interstate highways, **I-35** and **I-40**, cut Oklahoma into almost equal fourths and converge in the center of the state, which is also the middle of Oklahoma City, the capital. This division corresponds almost exactly with the state's four main geographical regions, and the four sections of this guide cover each area. Two additional sections cover the metropolitan areas of Oklahoma City and Tulsa.

Within each of these six sections, you will find chapters on all types of adventures to be taken On Foot, On Wheels, and On Water. Other chapters are geared toward the basics, including Where to Stay and Where to Eat. Each section also includes just enough history and geography to make your explorations interesting, a few tips to smooth your journey, some frank evaluations, and plenty of resources to consult for additional information.

The six regional sections begin with a quick start **Introduction** of relevant history, principal sites, and major activities. **Touring** actually puts you on the road and leads you along scenic routes to the best sites in that city or region. As the road trips progress, you are given valuable details such as addresses, directions, landmarks, phone numbers, prices and hours of operation. Contact information for city, state, and national agencies that provide useful maps and brochures is also given, either in the text or at the end of the chapter. These resources are listed again by category at the back of the book.

Chapters on specific adventures follow the driving-tour chapter in each regional section. **On Foot** suggests hiking/backpacking trails, interpretive walking paths, rock climbing locations, and public golf courses. **On Wheels** includes bike routes along back roads, information on mountain bike trails, and directions to areas open to motorcycles and off-road vehicles. **On Water** covers canoeing, rafting, kayaking, boating, and fishing on both rivers and lakes. Oklahoma is horse country, and **On Horseback** will guide you to camps and trails open to horse owners, stables that rent by the hour, and companies that run "city slicker" trips.

Sometimes, the same trail, river, mountain, or lake is mentioned in more than one chapter because a terrific hiking path through a forest may also be the best equestrian route, and a stretch of river that looks like a canoe trail to one reader may look like a fishing hole to another. If you're interested in a certain activity, turn directly to that chapter. If you want to investigate all an area has to offer, skim through the pages and search for that location in boldface type.

After the adventure chapters, you'll find **Where to Stay, Where to Eat**, and **Where to Shop**.

Oklahoma urban areas are as modern and convenient as the rest of North America, and you can find chain hotels, familiar restaurants, and shopping malls scattered throughout the state. At times, you will be advised to use these well-known establishments simply because they are the best places to eat, sleep or shop in that area. More commonly, you will be led to quaint bed & breakfasts, bucolic retreats, family-run cafés, and unique antique/craft shops. Camping information is sometimes mentioned in the adventure chapters when it relates directly to that activity, but a listing of campgrounds is included in the **Where to Stay** chapter for each region.

Oklahoma Parks and Resorts offers a **CEO (Customer With Exciting Opportunities) Card** free of charge; register by calling ☎ 800-654-8240, or apply at any state park. The card entitles you to free nights lodging and discounts on food and recreation. Also, with or without the CEO Card, when you stay seven consecutive nights at a state-owned resort, you receive a 15% discount off the total accommodation charges. Call for details.

Accommodations Prices

Where actual prices are not given in the text, $ symbols indicate the following prices ranges:

$	Up to $50 per day
$$	$50-$100 per day
$$$	$100-$175 per day
$$$$	$175+ per day

Prices in the listings are for a typical room with two adults. Always ask about weekend or mid-week specials. If you'll have more than two in a room, check with the desk about additional charges. Children usually stay free in their parents' room, but bed-&-breakfasts, cottages, inns, and campgrounds may charge for each person.

Restaurant Prices

Restaurants are keyed according to the following price ranges:

$	$10 or less
$$	$10-$20
$$$	$20-$30
$$$$	$30-$40

Prices given are the average cost per person for a complete meal. Specials may be priced higher. If you order dessert and alcoholic drinks, add those costs to the average price.

Finally, at the end of each section, there is a chapter listing outstanding **Annual Events**. Most festivals take place about the same time each year, and contact numbers are listed for each event so that you can call for exact dates and ticket prices.

Getting There

Many commercial airlines serve **Will Rogers International Airport** in Oklahoma City and **Tulsa International Airport** in Tulsa.

Airlines

Delta Air Lines, ☎ 800-221-1212, www.delta-air.com

Southwest Airlines, ☎ 800-435-9792, http://iflyswa.com

American Airlines, ☎ 800-433-7300, www.americanair. com/aahome/aahome.html

Continental Airlines, ☎ 800-525-0280, www.flycontinental. com

United Airlines, ☎ 800-241-6522, www.ual.com

Visitors arriving by car are greeted at **Travel Centers** near the borders on major highways leading into the state from all directions except the northwest Panhandle. These centers are staffed by knowledgable advisers who offer maps, brochures, information, and a hot cup of coffee. Stop at one of the following centers from 8:30 am to 5 pm any day except Christmas.

Travel Centers

- **Arriving from the north** – I-35, 10 miles south of the Kansas border
- **Arriving from the northeast** – (two centers) I-44, just west of the Missouri border and I-44 south of the Vinita exit inside McDonald's Restaurant
- **Arriving from the east** – I-40, 17 miles west of the Arkansas border

- **Arriving from the south** – (two centers) US-69/75, two miles north of the Texas border, and I-35, three miles north of the Texas border
- **Arriving from the southwest** – I-44, at the Elmer Graham Plaza
- **Arriving from the west** – I-40, nine miles east of the Texas border

Getting Around

Three interstate highways and a system of turnpikes cross Oklahoma, connecting Oklahoma City and Tulsa with every part of the state. Visitors who fly into either city can rent cars from the following companies.

Car Rental Companies

- Alamo, ☎ 800-327-9633
- Avis, ☎ 800-331-1212
- Budget, ☎ 800-527-0700
- Dollar, ☎ 800-800-4000
- Enterprise, ☎ 800-325-8007
- Hertz, ☎ 800-654-3131
- National, ☎ 800-227-7368
- Thrifty, ☎ 800-367-2277

Avis, Budget, Enterprise, Hertz, and Thrifty also have offices in other large towns.

Major freeways and toll roads connect Oklahoma City and Tulsa with each other and the rest of the state. If you plan to travel on the state's convenient turnpike system, consider purchasing a **PIKEPASS**, which will save you a little money and allow you to pass through the toll booth without waiting in line. Contact the **Oklahoma Turnpike Authority**, ☎ 405-425-3600 or 800-745-3727, for details on the pass, maps of the turnpikes, and individual toll costs. For **road conditions** and current **weather reports**, call ☎ 405-425-2385. Report emergencies to the **Highway Patrol** at ☎ 405-682-4343; from a cellular phone, dial *55.

Oklahoma Q & A

Q: What's a Sooner?

A: Before the US government fired the gun to officially open Indian-grant land for white settlement, some eager – if not greedy and criminal – folks claimed plots of ground for homesteads. Thus, the birth of two terms: "Jump-the-gun," meaning to be impatient, and "Sooner," meaning a person who crossed into Indian territory *sooner* than the official opening. Today, many natives and residents of Oklahoma proudly call themselves Sooners.

Q: Is mistletoe a flower?

A: Actually, mistletoe is an aerial parasite that attaches itself to other living plants and trees. It has evergreen leaves and white berries, but no true flowers.

Q: Is the redbud a tree?

A: Yep. Some argue that it's a shrub, and they're not wrong since several bushes, as well as small trees, belong to the genus *Cercis*. In the spring, all *Cercis* put on a glorious display of pinkish red blossoms before the leaves appear.

Q: What does a scissor-tailed flycatcher look like?

A: A bird with a mission.

You'll spot these aggressive little guys in late March or early April when they return to Oklahoma after wintering in Mexico and Central America. They do an amazing sky dance to attract members of the opposite sex, fearlessly harass larger birds, and dart about furiously snatching insects for dinner.

Of course, there's the scissor-tail – a long, deeply forked stalk of feathers that distinguishes it from other flycatchers. The body is gray, the wings and tail are black, and a bright red patch is visible under the wings when the birds are in flight. Ironically, the flycatchers' meal of choice is the grasshopper.

Getting Started

Use the interstates and toll roads to cut through the state from any direction, but, as quickly as possible, turn off onto less-traveled state highways or back roads – simply to see where they lead. This book will help you with the basic planning, and prevent you from wandering aimlessly, but the nature of adventrue requires a slow pace, insatiable curiosity, an open mind, and relentless enthusiasm.

The Top Adventures

If you're not sure where to begin, the Top Adventures you should not miss are:

- Horseback riding through the **Ouachita Forest**
- Rafting the **Illinois River**
- Climbing the sandstone walls at **Red Rock Canyon State Park**
- Hiking **Little Bugaboo Canyon**
- Fishing for ocean-bass in **Lake Texoma**
- Biking the buffalo paths in the **Wichita Mountains**
- Sailing **Grand Lake o' the Cherokees**
- Splashing in **Turner Falls**
- Camping in **Chickasaw National Park**
- Golfing all nine **State Resort Golf Courses**
- Driving historic **Route 66**.

Representatives of more than 100 Native American nations, bands and tribes gather in downtown Oklahoma City for the annual Red Earth Festival Parade. (Photo by G. Jill Evans)

However, this must-do list changes from season to season.

In winter, you may be happier lounging before the fireplace in the cozy **Tatonka Cabin** deep in the woods near **Beaver Bend State Park**, or attending the **Red Earth Winter Expo** or **An Affair of the Heart** craft show in **Oklahoma City**, or watching eagles feed below **Keystone Dam** on the **Arkansas River**.

Fall color is brilliant in the hardwood forests, and an early spring brings warm days and dazzling wildflowers to the countryside. At these times of the year, it's an adventure to simply be outdoors. If you happen, also, to be astride a frisky horse, or drifting downstream in a canoe, or at the highest point of a mountain range – so much the better.

OK History 101

- First there were ancient hunting tribes, who roamed the land in search of prey, followed by more advanced communities of farmers, weavers, and pottery-makers.

- About 2,000 years ago, people began building Oklahoma's first houses and religious structures. In the eastern part of the state, Mound Builders raised large piles of mud to serve as altars and hollowed out some mounds to serve as shelters. To the west, Slab-House builders began digging pits, lining them with stones, and erecting poles to support earth and reed roofs. Examples of ancient mounds are located in LeFlore County at Spiro Mound and Williams Mound.

- Many Plains Indians lived on Oklahoma land about the time Europeans began New World explorations. The largest tribes were the Wichita, Caddo, Cheyenne, Arapaho, Pawnee and Osage.

- In 1803, the United States gained control of western land, including what would become Oklahoma, as part of the $15 million Louisiana Purchase from France.

- The US government "relocated" The Five Civilized Tribes – Cherokee, Choctaw, Chickasaw, Creek and Seminole – from southeastern states to Oklahoma's Indian Territory beginning in 1830.

- After the Civil War, other tribes were granted rights to land originally promised to The Five Civilized Tribes.

- Cattle routes, such as the Chisholm Trail, lured whites to Indian Territory and by 1901 all of Oklahoma was open to white settlers.
- The Five Civilized Tribes contributed to the writing of the state constitution when Oklahoma became the 46th state in 1907.
- Indians have been elected to both the state and national legislatures.
- The discovery of oil in the late 1800s made Oklahoma a booming, wealthy state.
- During the Great Depression, the western part of the state suffered from the "Dust Bowl" drought that plagued parts of America. Many farmers lost their land and were forced to leave the state in search of work.
- Energy-related industries brought prosperity back to Oklahoma after World War II.
- Although the state's economy suffered during the oil-bust 80s, the state is once again gaining a reputation as a thriving Sunbelt location.

Adventures

On Wheels

Biking

Whether you're a "trailheader" or a "roadie," Oklahoma has a bike trip for you.

State parks recently opened most trails to bikes, and cycling clubs are pushing for more and better routes all the time. Since Oklahoma is less populated than many states, it is possible to find miles of sparsely traveled rural roads just outside urban areas, and many small towns are spaced ideally for two-wheel tours. Single-lane logging roads cut deep into forests, and old farm roads cover miles of wide-open countryside.

But Oklahoma is not a '90s-style bike-friendly state. Currently, there are no designated bike paths specifically maintained by the department of transportation. The highways are not signed for safe cycling, and many have no shoulders, much less bike lanes. And, the state's official bicycle route map is out of print.

All this makes for problems if you want to bike cross-country. It is far more worthwhile to gear your thinking toward day trips along back roads between small towns or rides within the confines of a state park. Once your plans take this form, the opportunities are endless. The chambers of commerce in most cities can supply a map and riding information for their area, and the Oklahoma Department of Parks and Recreation offers suggestions for bike trails in every part of the state. Phone ☎ 800-654-8240 and ask for information on trails that fit your skill level and bike-style.

Trailheaders with a love for steep climbs will find a challenge at the **Lake Elmer Thomas Recreation Area** in the **Wichita Mountains** of southwest Oklahoma. Those who prefer a more level site will enjoy the six-mile **Clear Bay Trail** near **Lake Thunderbird**.

Roadies will be happiest on the routes within the state's resort parks, or along deserted back roads. A 25-mile loop circles **Lake Murray** in the south central section of the state, and casual bikers can take their time going the distance, or turn around and retrace their route at any point. There are plenty of places along the way for sightseeing, picnicking, and napping.

The biking chapters in each regional section will suggest a few road trips and lead you to the best off-road trails. However, a road in *bikeable* condition one week may be full of potholes or holiday traffic the next, so check it out before you start. If you're not sure that a road or trail is open to the public, ask at a local bike shop or the Chamber of Commerce in a nearby town.

Since many trails in the park system are multi-use, yield to pedestrians and follow passing directions of horseback riders so you don't scare or injure anyone. And always – no excuses – wear a helmet.

Motorcycles & ORVs

Open spaces and rugged terrain make many areas of Oklahoma suitable for motorcycle and off-road vehicle (ORV) riding. Several designated trails are open to motorized vehicles in state parks, and these are listed at the end of biking chapters in those regional sections.

Sand dunes in two northwestern state parks provide opportunities for dune buggies, motorcycles, and four-wheel-drive vehicles. Lakes and parks in other parts of the state allow ORV driving in restricted areas.

If you find a spot that is not listed in this book, ask around before you ride there. You may need a permit or permission – or you may not be welcome at all. Go by the rules, or go on your way. When you use a multipurpose trail, keep the noise down, don't scare anyone (especially horseback riders), and stay on the trail. Clubs and ORV dealers are pushing for more and better riding areas, so it's important to present a good image to the tax-paying public.

On Foot

Hiking

 The system of trails in Oklahoma is too extensive to cover in detail within a comprehensive travel guide. There are more than 500 miles of trails in the **Ouachita National Forest** alone. In addition, most state parks feature interpretive nature trails with signs to tell you what lives and grows in the park. Many also maintain paths through the woods and along water sources for day hikes, and a few offer miles of wilderness-type backpacking routes.

Wildlife Management Areas and Public Hunting Grounds permit hikers to use their lands during non-hunting seasons. Sometimes they'll even send you a map and pretend they're glad to see you – just don't scare the fish or feed the deer. Call these dedicated folks at ☎ 405-521-3851.

The US Army Corps of Engineers oversees several major trails, including the 60-mile Jean Pierre Chouteau along the McCllellan-Kerr Navigational Channel and the 24-mile Platter-Lakeside near Lake Texoma. The Tulsa District Office puts out an informative brochure about all their trails, and you can get one by stopping at any project headquarters or calling ☎ 918-581-7349.

The hiking information in this book attempts to point out the best trails in each area of the state in a variety of lengths and difficulty levels. Directions are given to get you to the trailhead along with an overview of what to expect along the way. The rest is up to you. If one path leads off to another, and you are drawn in an unexpected direction, go with your instincts. Just be sure to carry a compass, and use it. One spot can look very much like another, especially when the sun begins to set in the forest or the open plains stretch identically in all directions.

Topography maps for the trails may be obtained from **Oklahoma Geological Survey**, 830 Van Vleet Oval, Norman, OK 73069. Less-detailed maps are available at every park or district office, and most will send you one by mail if you call the number listed with trail information in each section of this book.

In addition, the rangers ask that you:

- Carry plenty of water.
- Underestimate your limitations and endurance.
- Always let someone know where you plan to go and when you expect to return.
- Keep the trails clean.
- Respect all natural features and creatures of the land.
- Check with the park office or ranger in the area you plan to hike for specific restrictions and permits.

Golfing

Golf is a year-round sport in Oklahoma, and you don't have to be a member of a club to play some of the best courses in the state. **The Oklahoma Nine** are state-run golf courses, most with resort facilities, set in scenic locations. Every course is individually designed so golfers can play each and never encounter the same conditions twice. Nearby attractions and excellent facilities make them an ideal destination for weekend getaways or full-blown family vacations.

Besides state-run facilities, there are challenging public courses in most towns. This guide will direct you to the best possibilities in each region, give you a basic overview of the course, and list fees for play and equipment rentals. However, fee structures frequently change and facilities are continually upgraded, so ask for current charges and conditions when you call for a tee time.

Rock Climbing & Rappeling

You'll find a chapter on rock climbing in only one section of this book, so don't bother double-checking the index. Just the southwest region of Oklahoma has enough going on to keep a climber or rappeler busy for more than a couple of hours. Of course, there are mountains and rocky bluffs in other parts of the state, but they're more the excuse-to-get-out-of-the-car variety than real adventures. These climbing opportunities are mentioned in chapters dealing with more popular activities in that region, such as hiking and biking. The southwest, however, has some fine granite-faced mountains with developed climbing areas, and an out-of-the-way red-rock cliff popular with rappelers.

All over the world, environmentalists and nature-lovers are concerned with the negative impact the general public has on geological features. Most experienced sportsmen are committed to protecting the environment and accept the responsibility of practicing "minimal impact" techniques. Nonetheless, the following can't be stated too often:

- Travel in small groups and disperse your activities.
- Stay on established trails.
- Respect the wildlife. They were here first.
- Don't chip, chisel, or otherwise deface rock resources.
- Get a permit before you place or replace a bolt.
- Minimize chalk use.
- Clean up – even if it's not your mess.

On Water

 First time visitors may be surprised by the abundance of water and water sports in Oklahoma – especially east of Interstate Highway 35. The western portion of the state is drier, but even there you will find plenty of opportunities for fishing and boating. Eastern rivers are popular for easygoing floats by canoe, raft, or kayaks.

The rivers and lakes listed in each of the regional sections of this book are often the most popular of their kind, but you will also find smaller, lesser-known spots chosen for their unique beauty or untamed seclusion. Resource information and directions are given in each section for the best water adventures in that area. A statewide directory at the back of the book lists additional addresses and phone numbers.

Sail & Power Boating

It's possible to boat year-round in Oklahoma. The state has more than a million acres of surface water, 2,000 more miles of shoreline than the Atlantic and Gulf Coasts combined – and not a single natural lake. Every one of the 4,500 reservoirs dotting the state is a manmade attempt to control flooding and deliver water someplace it doesn't appear spontaneously.

Mild temperatures and steady breezes make Oklahoma a popular site for sailors, and several active clubs hold official regattas and just-for-fun rallies during most months. Water skiing and motor boating is allowed on almost every lake, and the larger reservoirs have marinas offering jet ski, paddleboat, and pontoon rentals. The state operates 52 parks and the US Army Corps of Engineers oversees another 26 – most near a lake or river with water sports. National and private organizations allow recreational use in a dozen other protected areas.

Boating information and lake maps are available from individual park offices or:

The **US Army Corps of Engineers Tulsa District**, ☎ 918-669-7366

The **Oklahoma Tourism and Recreation Department**, ☎ 405-521-2409 or 800-652-6552; www.otrd.state.ok.us

Rafting, Canoeing & Kayaking

The Illinois in northeastern Oklahoma is the major recreational river in the state. Outfitters along State Highway 10 rent canoes, rafts, and kayaks for float trips lasting from a few hours to a few days. The river is rated Class I and Class II, so even beginners and kids can manage a self-guided trip.

Rafts and top-riding kayaks are easier to keep upright, but most floaters prefer to travel the river by canoe. On hot summer days, tipping over is a refreshing part of the fun. Unless you're incredibly inept or the river is running high and fast, go for the two-man or three-man canoe. You probably can't do yourself much harm, and you'll get the best ride.

However, if you're looking for a leisurely dry excursion, ask for an inflatable raft for four to six passengers. They're more difficult to paddle. However, this isn't a race, so sit back and enjoy. Kayaks offer an agreeable compromise.

Rentals also are available on the Lower and Upper Mountain Fork Rivers around Broken Bow in the far southeastern section of the state. Other rivers are floatable, but none are as developed as the Illinois and Mountain Fork, and floaters must provide their own equipment.

Maps and river information are available from:

Oklahoma Scenic Rivers Commission, ☎ 918-456-3251

Fishing

State agencies operate four fish hatcheries and regularly stock reservoirs, ponds, rivers and creeks with several species of bass, catfish, sunfish, perch, and crappie. In addition, rainbow and brown trout are stocked in designated trout streams.

Each section of this book will guide you to great fishing spots and tell you about nearby facilities. However, there are professionals whose only responsibility is to keep up-to-the-minute records on which species are biting what bait where. If you're a serious angler, call the pros – ☎ 800-ASK-FISH.

You'll need a current Oklahoma fishing license before you even think about dropping a line into the water. Standard resident fees are $12.50 per year, and nonresident fees are $28.50 per year. A $7.75 license is required for everyone who fishes in stocked streams during trout seasons. Less expensive licenses may be purchased for periods of five and 14 days.

 *You're also responsible for knowing and following current regulations set by the **Department of Wildlife Conservation's Fishing Division**, ☎ 405-521-3721. Since regulations and fees are set by the state each year, check each season for current information. If you need an angler answer that 800-ASK-FISH can't handle, The **Oklahoma Tourist Information Office** will put you in touch with the right agency, ☎ 800-652-6552.*

Scuba

Oklahoma may be landlocked, but there's still plenty of water. Scuba diving is possible – and quite popular – at three lakes. Of course, a real scuba fanatic will dive anywhere, anytime, anyhow, but the following spots have full service shops, certification lessons, and good water conditions.

Broken Bow Lake, in the southeastern corner of the state, offers some of the cleanest water. Unless there has been a lot of rain, visibility is about 25 feet, and there are more islands to explore than in any other lake in Oklahoma. Because of its location near the Texas/Oklahoma border, **Lake Murray** is a popular dive site for residents of both states. Visibility is typically about 15 feet, depending on how much rain has fallen in recent days. In northeastern Oklahoma, **Lake Tenkiller** provides good visibility, island dives, and night diving. Divers can expect 15 to 20 feet of visibility, and by late summer, the water temperature warms to an average 80°. Dive shop information and scuba details are provided in the *On Water* chapters of the Southeastern and Northeastern sections of this book.

On Horseback

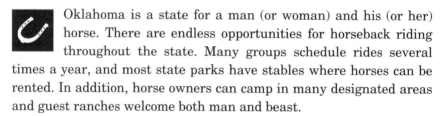 Oklahoma is a state for a man (or woman) and his (or her) horse. There are endless opportunities for horseback riding throughout the state. Many groups schedule rides several times a year, and most state parks have stables where horses can be rented. In addition, horse owners can camp in many designated areas and guest ranches welcome both man and beast.

The eastern half of the state offers more equestrian trails, and these are discussed in the *On Horseback* adventure sections of each region. The open space and rugged terrain of the western half of the state are ideal for exploration on horseback, and riders can often select a spot and head out in any direction. However, be aware of permit requirements on some federal and state land, and never cross private property without permission.

Information

For information about riding areas and events not listed in this book, contact **The Oklahoma Equestrian Trail Riders Association**, e-mail address: okierider1@aol.com. The address and phone number at press time are: Rt.4, Box 212, Seminole, OK 74868, ☎ 405-382-0613. However, this is a member-run organization, and all officers change each year, so call the **Oklahoma Tourism Department**, ☎ 800-652-6552, if you have trouble contacting the proper spokesperson.

Climate

Oklahoma has a mild climate with a mean streak. Most of the time, during most of the year, the weather is calm and pleasant. However, if you see a thunderstorm gathering in the distance, pay attention. Tune into a local radio or TV station to find out what is expected, and if you hear the word *tornado*, take it seriously. Lightning can also be a serious inconvenience. Follow the advice of local weather stations, if you have any questions about safety.

While the state's average high temperature is 71° F, summer temperatures can top 100, and high humidity sometimes turns eastern regions into steam baths. Winter is short, but below-zero temperatures are common at night, and parts of the state stay below freezing most of January and February. Spring comes early. Fall arrives late. Some years, winter hits hard and hangs on for weeks, but other years it never settles in at all. Summer is usually pleasant if you plan for water or air-conditioned activities in the middle of the day. Expect extremes of all types during any season in mountain areas.

It's difficult to predict what's "average" in Oklahoma. In a single day, one part of the state may be covered in snow while another part is sticky hot. The southeast may be flooding while the northwest is drier than a desert. However, the following are average high temperatures and rainfall for the state throughout the year.

Temperatures & Rainfall		
	Average High	Average Rainfall
January	47°	0.5
February	53°	1.3
March	61°	2.8
April	72°	4.5
May	79°	3.2
June	87°	1.6
July	93°	2.3
August	92°	2.3
September	84°	1.3
October	74°	1.4
November	60°	3.1
December	50°	1.3

Get a Pass

Oklahoma offers several money-saving programs, if you meet the requirements and apply in advance. The following are just a few examples. Call the Travel and Tourism Department, ☎ 800-652-6552, to ask about other offers.

The **State Parks and Resorts CEO (Customers with Exciting Opportunities) Card,** ☎ 800-654-8240, entitles you to receive fourth-night-free lodging at any park with cabins from September 16 through May 14, and up to 50% discount on tent camping from September 1 to March 31. Also, CEOs receive a fourth day of golf free from October 1 through February 28, a 15% discount on gift shop and pro shop purchases, and a 10% discount on box lunches at resort restaurants. The card is free – simply apply by phone or at any state park office.

The **Golden Age Passport** is for any citizen of the United States who is 62 years of age or older. The **Golden Access Passport** is for any citizen who has been medically determined to be blind or permanently disabled. Both allow entrance to national parks, monuments, historic sites, recreation areas and national wildlife refuges administered by the national government which charge entrance fees. It also gives a 50% discount on federal use fees charged for services such as camping, boat launching, and parking. Other benefits apply, so call ☎ 800-652-6552 for information. There is a one-time fee of $10 for the Golden Age Passport. The Golden Access Passport is free.

Senior Citizens who are Oklahoma residents or live in certain specified states, and all **Disabled Persons** may also receive a 50% discount on state-operated campsites. Proof of age or disability is all that is required to obtain the state discount.

Pikepass, ☎ 405-425-3600, allows card holders to save on tolls throughout the state without having to wait in lines at toll booths. Worth getting, if you plan to ignore the advice in this book about staying off these time-saving but monotonous roadways.

Who Ya Gonna Call??

Local information, such as chambers of commerce, visitors' centers, tour operators, and adventure outfitters are included in the regional sections of this book. National and state resources are listed below.

General State-Wide Information

Oklahoma Tourist Information

☎ 800-652-6552 or 800-909-710 or 405-521-2409

State Park Lodging

Oklahoma Resort Lodges and Cabins, ☎ 800-654-8240 or 405-521-2464, e-mail rsrtpark@mail.otrd.state.ok.us; www.otrd.state.ok.us/

Fishing Information

☎ 800-ASK-FISH or 800-521-3721

Fishing Licenses

Oklahoma Department of Wildlife Conservation, ☎ 405-521-3851

Miscellaneous

US Corps of Engineers, ☎ 918-669-7407

Oklahoma Bicycle Society, ☎ 405-943-5161

Highway Patrol/Emergency, ☎ 405-682-4343, cellular phones dial *55

Road and Weather Conditions, ☎ 405-425-2385

Turnpike Toll and Access Information, ☎ 800-745-3727 or 405-424-0473 or 405-425-3600

Oklahoma Department of Transportation, ☎ 405-521-2541

Public Transportation, ☎ 405-521-2584

Oklahoma Historical Society, ☎ 405-521-2491

Oklahoma Route 66 Association, ☎ 405-258-0008

Oklahoma Arts Council, ☎ 405-521-2931

Oklahoma Museum Association, ☎ 405-424-7757

Handicapped Concerns Office, ☎ 405-521-3756

Oklahoma Restaurant Association, ☎ 405-942-8181

Oklahoma Governor's Office, ☎ 405-521-2342

Oklahoma Bed and Breakfast Association, ☎ 800 676-5522 or 405-321-6221

Guided Wilderness Backpacking Trips

Outback Guides, ☎ 918-446-5956, Website: www.outbackguides.com

Guided Group Tours

Wild West Tours, ☎ 800-700-3928, organizes group tours for adventurous architecture fans and history buffs through Osage Country in north central Oklahoma.

Whirlwind Tours, ☎ 405-329-2308, offers tornado-chasing tours through *Tornado Alley* during season. Call for details and prices.

Kincaid Travel Tours, ☎ 800-998-1903, has several *Discover Oklahoma* tours. The trips are mostly one-day outings, but there are a few multi-day tours. Prices vary, so call for information and a schedule of trips.

Regional Tourist Information

Green Country (northeast), ☎ 800-922-2118

Kiamichi Country (southeast), ☎ 800-722-8180

Great Plains Country (southwest), ☎ 580-562-4882

Red Carpet Country (northwest), ☎ 800-447-2698

Frontier Country (central), ☎ 800-FUN-OKLA

Lake Country (south central), ☎ 405-369-3392

Eufaula Tourism Hotline, ☎ 800-4-EUFALA

Recommended Books, Magazines & Videos

Oklahoma Today, ☎ 800-777-1793, is an award-winning publication and the state's official magazine. A one-year subscription is $13.50; back issues may be ordered for $6.95.

Oklahoma II by photographer David Fitzgerald is a coffee-table book of beautiful pictures that show off the scenic wonders of the state. Cost is $40 at most large bookstores, or you may order a copy by calling ☎ 800-777-1793.

Oklahoma Video is a one-hour show produced by the Oklahoma Heritage Association and the Oklahoma Tourism and Recreation Department. Watch it before your visit to get an overview of the state's fascinating history. Order a copy by calling ☎ 800-777-1793.

Oklahoma Off the Beaten Path, by Barbara Palmer, published by The Globe Pequot Press, Inc., is a quick look at unusual and interesting sites and sights across the state. The list price is $10.95 and you can find it or order it from most large bookstores.

Exploring Oklahoma Together and ***Exploring Oklahoma With Children***, both edited by Sarah L. Taylor for Inprint Publishing, Inc., are informative directories for anyone who wants to visit the best places in Oklahoma. The cover prices are $9.95 for *With Children* and $12.95 for *Together*. Ask for them at most large bookstores.

Mountain Biking Texas & Oklahoma, by Chuck Cypert, published by Falcon Press, costs $14.95 at most large book stores and some bike shops. A dozen Oklahoma mountain bike trails are discussed in detail.

Roadside History of Oklahoma, by Francis L. and Roberta B. Fugate, published by Mountain Press Publishing Company, has a $15.95 cover price. It is an entertaining town-by-town history of the state, ideal for the passenger to read aloud to the driver on road trips.

The Story of Oklahoma, by W. David Baird and Danney Goble, is published by University of Oklahoma Press. It's a bit scholarly for most tourists, but if you're a history buff or student, you'll want to invest in this hardback book – or check it out from your local library.

Cimarron, by Edna Ferber, tells about the settlement of Oklahoma. The Pulitzer Prize winning author stayed in the T.B. Ferguson home in Watonga to gather information for this best-selling novel.

The Grapes of Wrath, by John Steinbeck, won a Pulitzer Prize and National Book Award, so you should read it. However, the author was a master at creating images of things he had never seen, and his description of Oklahoma is one excellent example. Unfortunately, many people still think the state is a dustbowl because of this book. Read it for its literary and social value, then come see the real Oklahoma for yourself.

Oklahoma City

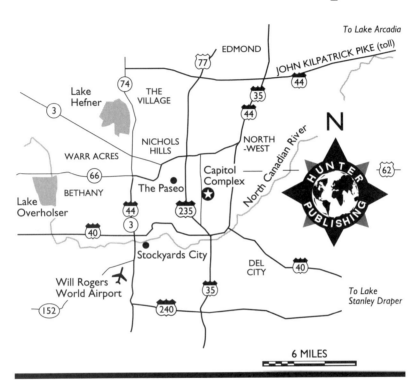

Oklahoma City

We know we belong to the land
And the land we belong to is grand!
And when we say – Yeeow! A-yip-i-o-ee-ay!
We're only sayin' You're doin' fine. Oklahoma! Oklahoma – OK

State song adopted from Rodgers and Hammerstein's *Oklahoma!*

The capital city stretches across the center of the state covering more land than any other city in the United States. You'll need a car and time. Don't rush through here doing 65 on one of the three interstates and think you've seen it. As with the rest of the state, you won't find the real city until you get off onto the side roads and ramble about a bit.

■ History

Oklahoma City didn't grow from a handful of settlers, it just happened – twice.

You probably know the story about the birthday of Oklahoma. It goes something like this: One fine spring day in 1889, the United States government opened "unassigned land" – that no one was really using anyway – to courageous fellows who ran, at the sound of a starting gun, to stake a claim on free-for-the-taking townsites and quarter-sections where they built homes for their families and lived happily ever after.

In reality, white settlers were stealing land promised to Native Americans by official treaties for "as long as grass grows and the rivers run," years before the sound of a run-gun.

Railroad officials may have sparked the idea of "free" land when they spread stories around the country of unoccupied prairies in America's midsection. However, cowboys driving their herds to market had been loitering around watching their cattle graze in Indian Territory before that. The railroad rumors simply jump-started a demand from easterners for legal access to the West. Groups of organized "Boomers" congregated along the borders of the future state; then, when their numbers were large enough to give them courage, they marched brazenly and covetously onto restricted land, knowing that existing laws did not allow prosecution for trespass on Indian soil.

By the time President Benjamin Harrison issued a proclamation for the opening of unassigned land, the site that became Oklahoma City already had a Santa Fe Railway depot, a post office, a boarding house, and an assortment of "Sooners" who had taken the liberty of laying out Main Street. When the gun sounded to start the land run at noon on April 22, 1889, perhaps 100,000 people rushed across the border to claim a plot, and by nightfall 10,000 of them were camped in what is now the capital city.

So, that's how Oklahoma City happened the first time. The second time was on December 4, 1928 when a drilling company hit oil – a lot of oil. Immediately, a greedy race for black gold roared full speed through the town, inflating the population, and Oklahoma City was born "full grown" again.

At one time, 24 working wells pulled oil from the grounds around the state government offices, and you can see Petunia Number One still pumping in front of the capitol building. You may be disappointed to know that it's just faking. After producing for 44 years, the well was plugged in the 1980s and now just goes through the motions under the protective eye of the Oklahoma Historical Society.

■ Touring

The Capitol Complex

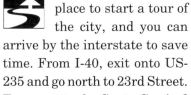

The capitol is a fine place to start a tour of the city, and you can arrive by the interstate to save time. From I-40, exit onto US-235 and go north to 23rd Street. Turn east to the **State Capitol** at 2300 Lincoln Blvd. Don't look for a dome. There isn't one. When the building was built in Roman Corinthian style between 1914 and 1917, the state legislature couldn't justify the expense of adding a dome. During the depression and two world wars, a dome was out of the question. Various proposals have been debated over the years, but, at this time, there are no plans for putting anything on top of the rather austere building. Most Oklahomans like the familiar appearance – and feel just fine leaving things the way they've been for over 80 years.

State Capitol, Oklahoma City, built 1914-17. (Fred W. Marvel)

There is a domed ceiling – and a rotunda – inside the building. Tours through the Capitol are conducted free of charge and begin on the hour from 8 am to 3 pm Monday through Friday. A brochure for self-guided tours is also available, and the doors are open every day except Christmas and Thanksgiving. ☎ 405-521-3356 for information.

Oklahoma City

From February 1 to May 31, the legislature is in session, and visitors are allowed to watch the proceedings from the galleries. Year-round, the tour stops at the governor's office, the state Supreme Court, and the House and Senate chambers. Historical events such as the Trail of Tears and the Land Run are depicted in murals by Charles Banks Wilson throughout the building, and the wall of the fourth-floor rotunda is covered with a semicircular mural of five world-famous Native American ballerinas.

If it's humid and hot outside, it will be humid and hot inside the rotunda because there is no air-conditioning (or heating). All other areas of the building are climate-controlled, and visitors can move between the Capitol and the **State Museum of History** by tunnel. The museum, at 2100 North Lincoln, has exhibits in five galleries which visitors can tour on their own. Some of the more memorable displays include articles from old forts, a tepee made from buffalo hides, a wagon that made the land run, and oil field gizmos. Visitors are welcome free of charge Monday through Saturday from 8 am to 5 pm. ☎ 405-521-2491 for information.

The Harn Homestead presents a realistic view of the lifestyle of land-run settlers. Located south of the Capitol building at 313 NE 16th, the historical complex includes a restored and furnished home, a one-room schoolhouse, an outfitted barn, and an authentic farmhouse. Guided tours of the Harn House, a typical middle-class home during the pre-statehood period between 1889 and 1907, take place on the hour from 10 am to 3 pm, Tuesday through Saturday. Visitors tour the other buildings on their own following a brochure and map. Admission to the Harn complex is $3 for adults and $1.50 for children. ☎ 405-235-4058 for information.

The Paseo

After all this history, you may be ready for **The Paseo**, a struggling-to-revive inner-city shopping and arts district that was originally named Spanish Village. Find this area by driving west from the Capitol complex on 23rd Street to the other side of US-235/77. Turn north on Walker and follow it to the entrance markers where Dewey Road curves into Paseo. You'll know you're in the right place when you see the multicolored stucco buildings, red-tiled roofs, and wrought-iron railings. Each single-story shop is molded into its allotted space and painted some shade of purple, yellow, blue, or terra-cotta. The Paseo is a work in progress, and the edges are still a little ragged, but you'll be impressed if you focus on the craftsmanship and beauty of each restored shop. The entire area covers only a couple of blocks, so park your car and walk.

Individual artists, photographers, writers, dancers, and restaurateurs have bought many going-to-decay buildings built in the 1920s. Most work on-site in their studios and welcome visitors to watch or browse during shop hours. At 2927 Paseo, a group of artists and an architect share space. Down the street, at 3001, Chickasaw artist **Mike Larsen** has a studio and gallery. Next door at 3003, **Diane Coady** hand paints silk and turns it into clothing. At the nearby Paseo Market, **Craig Travis** makes jewelry and Tiffany-style lamps while **Subherbs Hemp Company** makes and sells natural soaps formulated with herbs and hemp oil. You can watch **Collin Rosebrook** turn out original pottery, or listen to poetry readings while you sip cappuccino at Medina's, or.... Well, you get the point. It's a unique, interesting, fun place. Allow plenty of time to linger.

In Town

Go south on Walker when you leave the Paseo and drive by the **Overholser Mansion**. It's a Victorian house built in 1903 at 405 NW 15th Street. The surrounding neighborhood is called Heritage Park, the home of "old money," and the lovely old houses sit on spacious lawns shaded by towering trees. Tours are held hourly Tuesday through Friday between 10 am and 4 pm. On weekends, three tours are given between 2 pm and 4 pm. The home holds some of its original furnishings, and some walls are covered with hand-painted canvas. ☎ 405-528-8485 for information.

Farther south, Walker runs into downtown. History and architecture fans will be interested in the buildings listed in the National Register of Historic Places. Get a walking map and information from the **Convention and Visitors Bureau at 189 West Sheridan**, ☎ 800-225-5652. Among the more interesting are two churches which were built at the turn of the century and damaged in the April 19, 1995 bombing. **Saint Paul's Cathedral** on Robinson at 7th Street, is Norman Gothic with a lovely garden. **Saint Joseph's Cathedral**, on Harvey at 7th Street, is built in the Victorian Gothic Revival style.

Oklahoma City

What's New In Town?

The **Civic Center Music Hall** at 201 Channing Square is closed for major remodeling. Improvement to the Depression-era concert hall is expected to cost $46 million, and a gala grand opening is scheduled for the fall of 2000. Call ☎ 405-297-2584 for updates on the progress.

The **Myriad Convention Center**, on Sheridan between Robinson and Gaylord, has an additional 200,000 square feet under construction, which will extend its total space to 1,200,000 square feet. The $47 million expansion is expected to open in the summer of 1999. New hotels planned near the center, such as Marriott Renaissance and Embassy Suites, will double the number of luxury accommodations in the downtown area.

Even if you don't like either history or architecture and you hate the idea of driving in downtown areas, try **Myriad Gardens**, ☎ 405-297-3995. It's on the southern edge of downtown, a turn to the east off Walker onto Reno, with parking on the left past Hudson Avenue. You'll spot the building easily. It's a giant glass-like tube built over a spring-fed lake surrounded by 17 acres of lush gardens. You can walk the outdoor paths at no charge, but there's a $2 admission fee to go inside the Crystal Bridge, which is open from 9 am to 6 pm daily. Inside you'll find a 224-

Myria Botanical Gardens / Crystal Bridge Tropical Conservatory, Oklahoma City. (Fred W. Marvel)

foot-long enclosed tropical conservatory with a rainforest, butterflies, waterfalls, orchids, palm trees – Eden in the middle of the city.

Bricktown is nearby, and you can hop a shuttle next door at the northeast side of the Myriad Convention Center. Other downtown shuttle-stops are marked by a Coca-Cola/Bricktown sign at curbside. A ride costs 50¢ each way, and visitors who park at the Main Street Santa Fe Garage Friday or Saturday nights get a $1 parking discount plus one round-trip shuttle ride free of charge.

Bricktown is a refurbished warehouse district along Sheridan Street east of Broadway with trendy restaurants and clubs. Near lunch time, find it by following the crowds. At night, it's the only downtown spot with action. Restaurants, comedy clubs, a micro brewery, music clubs, and specialty shops are housed in remodeled red brick warehouses built between 1890 and World War II.

What's New In Bricktown

Southwestern Bell Bricktown Ballpark opened in April, 1998. It is a $32 million retro-style stadium and the cornerstone of a downtown redevelopment program aimed at making Oklahoma City a first-class American urban center. It is home to the Oklahoma RedHawks, the top minor league affiliate of the Texas Ranger baseball team. Bricktown Ballpark is a smaller version of new retro parks built in Baltimore for the Orioles and Arlington, Texas (near Dallas) for the Rangers. Architecturally, the park reminds fans of baseball's glorious past. There is an asymmetrical playing field like the old city ballparks that were squeezed into random vacant space in crowded commercial districts. A 24-foot green fence in right field is Oklahoma's version of the Green Monster at Fenway Park in Boston.

Canal-Riverwalk is planned to connect Bricktown with development along the North Canadian River. The canal, when complete, will be about four feet deep and a mile long, and is expected to cost approximately $20 million. Developers hope to make the area a successful imitation of the popular restaurant/shopping/entertainment walkway built along the river in downtown San Antonio, Texas. Check with the tourist office for an update on the progress of the canal.

Oklahoma City

On pleasant weekend evenings, patrons take a horse-drawn carriage ride or stroll the streets in the glow of the gaslights. Most holidays are celebrated with decorations and special activities such as a parade on St. Patrick's Day, a visit from Santa during the Christmas Festival of Lights, an old-fashioned block party on the Fourth of July, and Opening Night festivities on New Year's Eve. ☎ 405-236-8666 for directions and information.

Stockyards City

History doesn't get any more authentic than at **Stockyards City**. Cattle were the purpose in 1910, and cattle are the purpose today – with very few changes. Cowboys still control their stock on horseback, auctioneers still bellow out bids in a rapid monotone chant, and money still makes all the rules. Visitors are welcome, but sacred business is being transacted, and you'll know it when you drive through the gate. From downtown, drive west on I-40, turn south on Agnew then west on Exchange. The gateway to Oklahoma National Stockyards is straight ahead.

Built as a meat processing and packing district, Stockyards City was once home to Morris, Wilson, and Armour. However, as technology advanced, the packing plants closed and left the district to cattle traders and related businesses. Some of the best Western apparel and ranching equipment in the country is still sold here in wooden-fronted stores that date from the early 1900s. Over the years, this district has shunned all things "touristy," so you won't find souvenir trinkets and cute T-shirts on the shelves. What you will find are genuine cowboy working boots, custom-made hats, work-of-art saddles, and Western wear to fit everyone in the family. Several artists and craftsmen have studios in the district and welcome visitors to watch them work.

The best day to visit is Monday when tours are available, but Tuesday are a good second choice. Both are auction days, and the pens will be full. You can walk through the holding area and sit in on the auction. Then walk over to **Cattlemen's Steakhouse** for a hand-cut, perfectly aged steak. Walk off your meal by touring the shops and galleries, or stop by the headquarters of the **International Professional Rodeo Association**.

Several special events take place in the Stockyards during the year. "**Stampede**" is a Western street party with bull riding, barbecue, and music, held the first full weekend in June. Every weekend between Thanksgiving and Christmas, carolers and a Western Santa appear at "**Cowboy Christmas**." The **International Final Rodeo** hosts a large parade featuring horses, wagons, and entertainers every January. ☎ 405-235-7267 for exact dates and information.

Northeast OKC

The National Cowboy Hall of Fame is enormous and beautiful. Opened in 1965, it is more like a world's fair than a museum, and more like a tribute to the West than a cowboy collection. Individual galleries cover every aspect of the Old West, from explorers Lewis and Clark to entertainers Roy Rogers and Will Rogers.

Visitors can go inside a sod house like those built by the pioneers, walk through a silver mine, explore a typical Western territorial town, and see authentic 19th-century artifacts. Five triptychs (16 by 40-foot paneled landscape murals) by Wilson Hurley dominate the 1,200-seat Sam Noble Special Events Center, and several larger-than-life statues tower over thousands of other exhibits throughout the hall. One of the most impressive works – and proof that this is more than a cowboy museum – is an immense statue of a weary Indian slumped on his exhausted horse – "The End of the Trail" by James Earle Fraser.

Paint Mare & Filly by Veryl Goodnight at the National Cowboy Hall of Fame.

Find the Hall of Fame at 1700 Northeast 63rd Street off Martin Luther King Boulevard, north of I-44. If you visit the third weekend in April, you can hear cowboy poets and singers perform at the **Cowboy Poetry Gathering**. The **Cowboy Chuck Wagon Gathering** is held on Memorial Day weekend. The National Cowboy Hall of Fame is open daily from 8:30 am to 6 pm during the summer and from 9 am to 5 pm during the rest of the year. Admission is $6 for adults and $3 for children. ☎ 405-478-2250 for additional information.

Oklahoma City Zoological Park is nearby at 2101 Northeast 50th Street off Martin Luther King Boulevard, south of I-44. It is one of the best zoos in the country – first-class in every respect. Some of the most outstanding exhibits are:

- *Island Life,* where a 600-pound Galapagos tortoise shares space with a Sulawesi grosbeak starling that communicates with his tail feathers;

- *The Cat Forest / Lion Overlook,* where trails lead through 2½ acres of natural habitat featuring lions, tigers, jaguars and leopards;

- *The Great EscApe,* where 3½ acres of tropical forest house a major collection of gorillas, chimpanzees, and orangutans.

A view into the Children's Zoo at the Oklahoma City Zoo, featuring the azalea collection in full bloom.

In addition, a Sky Tram travels over the entire area so riders get an overview of the zoo's inhabitants, and there are many shady spots in the 110-acre spread for a picnic or rest. The zoo is open daily except Christmas and New Year's Day from 9 am to 6 pm during the summer and 9 am to 5 pm from October 1 through March 31. Admission is $4 for adults and $2 for children with additional charges for rides and special shows. Call the zoo office for information about special exhibits and events, ☎ 405-424-3344.

The Kirkpatrick Center Museum Complex is the perfect place to spend a rainy or too-hot day because seven museums are located under one roof and one admission fee gets you into all the exhibits. Exit I-44 onto Martin Luther King Avenue and go south to 2100 Northeast 52nd Street. One toll-free number provides information about all the museums in the Center, ☎ 800-532-7652.

Part of the Kirkpatrick Center, **The Oklahoma Air and Space Museum**, ☎ 405-242-0203, has several hands-on exhibits such as an F-16 Fighting Falcon simulator and audio recordings of the moon landings. A tropical garden, topiary plants, and a waterfall are the highlights at the **Kirkpatrick Conservatory and Botanical Gardens**, ☎ 405-427-7529. Native American heritage is the theme of **The Red Earth Indian Center**, ☎ 405-427-5228, where nationally recognized Oklahoma In-

Downtown Oklahoma City is ablaze with color as more than 1,500 Native American dancers from throughout North America participate in the Red Earth Festival opening day parade. (G. Jill Evans)

Oklahoma City

dian artists display their work, and visitors can tour a full-size Indian home and a kid-size tepee filled with artifacts. **The International Photography Hall of Fame**, ☎ 405-424-4055, honors Ansel Adams, George Eastman, and other early photographers. There are exhibits of antique photographic equipment and award-winning photographs, including a 360° laser-produced mural of the Grand Canyon. **The Omniplex Science Museum**, ☎ 405-424-5545, includes a planetarium with shows every hour on weekend and summer afternoons. ☎ 405-424-5545 for show hours at other times of the year. In addition, there's a virtual reality trip through the human digestive system, a simulated earthquake experience, and 300 other scientific exhibits.

If you're interested in military equipment and history, **The 45th Infantry Division Museum**, ☎ 405-424-5313, at 2145 Northeast 36th Street, offers fine displays. Military weapons, aircraft, tanks, and trucks spread over 12 acres of land surrounding the museum. Inside, one of the most interesting exhibits is a collection of more than 200 original World War II cartoons by Pulitzer-Prize winner, Bill Mauldin. Rare artillery pieces, including weapons from the Revolutionary War and Vietnam, are housed in the Jordan B. Reaves wing. The museum is open Tuesday through Friday from 9 am to 5 pm, Saturday from 10 am to 5 pm, and Sunday from 1 pm to 5 pm. Admission is free.

Pickin' 'n Singin' Honky-Tonk

Here are a dozen popular Country and Western music stars from Oklahoma:

- Vince Gill
- Garth Brooks
- Reba McEntire
- Ronnie Dunn of Brooks and Dunn
- Bryan White
- Joe Diffie
- Toby Keith
- Bob Wills
- Merle Haggard
- Conway Twitty
- Roy Clark
- Woody Guthrie

■ Adventures

Lakes, Parks, Golf Courses & Trails

 Lake Hefner is in the northwestern part of the city off Northwest Expressway. Turn into the park onto Lakeshore Drive near the golf course. Drive around the east side of the lake until you come to the junction of Britton Road, where you'll find a parking area on the right as you face the lake. A newly completed nine-mile trail extends almost entirely around the lake, offering opportunities for biking, skating, walking and jogging.

The Hefner Trail is part of a $2.4 million project to add 200 miles of multi-use pathways to the city over the next few years. Immediate plans include a trail to circle nearby **Lake Overholser**, with a third trail intended in the future to connect the two lakes. When the three trails are complete, residents and visitors can enjoy the facilities of both recreation areas and also bike, hike, or skate an extended distance.

More construction was underway at press time on an East Wharf restaurant area. When complete, a complex of restaurants will overlook a new harbor with docks and a lighthouse. Check the progress of construction and request maps by calling ☎ 405-525-8822. **Wheeler Dealer Bicycle Shop**, ☎ 405-947-6260, is also a good source for information and maps.

Sailing is popular at the lake and two clubs sponsor competition. For information about membership or scheduled events, call **Central OK Sailing Association** at ☎ 405-720-1001 or **OKC Boat Club** at ☎ 405-752-9597. Fishermen will want to try for the elusive walleye. They're down there, but hard to catch. Sand bass and crappie aren't sure bets either, but it's worth putting a minnow on a line to test your luck.

Martin Park Nature Center, ☎ 405-755-0676, north of Lake Hefner at 5000 West Memorial Road, houses a wildlife sanctuary. You can explore the 140-acre park on your own at no charge, and naturalists give guided tours at certain times. Deer roam through the sanctuary. However, they are shy, so be prepared to watch prairie dogs and birds (who expect an audience) and turtles (who are too lazy to care).

Lake Overholser, south of I-44 on the North Canadian River, is surrounded by beautiful scenery. The clear water is popular with fishermen because of the large hybrid striped bass that are often pulled from the depths. Picnic facilities and the Stinchcomb Wildlife Refuge are located near the lake, but there are no camping or swimming sites. A 1¼-mile jogging trail is located west of Council Road at Northwest 23rd Street, and a new trail circling the lake may be complete by the time you read this book. For directions and information call ☎ 405-789-3746.

The **Lake Hefner Golf Course**, ☎ 405-843-1565, 4491 South Lake Hefner Road, is a 36-hole two-course facility with 7,000 total yards on the North Course and 6,305 total yards on the South Course. The North Course slope rating is 128, the South Course rating is 111. Carts and clubs are available for rental, and there are putting greens, practice holes, a driving range, and a restaurant. Green fees are $14.63 both weekends and weekdays

Earlywine Park Golf Course, 11600 South Portland, ☎ 405-691-1727, is a two-course, 36-hole facility. The North Course is 6,173 yards with water on half the course and a slope rating of 121. The South Course is 6,295 yards with water on a third of the course and a slope rating of 107. There are putting greens, chipping and pitching areas, and a driving range. You may rent clubs. Green fees are $14.63 daily.

Lincoln Park Golf Course, 4001 North East Grand Boulevard, ☎ 405-424-1421, is also a two-course 36-hole facility. Both courses have 6,508 total yardage with a slope rating of 120 on the East Course and a slope rating of 121 on the West Course. Carts and clubs are available for rental, and there are putting greens and a driving range. Green fees on weekdays and weekends are $14.63.

Silverhorn Golf Club, 11411 North Kelley Avenue, ☎ 405-752-1181, is an 18-hole course with a total yardage of 6,071 and a slope rating of 123. There are practice areas and putting greens. Green fees on weekdays are $22; $30 with a cart. On weekends, the fees are $27; $35 with a cart.

Trosper Park Golf Course, 2301 South East 29th Street, ☎ 405-677-8874, is an 18-hole course with a total yardage of 6,800 and a slope rating of 116. There are putting and chipping areas and a driving range. Daily green fees are $13.50 plus tax.

If you prefer to do your walking off the golf course, try **Soldier Creek Nature Trail** which begins at **Tom Poore Park** on 10th Street (south of the city, across the North Canadian River in the suburb of **Midwest City**). This 2½-mile gravel path follows the creek, crosses over footbridges, and runs along an inscribed-brick stretch called Memory Lane in Regional Park at 15th Street. This is an easy hike/bike for all ages and all levels of experience. For directions or information about the trail, phone **Joe B**. **Barnes Regional** Park, ☎ 405-739-1293.

The John Conrad Regional Golf Course, 711 South Douglas Boulevard, Midwest City, ☎ 405-732-2209, is an 18-hole course with a total yardage of 6,854 and a slope rating of 115. Call the pro shop for current green fees.

Near Tinker Air Force Base, **Lake Stanley Draper** has 34 miles of shoreline, gorgeous scenery, and miles of trails. Mountain bikers share fast, technical, single-track trails with motorized bikes and four-wheel ORVs. Turns are tight and the terrain is hilly through the creek system, so only advanced-intermediates and expert bikers will enjoy the pace. Find the trails about one-fourth mile east of Douglas Boulevard on South East 74th Street between Tinker AFB and the lake.

Elsewhere on the lake, the fishing is fair to good most of the year and water skiing is allowed. On the south shore there's a model airplane flying field. Bring a picnic – or pick up lunch at the bait shop/convenience store/restaurant on the corner of Douglas and 74th Street – and eat at one of the shaded tables near the water. From Oklahoma City take I-35 south to US-240, turn east and go to Douglas Boulevard, then follow the signs to access roads. Call ☎ 405-794-5010 for maps and information.

■ Where to Stay

Hotels

 The Waterford at 6300 Waterford Boulevard, Oklahoma City's only four-star hotel, was completely refurbished in 1996. There are beautiful public areas, a full service health spa, an Executive Level floor, and all the usual amenities of a first-class facility. For reservations, ☎ 800-992-2009, fax 405-848-7810.

The Fifth Season, 6200 North Robinson a block west of NW 63rd Street and the Broadway Extension, ☎ 800-682-0049, fax 405-840-8410. Guests enjoy big rooms, an indoor pool and hot tub, and a full breakfast. Rates are $79 to $95.

The Embassy Suites Hotel, 1815 South Meridian Avenue, ☎ 800-362-2779, fax 405-682-9835. Guests are assigned two-room suites and enjoy a cooked-to-order breakfast each morning. There is a happy hour each evening. Suites are $135.

Chain Hotels

Oklahoma City is a large, modern city with all the usual hotel/motel chains, so if you just want a good bed in a clean room call **Best Western's** national number at ☎ 800-528-1234. The **Best Western Santa Fe** at 6101 North Santa Fe serves a complimentary breakfast and room rates are about $65. **Holiday Inn's** national number is ☎ 800-HOLIDAY. Oklahoma City Convention and Visitors Bureau will send a list of hotels and rates, or offer assistance if you contact them at ☎ 800-225-5652.

In addition, **Marriott,** ☎ 800-228-9290, **Hilton,** ☎ 800-848-4811, and **Medallion,** ☎ 800-285-2780, have lovely properties in the city with rates in the $89 to $139 range.

Bed & Breakfasts/Small Inns

The Gradison at Maney Park, 1200 North Shartel, ☎ 405-232-8778. There are nine bedrooms with private baths, fireplaces, Jacuzzis, and cable TV. The original home was built in 1904, and still has some of its original woodwork, plus a grand staircase and a balcony hallway overlooking the lower floor. Rates are from $75 to $150.

Flora's Bed and Breakfast, 2312 NW 46th Street, ☎ 405-840-3157, offers a quiet neighborhood retreat near Penn Square Mall, one of the largest and nicest shopping areas in the city. Flora's offers a spa on the outdoor deck, a fireplace, antique furnishings, and a full breakfast every morning. This is an ideal place to stay when you come to town to shop. Rooms rent for $70 and up.

The Gradison, 1841 North West 15th, ☎ 405-521-0011, 800-240-4676, fax 405-521-0011, was built in 1912 and still has original woodwork, crystal chandeliers, and Belgian stained glass. There are five bedrooms with private baths, a large front porch, and a gazebo in the garden. Guests may have breakfast served in bed or eat in the main dining room. Rooms range from $55 to $125.

Country House Bed and Breakfast, 10101 Oakview Road, ☎ 405-794-4008, a mile east of Lake Stanley Draper. If you're celebrating a special occasion, ask for the honeymoon suite – it has a heart-shaped Jacuzzi. Fresh fruit and Godiva chocolates will be in your room when you arrive. Breakfast is served by candlelight on Spode china, either in your room or on the balcony. Rooms rent in the $50 to $150 range.

Willow Way Bed and Breakfast, 27 Oakwood Drive, ☎ 405-427-2133, fax 405-427-8907. If you're looking for a unique experience, ask to stay in the "Glass House," a fantastic greenhouse away from the main house. Conventional rooms with private baths are inside the two-story English Tudor country house, but the greenhouse is truly an adventure. All guests are served a gourmet breakfast each morning near a large picture window. Rooms rent for $50-$150.

■ Where to Eat

Some of the best food and ambience are found at Stockyard City, Bricktown, and the Paseo. Of course, the usual chains and imitators serve good meals all over town, but if you want an experience to go with your dinner, head for one of these three districts.

In Stockyard City, the historic $$ **Cattlemen's Steakhouse** charcoal-broils the best cuts of beef in town. Located at 1309 South Agnew, one block south of I-40, the restaurant started as a little coffee shop called Cattlemen's Café in 1910. Cowboys would come in for a cup of strong, black brew, and linger to chat with friends about cattle prices and "tha dang weather." In 1945, Gene Wade won the cafe from its original owner in a spirited crap game, enlarged the building, and began serving steaks a hungry cowboy could sink his teeth into.

When you order a steak here today, you'll know it's been hand cut and aged right on the premises, then cooked over blazing coals. To a cowboy, anytime is the perfect time for a fine steak, so Cattlemen's opens at 6 am every day and cooks up some beef to go with the eggs and grits. The restaurant is open until 10 pm during the week, and until midnight on the weekend. Give 'em a call at ☎ 405-236-0416.

New restaurants are opening and old ones are remodeling on the Paseo, but one establishment is consistently worth a visit. $ **Medina's Coffeehouse & Gallery** has a state-of-the-art cappuccino machine that turns out a wonderful brew. There's a limited lunch selection, but the real standouts are the coffees, cookies, and cakes. Even if the java weren't first-rate, the little coffeehouse deserves a visit because of the art, music, and poetry. The works of Oklahoma artists – including decorative masks created by owner Paul Medina – are displayed on the walls.

On weekends, a variety of ready-to-hit-the-big-time musicians perform, and Wednesday nights poets read their poems. And always, there is coffee – delicious, fresh-roasted, just-brewed, Oklahoma-grown coffee. There's a bar, if you prefer, but most customers don't leave without a steaming cup of their favorite drink. Medina's opens at 9 am every day except Sunday and Monday. On Sunday the hours are noon until midnight. Monday, they're closed. During the week, things close down about midnight, but on the weekends it's about 2 am before the last customer leaves. Call ahead to find out who's playing or reading, ☎ 405-524-7949.

Bricktown is about eating – and drinking, and making merry – so there's no shortage of restaurants. The best plan is to park at the Santa Fe Garage after the work crowd has gone home, take the shuttle down to Bricktown, and stroll-n-sniff your way to dinner. The aromas wafting up the street will rev up your appetite, then you can follow your cravings to the perfect meal. If you can't decide, make it a progressive dinner. Cocktails at one place, appetizers at another, until you waddle back to your car after a to-die-for dessert.

You can't go wrong with the $ **Spaghetti Warehouse** at Sheridan and Broadway, ☎ 405-235-0402. For under $10 you can fill up on pasta, garlic bread, and atmosphere. Dress is casual, and the kids have a special menu of their own. Open at 11 am for lunch, the Warehouse closes at 10 pm during the week and 11pm on weekends.

$$ **Bricktown Brewery**, around the corner at 1 North Oklahoma Avenue, is one of the largest brewpubs in the nation. The Copperhead Amber Ale is a perennial favorite, but there are always three to five fresh brews on tap each day. You can't buy it anywhere else, and you can't take it with you, so try a couple of different flavors. There's also a variety of food items ranging from burgers to fresh fish, and even a kid's menu. The Brewery is open from 11 am to midnight during the week, and to 2 am on Friday and Saturday. Phone ☎ 405-232-2739 to ask what's in the vats on the day you plan to visit.

If you order the Cajun Crab Boil at $/$$ **Crabtown**, 303 East Sheridan, your dinner will be spread out in front of you on butcher paper. You just lean over, rest your elbows on the table, and chow down. Delicious.

There are also other crab dishes plus some fresh fish and non seafood items. The doors open at 11 am every day, and the cigar-smoking, cognac-sipping crowd stays on in the Cigar Room until late into the night. ☎ 405-23-CRABS for information about off-track wagering and other activities related in no way to crabs.

There are many other choices in Bricktown. A couple of great Mexican restaurants, a coffeehouse, a burger place, a pizza parlor – something to please everyone. If you're in town a while, consider making several trips to this area, even if you just stop in for a freshly brewed glass of beer or cup of coffee.

Two other restaurants are worthy of mention because of their popularity with the locals. $/$$ **The County Line**, ☎ 405-478-4955, at 1226 Northeast 63rd Street, opens every day at 11 am, and lists their barbecue menu on a Big Chief writing tablet. How simple could it be? The servings are large, and come with a loaf of fresh bread and down-home-good side dishes. $$ **Applewoods**, ☎ 405-947-8484, at I-40 south of Reno and east of Meridian, has a Sunday brunch, fresh-from-the-oven baked goods, and some health-wise menu choices. Closed mid-afternoon, they are open for the lunch and dinner hours every day.

■ Where to Shop

 If you're into antiques – or if you just like to snoop through other people's old stuff – Oklahoma City has some remarkable shops. Between Northwest 9th and Northwest 36th Streets, 350 dealers sell from 19 shops clustered along May Avenue. The old May Theater is the landmark location, but other shops extend down the street and around the corner on Northwest 10th. **The Buckboard** at 1411 North May has 500 quilts displayed in 10 rooms, ☎ 405-943-7020; **Trademark Historical** at 2800 Northwest 10th inside **Crow's Nest Mall** has an extensive collection of military items, ☎ 405-947-4343; and inside May's you'll find everything from fine-wood furniture to music boxes, ☎ 405-947-3800.

On Western Avenue, north of 63rd Street, another group of shops lines both sides of the street. Both **Jody Kerr** at 7908 North Western, ☎ 405-842-5951, and **Sara Treadway** 7632 North Western, ☎ 405-840-2894, handle antique furniture and porcelain. **Arthur Graham** at 7118 North Western, ☎ 405-843-4431, sells imports from England. Just south, at 1433 Northwest Expressway, **The Antique Centre**, ☎ 405-

842-0070, houses 50 fine dealers in a 15,000-square-foot mall. The specialty here is American and European furniture and a huge variety of collectibles.

South of The Antique Centre on North Western between 42nd and 51st Street, **The Colonies** has a tea room called **The Boston Tea Party**, ☎ 405-842-3477, inside its 13,000-square-foot mall. The tea room is New England quaint and proper – cloth tablecloths, flavored teas, soup, sandwiches, and nice desserts. The mall itself houses dealers of antiques and gifts.

Other individual shops are scattered around town, and the Convention and Visitors Bureau will send lists and information if you call them at ☎ 800-225-5652.

Twice a year, **"An Affair of the Heart"** arts and crafts show takes place at the Oklahoma City Fairgrounds, Northwest 10th at May Avenue, ☎ 800-755-5488. This three-day indoor event, usually in February and October, has more than 1,000 exhibitors offering every imaginable type of craft, antique, and collectable. The $4 admission covers entry to all building during every day of the show.

Old Paris Flea Market, ☎ 405-670-2611, is held in 124,000 square feet of air-conditioned shopping space at 1111 South Eastern just off I-40 on Saturday and Sunday from 9 am to 6 pm. More than 400 dealers offer

Native American artifacts are displayed and sold throughout the state.
(Lynne M. Sullivan)

unusual gifts, collectibles, and new or pre-owned furniture, jewelry, hobby supplies, and plants. Admission is free, and a little bit of everything is for sale.

The Choctaw Indian Trading Post, 1500 North Portland, six blocks northwest of the Fairgrounds, ☎ 405-947-2490, is the oldest Indian store in the city. People come from all over the world to view the unique collections of authentic Native American goods and artifacts. The trading post is open Monday through Saturday from 10 am to 6 pm, and Sunday from 1 pm to 5 pm. Navajo rugs, Kachina dolls, handmade beadwork, sand paintings, and handwoven baskets are a few of the most popular wares.

The best new-stuff shopping is at the indoor malls. **Crossroads Mall** at I-35 and I-240, and **Penn Square Mall** at 1901 Northwest Expressway, each have 140 stores including J.C. Penney and Dillard's. **50 Penn Place** on Northwest Highway at Pennsylvania has upscale stores such as Talbots and Williams-Sonoma.

■ Touring Nearby Towns

Norman

Norman is 19 miles south of Oklahoma City, but the two towns overflow into each other so subtly that you may not know when you cross from one into the other. **The University of Oklahoma** is here, and its presence is seen and felt all over town. Besides taking up 3,000 acres of prime real estate just east of I-35, the university has influenced the development of first-class museums, art exhibits, cultural events, and a rabid Sooner fever that grips residents and students each Fall.

❐ What to See & Do

 Get organized by stopping at the Convention and Visitors Bureau in the old **Santa Fe Depot**, downtown at 200 South Jones, ☎ 405-366-8095 or 800-767-7260. The train station is a nationally registered historic building constructed in 1909, but the first train chugged through "Norman's Camp" in 1887 – two years before the land run. Today, Norman is Oklahoma's third largest city, and there is plenty to keep you busy for a day or two.

See the university first. It's the heart and soul of the town. Traveling south on I-35, reach **The University of Oklahoma** by exiting east at Lindsay Street, then turning north toward campus on Chautauqua. Find parking by turning right onto Boyd and looking for Jacobson Hall at the corner of Boyd and University. The Visitor Center is inside. A parking lot is behind Boyd House, the president's home. Students lead tours Monday through Friday at 2 pm, but, unless you're a prospective freshman, you will probably prefer to pick up a map and amble about on your own. In spring and summer, the flower gardens are gorgeous, especially around Van Vleet Oval. Kids like to walk through a dorm and have a snack at the student union. If you've been-there-done-that, just stroll and soak up the spirit.

Norman offers small-town charm left over from a provocative past. (Lynne M. Sullivan)

Then it's on to **The Fred Jones Jr. Museum of Art** on the campus at 410 West Boyd and Elm Street, ☎ 405-325-3272. This is one of the best university art museums in the country, so there's a great deal to see. Pay special attention to the Native American works by a group of talented Kiowa artists who were brought to the university to study painting in the 1920s. These students became well known as the **Kiowa Five** when their work was displayed internationally, and they are credited with being the founders of modern Native American painting.

The art professor who took charge of the Kiowa Five when they arrived from Anadarko was Oscar B. Jacobson. His former home, **The Jacobson House**, at 609 Chautauqua and Boyd, ☎ 405-366-1667, is now an art center listed on the National Register of Historic Places. The permanent art collection is outstanding, and guest exhibits appear often. Besides paintings, the center displays examples of Native American music, poetry, photography, sculpture, and crafts, Tuesday through Saturday from 1 pm to 5 pm. Admission is free.

Another nationally registered historic house is located at 508 North Peters. This Queen Anne-style house was built in 1900 by an investor named William Moore – at a cost of $5,000, when a typical family home ran about $400. The Lindsay family bought the house in 1908, and the structure was known as the **Moore-Lindsay House** until 1973, when the city of Norman bought it and turned it into **The Cleveland County Historical House**. Gables, stained glass windows, carved woodwork, a turret, and a grand staircase make this house an architectural treasure. It is open to the public free of charge on Wednesday and Saturday from 10 am to 5 pm.

If you came to shop, try **Campus Corner**, covering five blocks north of the university. This is a terrific place to pick up OU souvenirs and unusual gifts. The major department stores are at **Sooner Fashion Mall** off I-35 at the Main Street exit, ☎ 405-360-0360. Most of the antique shops and flea markets are in the downtown area on Main Street between Flood and Porter.

The United Design Corporation south of Norman in Noble (south on I-35 to SH-9, east to US-77, then south two miles to the factory, which is on the west side of the highway) makes well-known, unique, and adorable figurine critters sold all over the country. Each animal is sculpted, molded, cold cast, and painted by master craftsmen using a technique perfected by two Oklahoma University students more than 15 years ago. The process takes several months and allows an amazing amount of detail to survive the heat of the kiln. Tours of the factory are given at 10 am and 1 pm Monday through Friday, and the gift shop is open Monday through Friday from 9 am to 5 pm and also from 10 am to 4 pm the first Saturday of the month. Call ☎ 405-872-7131 to arrange group tours or verify times.

Lake Thunderbird and **Thunderbird State Park** (formerly called **Little River State Park**) is 12 miles east of Norman on SH-9. A new feature here is the lake hut, an elevated form of camping. Eight log structures are located in a wooded area on the eastern shores of the 6,000-acre lake, and more are planned. Each hut has a wooden floor, paneled walls, ceiling fans, a screened back porch, electricity, and a fireplace. No kitchen. No bathroom. No running water. No furniture. This is camping, after all. You bring a sleeping bag or cot, cook outside on the grill, and pump your own water. All for $25 a night with a two-night minimum on weekends. Call ☎ 405-360-3572 up to a year in advance for reservations.

Tent and RV camping also is available on the east side of the lake at Little Axe and Post Oak campgrounds. On the north shore, try **Indian Point Campground**, and on the south, you can camp at Clear Bay. Each area has its good points, and there are swimming beaches and boat launches nearby.

There are short nature trails at Indian Point Campground on the north shore and Clear Bay, and a 4½-mile multi-use trail that loops from Area A Campground at Clear Bay to the south dam. If you're hiking, start at the trailhead near Campground A – bikes are not allowed to enter there. Obviously, if you're on a bike, start at the trailhead near the dam. When you get near Clear Bay, there will be signs directing bikers to the nearby roads. At times, the ranger station off SH-9 is out of maps. Avoid delays by calling ahead to ask the park office for maps and information, ☎ 405-360-3572.

Another way to explore the lake and park is on horseback. **Thunderbird Riding Stables** on SH-9 offers trail rides through 500 acres of wooded trails for $9 per hour. Call ☎ 405-321-5768 for information or reservations.

Westwood Park Golf Course, 2400 Westport Drive, ☎ 405-321-0433, is an 18-hole course with 6015 total yards and a slope rating of 108. Green fees are $13.98 daily. There are also tennis courts, a swimming pool, and a restaurant in the park.

❑ Where to Stay

A number of pleasant chain motels are located around town, but if you want an overnight experience, stay at an historic bed & breakfast.

The Holmberg House, 766 DeBarr Avenue, ☎ 405-321-6221, fax 405-321-6221, was built in 1914 by Fredrik Holmberg, the first dean of the University of Oklahoma College of Fine Arts. There are four guest rooms with private baths upstairs and a parlor and dining room downstairs. The rooms are furnished with period craft-style pieces, and a full breakfast is served each morning. Rates range from $65 to $85.

The Montford Inn, 322 West Tonhawa, ☎ 405-321-2200 or 800-321-8969, fax 405-321-8347, was built new in the historic prairie-style in 1993 with 10 guest rooms in the large, two-story main house and two suites in a cottage across the street. All the rooms have a private bath, fireplace and cable TV, but some furnishings date from the early 1900s to provide an historic ambience. Prices are from $75 to $125.

Whispering Pines, 7820 East Highway 9, ☎ 405-447-0202, is another built-new-to-look-old inn set on 20 acres. There are four rooms with private baths, a large indoor hot tub, and a pond shaded by tall pines and oak trees. A full breakfast is served. Rates are $75 to $125.

Cutting Garden Bed and Breakfast, 927 West Boyd Street, ☎ 405-329-4522. You will be tempted to spend most of your time outdoors at this B&B surrounded by an acre of beautiful gardens. Inside, there are three rooms with queen-size beds and private baths. A hearty, health-conscious breakfast is served each morning, featuring fresh herbs from the garden. Room rates are $55 to $75.

❒ Where to Eat

For lunch or dinner, try $ **The Mont** at the corner of Classen and Boyd near the OU campus, ☎ 405-329-3330. Mexican food is popular and the chicken-fried steak is locally famous. $ **Legend's** at 1313 West Lindsey, ☎ 405-329-8888, has a varied menu and homemade desserts. $ **Interurban** at 105 West Main, ☎ 405-364-7942, is both a restaurant and brewpub. Sit outside on the patio and enjoy a wood-fired brick oven pizza and freshly brewed beer. If you're not sure what you're hungry for, cruise through **Campus Corner** north of Boyd Street between University and Jenkins. There are outdoor cafés, pubs, and ethnic restaurants serving everything from German to Chinese.

Shawnee

State Highway 9 goes east from Norman to Shawnee and Tecumseh. The two towns waged a nasty little name-calling, morals-challenging, 23-year battle for the right to be known as the county seat of Pottawatomie County. Finally, in 1930, the Supreme Court shouted "enough already" and declared Shawnee the title holder. As a result, Shawnee has all the interesting tourist stops.

❒ What to See & Do

An amazing quilt is on display at the **Chamber of Commerce Office**, ☎ 405-275-9780, downtown at 131 North Bell. Members of the "Spinning Spools" quilting guild made the quilt,

In downtown Shawnee.
(Lynne M. Sullivan)

which depicts 30 of the city's historic homes and buildings. Once you see the quilt, you'll want to see the real structures, and the chamber office has brochures and maps to guide you.

The **Santa Fe Depot Museum** is worthy of a drive-by, and memorabilia fans will want to stop for a while. Off US-177 take the Farrel Avenue exit, continue to Main Street, turn left; after four blocks begin looking for the depot on the north side of the street. It's a stunning Romanesque Revival structure built in 1903 of limestone imported from Bedford, Indiana, with a tower displaying the Santa Fe Railroad logo rising 40 feet above the roof line.

Inside, every corner is filled with a mix of relics including antique doctors' equipment, dolls, Indian arrowheads and ceremonial pipes, railroad engineer uniforms and timetables, and a pump organ that survived a tornado in 1924. The museum is open Tuesday through Friday from 10 am to 4 pm and Saturday from 2 pm to 4 pm. There is no admission fee, but the Pottowatomie County Historical Society appreciates all donations. For information, ☎ 405-275-8412.

Snoops will want to stop at **The Beard Cabin** north of the depot, on the corner of Broadway and Highland, in the middle of Woodland Park. The town's first postmaster, Etta Ray, built this home in 1891 and later shared it with her husband, Henry Beard, who was Shawnee's first mayor. The two-story house is furnished with interesting old household articles such as a pie safe, stove, spinning wheel, rocking chair, and bed. Visit the cabin free of charge on Tuesday through Friday from 10 am to 4 pm and weekends from 2 pm to 4 pm. ☎ 405-275-8412 for information.

St. Gregory's College, on West MacArthur off US-177, is a lovely little campus with an unlikely pyramid-inspired building which houses an even more unlikely collection of Egyptian artifacts – including two mummies. There's also an enjoyable display of Renaissance paintings,

American landscapes, and Native American art, but the Egyptian collection is the most fascinating. Princess Menne, one of the mummies, is wrapped and hanging next to X-ray proof that someone's really in there. She probably lived between 400 and 300 BC, and how she came to be hanging around Shawnee, Oklahoma is an interesting tale.

Father Gregory Gerrer

St. Gregory's College evolved from a mission started in Indian Territory in 1876 by monks from the Benedictine order. When the railroad came through Shawnee early in the 20th century, the college was moved close by. One of the first priests, Father Gregory Gerrer, was a free-spirit who liked to play the clarinet while riding a bucking bronco before he became a monk. Art became one of his priestly passions, and he put together an extensive collection – including rare Egyptian pieces –that grew into the **Mabee-Gerrer Museum and Gallery**. The museum is open from 1 pm to 4 pm Tuesday through Sunday. Admission is free, but donations are welcome. The phone number is ☎ 405-878-5300.

Oklahoma City

The Potawatomi Tribal Museum is south of downtown on tribal grounds at 1901 South Gordon Cooper Drive. Stop in to see artifacts of the Potawatomi Nation, whose name means "People of the Place of the Fire." Admission is free and there is a gift shop with Native American articles. ☎ 405-275-3121 or 800-880-9880.

North of town, on SH-18 (exit 186), three buildings hold 242 antique and special cars at **Bob Townsend's Antique and Classic Cars**. Mr. Townsend began collecting cars 40 years ago, and his museum holds Mae West's 1938 V-16 Cadillac, Elvis Presley's 1956 Lincoln Mark II V-8, a 1901 Oldsmobile, and a 1906 Maxwell Roadster. Admission for adults is $3, but only $2 if you're a senior citizen or part of a car club group. Groups can make appointments for a tour, but the museum is open to the public Friday, Saturday, and Monday from noon to 6 pm, ☎ 405-275-1930 or 405-273-0330.

Firelake Golf Course, 1901 South Gordon Cooper Drive, ☎ 405-275-4471, is an 18-hole course with total yardage of 6,211 and a slope rating of 121. Weekday green fees are $13.50, but fees vary on weekends and holidays, so call for information.

❏ Where to Stay & Eat

 A large shopping mall is north of Shawnee, south of Townsend's car museum, on I-40 between SH-18 and US-177. Small shops offer antiques and unique gifts in the downtown area. Stop for lunch or an afternoon break at $ **Country Indulgence Tea Room and Bakery**, 12 East Main, Tuesday through Saturday from 10:30 am to 2:30 pm, ☎ 405-275-4544.

The best overnight is offered at **Mayne Harber Inn**, 2401 East Highland, ☎ 405-275-4700. This colonial-style home with four bedrooms, private baths, a wood-burning fireplace, swimming pool and Jacuzzi tub serves a gourmet breakfast each morning. There is a choice of king, queen, or twin beds. Room rates are $75 to $175.

Most of the chain hotels are clustered around the junction of SH-18 and I-40, near the shopping mall. Contact the **Convention and Visitor Bureau** at ☎ 405-275-9780 for information and phone numbers.

Edmond & Arcadia

❏ What to See & Do

 The historic **Round Barn** has been restored, and Route 66 is a popular alternative for "shunpikers" who don't want to pay a toll. So the little town of Arcadia, north of Oklahoma City and east of Edmond, is trying hard to regain its former life. For years, the round red barn on Route 66 was a landmark and happening place with barn dances, cookouts, and festivals. When the roof fell in, it sat abandoned for years, before a community effort restored it and won a National Preservation Award. Now the four-story barn is used to design and produce Round Barn/Route 66 souvenirs such as T-shirts and coffee mugs. Visitors can tour the barn Tuesday through Sunday from 10 am to 5 pm, ☎ 405-396-2398.

Nanitta Daisey

The town of Edmond had an interesting beginning. When the land run began in 1889, a woman named Nanitta Daisey who worked with *The Dallas Morning News* in Texas rode on the cowcatcher attached to the front of a Santa Fe Railway train engine as it chugged through unassigned land. When the train approached a little cattle-watering stop called Edmond, she jumped from the front of the engine, planted a stake in a plot of ground, fired a gun in celebration, then raced back to the slow-moving train where she was hoisted aboard.

Today, the town, which is west of Arcadia Lake and about 15 miles north of Oklahoma City, is a shady, upscale community with several golf courses, a fast-growing university, quaint downtown shops, and a whole range of interesting new restaurants.

Lake Arcadia is within the Edmond city limits and owned and operated by that city, but it's only 2½ miles north of Turner Turnpike in far northeast Oklahoma City. The terrain is wooded and rolling, and the lake covers part of old Route 66. Since swimming is not allowed in Oklahoma City lakes, residents flock to Arcadia's three sandy beaches on summer weekends. Each year before Memorial Day, 500 tons of sand is brought in from area rivers and spread along the lake shore.

The park has campsites, picnic tables, volleyball courts, playgrounds, and restrooms. Sailing is popular, and a regatta is sponsored by the Edmond Chamber of Commerce the first weekend of August each year. The lake is stocked with catfish, bluegill, sunfish, and largemouth bass, and you can fish from the shore or launch a boat. Either way, watch for deer, opossums, red-winged blackbirds, and woodpeckers.

A multi-use trail winds along the north shore, parallel to Route 66 through Central and Edmond Parks, then crosses Spring Creek and heads south to the fee booth at **Spring Creek Park**. Mountain bikers and hikers share the trail that runs 7½ miles one way and varies from wide-and-easy to narrow-and-difficult. Get maps and trailhead directions at entrances to the parks, or ☎ 405-396-8122. Admission is $6 per vehicle, but you pay only $1 per person if you walk or bike in.

Campsites are available on a first-come basis for $8 to $15. There are only 145 spaces, and on holidays and summer weekends they fill early.

Take I-35 north from Oklahoma City to 15th Street in Edmond. The entrance booth is on the right as you enter Spring Creek Park. Another entrance is located on Historic Route 66 about a mile east of I-35.

Coffee Creek Golf Course, 4000 North Kelly Avenue in Edmond, ☎ 405-340-4653, is an 18-hole golf course with a total yardage of 6,600 and a slope rating of 129. Green fees Monday through Thursday are $17.50; $27.25 with cart. Friday through Sunday and holidays, the green fees are $23.75; $33.50 with cart.

❏ Where to Stay & Eat

Arcadian Inn Bed and Breakfast, 328 East First in Edmond, ☎ 405-348-6347, is an historical Victorian-style home. The six guest rooms have private baths – some with Jacuzzi tubs – and the house features a large front porch, outdoor spa, and cable television. The Zeimer Master Suite has a four-poster bed, fireplace, and a crystal chandelier hanging over a double Jacuzzi. It's perfect for any special occasion. A full breakfast is served each morning in the dining room or in your guest room. Call ☎ 405-348-6347 or 800-299-6347 for reservations. Room rates begin at $85.

Across the street, $ **Hillbillies 66 Café**, ☎ 405-396-8177, serves fried chicken and chicken-fried steak, followed by homemade fruit cobbler. There's usually some sort of band playing foot-tappin' music. If you're too full to drive on, you can rent a rustic cabin out back and wake the next morning to a full country breakfast.

Guthrie

❏ What to See & Do

Farther north on I-35, the town of Guthrie is a history nut's dream, with over a thousand pre-1910 houses and 22 blocks of commercial buildings listed on the National Register of Historic Places. Everything, everywhere appears antique, and stained glass seems to fill every window frame. All of this terrific "old stuff" was built from 1890 to 1910, when Guthrie was the capital of Oklahoma Territory and then the state of Oklahoma. It has survived in top condition because the town was deserted in a flash when Governor Charles N. Haskell moved the state seal from Guthrie to Oklahoma City on the night of June 11, 1910 and proclaimed the Lee Huckins Hotel the new capitol.

Though the governor was backed by a solid popular vote, the words "stolen" and "pilfered" come up often when residents of Guthrie talk about that night. But the fact is, losing the state capital turned out to be a huge advantage to preservationists. Over the years, no one has pressured the town to tear down the old to make room for the new, and as a result, 400 city blocks containing 2,169 buildings cover 1,400 acres – to make up the largest contiguous urban historical district on the National Register. Get a map from the **Convention and Visitor's Bureau** by calling ☎ 405-282-1948 or 800-299-1889 or dropping by 212 West Oklahoma Avenue. Then drive or walk around town on your own, or take a trolley tour.

Guthrie has the largest urban district listed on the National Register of Historic Places, with more than 1,000 Victorian buildings. (Lynne M. Sullivan)

Mahogany and brass trollies give 45-minute tours on the hour from 10 am to 5 pm, Monday through Saturday, and on the quarter-hour from 1:15 pm to 5:15 pm on Sunday. Tickets are $2 for adults and $1 for senior citizens and kids. **First Capital Trolley** is located at 1st Street and Vilas Avenue, and you can park at a lot on the corner of 1st Street and Harrison.

❑ Golf

Cimarron National Golf Club, one mile west of Guthrie on SH-33, ☎ 405-282-7888, is a 36-hole double course with driving range, putting greens, and club rentals. The Aqua Canyon Course has a total of 6,500 yards and a slope rating of 112. Cimarron National Course has a total of 6,600 yards and a slope rating of 118. Green fees on both courses are $12 on weekdays and $16 on weekends and holidays.

Cedar Valley Golf Club, 210 Par Avenue, seven miles west of Guthrie on SH-33, ☎ 405-282-7529, is a 36-hole double course with a driving range, club rentals, a pro shop, and putting greens. The Augusta Course has 6,602 total yards with a slope rating of 108. The International Course has 6,520 total yards and a slope rating of 112. Green fees on weekdays are $11; $12 on weekends and holidays.

❐ Where to Stay

 When all the museums and buildings start to look the same, stop at one of the town's inns for the night. Guthrie is the undisputed "Bed and Breakfast Capital of Oklahoma," with more than a dozen renovated turn-of-the-century houses to choose from. Get a list from the **Bed and Breakfast Association of Guthrie**, ☎ 405-282-7497, or contact the **Oklahoma Bed and Breakfast Association** at ☎ 800-676-5522. Several inns host special programs such as murder-mystery weekends or Victorian weekends.

Harrison House Inn, 124 West Harrison, ☎ 405-282-1000 or 800-375-1001, is known as the pride of Guthrie. Thirty rooms are named for people and groups related to the city and decorated with historical items. A hearty breakfast is served to guests each morning. Rooms are $65 to $100.

Rosewood Manor, 401 East Cleveland Avenue, ☎ 405-282-8431, has gorgeous woodwork interiors and lovely stained glass. Rooms with private bath are $70 to $85.

$$/The Seely House, 701 East Mansur, ☎ 405-282-8889, was moved and renovated in 1987, but it was built in 1893. Rooms with private bath are about $60. The Honeymoon Cottage is in the $125 range.

The Victorian Rose, 415 East Cleveland, ☎ 405-282-3928, was built in 1894 in the Queen Ann style. Rooms with queen-sized beds and private baths are $60 to $90 and include a three-course breakfast. Ask about the Victorian Package for special occasions.

❐ Where to Eat

When downtown, try one of these restaurants on West Harrison.

$ Granny Had One, at 113 West Harrison, has wonderful home cooking and sinful desserts, ☎ 405-282-4482. Serving Monday through Saturday from 11 am to 9 pm and Sunday from 11 am to 3 pm, the place is known to have karaoke well into the early morning hours on weekends.

$$/$$$ George's, at 202 West Harrison in the Victor Building, serves an elegant dinner accompanied by piano music, Thursday through Saturday from 6 pm to 9 pm, ☎ 405-282-1000.

$ Daily Grind, 212 West Harrison, ☎ 405-282-4960, serves basic, delicious, high-quality meals at low prices. Hours are Monday through Friday from 7:30 am to 2 pm.

$$ 5W's Sunrise Ranch, southeast of Guthrie, ☎ 405-282-2605, runs a 12-person bunkhouse. There's no running water or electricity, but a cowboy-sized breakfast is served in the morning. The cost is $50 per person. This is a true adventure for groups or family reunions. Even if you can't handle the bunkhouse, you can schedule a hayride/cookout ($10 to $20 per person) or a horseback ride ($10 per person).

Oklahoma City

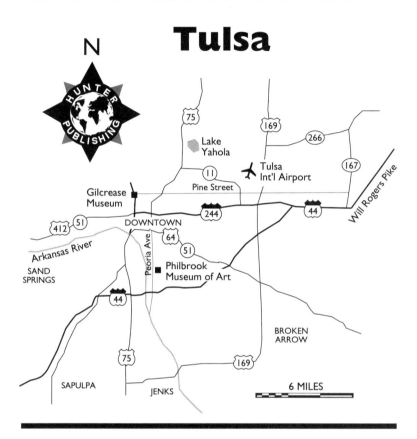

Tulsa

Tulsa

Tulsa is a beautiful city of culture and grace, due mainly to its former status as "Oil Capital of the World." First-class museums. Gorgeous gardens and parks. Unmatched architecture. It all glistens with wealth made possible by oil.

The city is noted among architecture fans as "Deco Mecca" because of its excellent examples of three types of art deco design. "Zigzag" is a style popular in the 1920s, when Tulsa began an oil-induced $1 million-a-month building boom exemplified by the grand lobbies and towers still standing downtown. "PWA" style took over when the depression brought frivolity to a halt all over the country and the Public Works Administration gave people jobs building sturdy structures such as Union Depot and Will Rogers High School. "Streamline" is the familiar style of rounded corners and horizontal lines fashioned after modes of transportation in the early 1940s; it has survived in local gas stations and private homes.

Pick up a walking-tour map at the **Convention and Visitors Bureau** (616 South Boston, Suite 100, ☎ 918-585-1201) and follow its directions to the many "deco'd-out" buildings built between the two world wars. Tulsa is so compact and well-planned, out-of-towners quickly grasp the layout and zip around like natives. Downtown, east-west streets are numbered, north-south streets are named for major US cities – in alphabetical order, with Main Street standing in for the Mississippi River, so eastern cities are east of Main and western cities are west of Main. It couldn't be simpler.

■ Touring

Tulsey Town

When the Creek Nation set up housekeeping in Indian Territory in 1836, they called their little settlement "tallasi" which means "town." Tallasi quickly became Tulsey on the white man's tongue, and, when the first federal post office was built in 1879, the name was dignified to "Tulsa."

You'll find a grand choice of attractions here, and two of the most impressive are the garden/museums of **Gilcrease** and **Philbrook**. These gorgeously landscaped buildings are so doubly spectacular, it's difficult to decide whether to spend more time indoors or out.

Gilcrease Museum is a rambling, modern-day structure on a knoll overlooking the Osage Hills. Next door, the historic home of oilman Thomas Gilcrease serves as headquarters for the Tulsa Historical Society, and the surrounding 440 acres encompass Stuart Park. The entire compound is captivating. Inside, the museum holds one of the best collections of Western art in the country, including work by Frederic Remington, Charles Russell and George Catlin. Several galleries show off art and artifacts dating from 500 BC to the present, and rotating exhibits make this a place you can return to often. On your first visit, try to arrive for the daily 2 pm tour. This free guided walk-through will orient you to what's available and point out the most important pieces of art. If you covet a particular painting, buy a print in the Museum Shop.

Gilcrease Museum.

Standing on the grassy front lawn of the museum, you can see Tulsa's skyline through the trees. Historic theme gardens connect around the grounds, and walking paths wind down through shady Stuart Park. Lunch and Sunday brunch are served in the Rendezvous Restaurant until 2 pm every day except Monday, and you can call ☎ 918-596-2720 for reservations. There's no charge for visiting either the museum or grounds, but a $3 donation is recommended for each adult. The estate is located at the west end of Pine Road at 1400 Gilcrease Museum Road (25th West Avenue on older maps); the museum is open Monday through Saturday from 9 am to 5 pm (until 8 pm on Thursday), and from 1pm to 5 pm on Sunday and federal holidays. ☎ 918-596-2700 for information.

While you're in the neighborhood, stop at the mansion at 628 North Country Club Drive (south on Gilcrease Museum Road, east on Edison past the Tulsa Country Club golf course, north on Country Club Drive) to see the **Ida Dennie Willis Museum**. You don't have to be a child to love this collection of toys – mostly dolls. Anyone who's ever collected anything will recognize the loving attention given to every detail. If you're not a collector now, you probably will be after Ms. Willis gives you the $3 tour. Allow about an hour when you stop in. It's open Wednesday through Saturday from 10:30 am to 4:30 pm. Call ☎ 918-584-6654 for more information.

The Italianate villa and extensive gardens of Villa Philbrook were home to
Waite and Genevieve Phillips from 1927 to 1938. Donated to the city in 1938,
it became Tulsa's first art museum.

Villa Philbrook was built in 1928 in the Italian Renaissance style as a private residence for Waite Phillips, one of Tulsa's richest oilmen. After living in the mansion with his wife, Genevieve, for 11 years, Phillips donated his home to the city to be used as an art museum. Today, **Philbrook Museum of Art** is one of only three public museums in the country which are also historic homes and lavish gardens.

Arriving at Philbrook is as pleasant as actually touring it. The museum is situated in a lovely neighborhood full of interesting homes on spacious lawns. Classy. Chic. The fragrance of old money dipped in oil whiffs through the air. Turn east onto 27th Place off Peoria Avenue and cruise down the block until it dead-ends at Rockford Road and the Philbrook parking lot. The museum is open Tuesday through Saturday from 10 am to 5 pm (8 pm on Thursday) and Sunday from 11 am to 5 pm.

In 1990, the new Kravis Wing was added to the original mansion, and the combined galleries display an international collection of art. Philbrook's publicity declares the museum is "our window on the world," because the exhibits give visitors insight into the culture of each represented country. One $4 admission allows you to tour both the mansion, which is beautifully furnished with many of its original pieces, and the Kravis Wing.

Twenty-three acres of landscaped grounds surround the museum, and there is no charge to wander along the flagstone paths leading to formal gardens and ponds. Bring your camera if you don't want to look like a tourist. This is a favorite spot among the locals for special occasion portraits. The Museum Shop features guidebooks, fine gifts, and souvenirs. An upscale restaurant overlooking the gardens serves lunch and Sunday brunch. You can make reservations by calling ☎ 918-748-5367. For information about the art galleries, ☎ 918-749-7941 or 800-324-7941.

In addition to the Gilcrease and Philbrook super-museums, Tulsa has three other collections worthy of a stop.

Fenster Museum of Jewish Art displays a huge collection of Jewish artifacts from the past 4,000 years. The Torah scrolls are marvelous, and the articles recovered from the Holocaust are heartbreaking. If you have questions or want more details about any of the exhibits, the museum staff is friendly and well-informed – and they don't show the slightest impatience when answering one elementary question after another. Park in the lot on the west side of B'nai Emunah Synagogue at 1223 East 17th Place, on the corner of Peoria and 17th Place. A sign directs you to the museum, which is open Sunday through Thursday from 10 am to 4 pm, except on Jewish holidays. There is no admission fee, but donations are always appreciated. ☎ 918-582-3732 for information.

If you've been out rock hunting and haven't found a thing worth keeping, make a humbling visit to Willard Elsing's little place in Oral Roberts University Retirement Village. The **Elsing Museum** is the life-long collection of all sorts of precious gems, minerals, and interesting stones – and Mr. Elsing himself is happy to show you around. Find this treasure in Cottage 28-A at University Village on the ORU campus at 8555 South Lewis off I-44. A small sign in the back of the complex directs you to the museum, which is open Wednesday through Sunday from 1 pm to 4 pm. There is no charge to see the collection, but donations are welcome. ☎ 918-299-2661, extension 628 for information.

While you're on campus, drive down the Avenue of Flags, past the Praying Hands sculpture and the landmark Prayer Tower. The **Visitors Center** inside the tower has maps and shows two slide presentations about the university. If you want more information, call ☎ 918-495-6807.

Mac's Antique Car Museum has a grand collection of vintage cars including LaSalles, Auburns, Rolls-Royces, and a 75-year-old truck called a Tulsa Four Oil Field Runabout. Of the 44 cars on exhibit, the red and black truck manufactured by the Tulsa Automobile Corp. in 1922 is one of the most unusual. Mac McGlumphy, owner of the perfectly restored car collection, also has a 1912 Model T and a Packard valued at $400,000 in his 2,000-square-foot building at 1319 East Fourth Street, a block east of Peoria. The museum is open on Saturday and Sunday from noon until 5 pm. Admission is $3.75 for adults and $2 for children. ☎ 918-583-7400 for more information.

The Tulsa Zoo is among those nationally recognized as a living museum, which means its exhibits integrate the animals with their natural environment. The 15,000-square-foot Tropical American Rain Forest, the newest addition to the zoo, is an outstanding example of this concept of integration. Visitors step into the exhibit and immediately see, hear, and feel the rain forest – 85% humidity, colorful birds chirping, 250 species of plants giving off heady oxygen, and 500 types of creatures swimming and slinking about. Two of the biggest "slinkers" are Tikal and Ix-chel, a husband-and-wife pair of rare black jaguars.

Admission to the Rain Forest is included in the zoo's general ticket, which costs $5 for adults, $4 for seniors, and $2 for kids. Another part of the 70-acre zoo includes the Robert J. LaFortune buildings, a representation of four different geographical regions on the American continent: desert, Arctic tundra, forest, and lowlands. The zoo is open daily from 10 am to 5 pm, ☎ 918-669-6600.

■ Adventures

Lakes, Parks, Trails & Golf Courses

The Tulsa Zoo is just one part of 2,800-acre **Mohawk Park** which also includes the 800-acre **Oxley Nature Center**, two golf courses, a polo field, and multi-use trails. Find this spread at 36th Street North and Sheridan Road, ☎ 918-596-7275. The nature center is on the main park road just past the zoo. Stop inside the building for a trail map and general information, then hike along one of seven trails. Red Fox and Blue Heron Trails are well developed and marked with interpretive signs. The other five trails are more primitive. You can hike the trails daily from 8 am to 5 pm, and the nature center is open Monday through Saturday from 10 am to 4:30 pm and Sunday from noon to 4:30 pm.

More than 80 other parks dot the city, so you're never far from fresh air, green grass, and tall trees. **River Parks** run along both sides of the Arkansas, from 11th Street to 81st Street on the east and from 11th Street to 31st Street on the west. Except during curfew from 11 pm to 5 am, joggers, bikers, and skaters travel the 10-mile trail along the river, crossing from one side to the other on the Pedestrian Bridge built in 1895. A small lake under the bridge is popular for canoeing, and lighted fountains shoot jets of water into the sky above the parks. Several playgrounds, concession stands, and picnic tables are located in the parks, and free weekly starlight concerts are held during the summer. Call the River Parks Authority at ☎ 918-596-2001 for a schedule of events.

LaFortune Park and **Woodward Park** are especially fine spots for hiking, picnicking, or watching the kids play. LaFortune has a pond, garden, and 3.2-mile jogging path. It's located at 5501 South Yale between 51st Street and 61st Street, ☎ 918-596-8627. Woodward, on 21st Street at Peoria, ☎ 918-746-7877, has a rose garden, a creek, and walking paths.

Redbud Valley Nature Preserve is outside the easy-to-locate realm of the city, but it's worth the drive. From town, take US-244 east or I-44 northeast. The two highways merge in the far northeast part of town, and soon after that merge, you will see the 161st Street exit, which you take. Turn left at a stop sign after you exit, and at another after you pass under the highway. Then take a right onto 161st Street and travel north about four miles to the preserve entrance. Beyond the gate, you'll find 80 acres of woods with a variety of trees as well as limestone bluffs with *explorable* caves overlooking grassy prairie. A rugged one-mile trail winds through it all, and you'll make better time if you're wearing hiking boots. The Visitors Center is open from 11 am to 3 pm and the trail is open from 8 am to 5 pm, Wednesday through Sunday. Admission is free. For more information, ☎ 918-669-6460.

Tee times for all **public golf courses** in Tulsa can be made through an automated reservation system at ☎ 918-582-6000 up to a week in advance of play. To check same-day tee time availability, call the individual pro shops listed for each course below.

LaFortune Park Championship Course at 5501 South Yale, is an 18-hole, 6,970-yard course with a par of 72, a slope of 123, and a USGA rating of 72.8. Nearby, and also in LaFortune Park, the 18-hole **Par-3 Course** is short but demanding, and lighted for night play. The park also has a driving range, putting green, club house, and restaurant. For tee times, phone the pro shop at ☎ 918-596-8627. Green fees are $16.19 on the Championship Course and $11.87 on the Par-3 Course. Motor-powered carts rent for $19.43, and pull carts for $3.

Woodbine and **Pecan Valley** are both in **Mohawk Park**, near the Tulsa Zoo and Oxley Nature Center at 36th Street North and Sheridan Road. Woodbine has 6,577 total yards with a par of 72, slope of 115, and USGA rating of 71. Pecan Valley has 6,499 total yards with a par of 70, slope of 124, and USGA rating of 71.6. The park also has a practice green and restaurant. Green fees are $13.60 weekdays, and $15.61 weekends. Motor-powered carts rent for $19.43, and pull carts for $3. Phone the pro shop at ☎ 918-425-6871 for information and same-day tee times.

■ Where to Shop

 The seven blocks between Peoria Avenue and Utica Avenue along 15th Street offer some of the most innovative shops and restaurants in town. The strip is known as **Cherry Street**, the road's original name, and has been converted from a shabby downtown district into a trendy urban restoration. Old buildings with sturdy physiques and classic features have become one-of-a-kind businesses frequented by chic clientele.

Shoppers can browse through specialty stores for the latest music and book releases, an out-of-the-ordinary gift, fashionable clothing, or antique furniture. This is also one of the best streets in town for trendy bakeries, coffee shops, and restaurants. Depending on the time of day and your appetite, try freshly-baked breakfast muffins, Chinese or Mexican cuisine or late-night coffee drinks.

The newest mega-mall experience is at the 540,000-square-foot **Southroads Power Center**, where major department stores and local shops share space with a 20-screen movie theater featuring stadium seating and state-of-the-art projection and sound. Find Southroads at 41st Street and Yale across from the smaller, art deco-style **Promenade Mall**. For information on Southroads, call ☎ 918-587-1700. The number for Promenade Mall is ☎ 918-627-9224.

Probably the most sophisticated stores and restaurants are located in **Utica Square** a little village of upscale shops on tree-lined streets between Utica Avenue and Yorktown Avenue on 21st Street. Special events often take place at the Square, and you can get a list of upcoming activities by phoning ☎ 918-742-5531. **Woodland Hills Mall** has been the sure-to-have-it shopping spot for Tulsa residents and visitors for more than 20 years. You'll find most national retailers here, along with more than 150 smaller shops. Woodland Hills is at 71st Street and Memorial Drive, ☎ 918-250-1449.

The largest selection of boots and jeans in all of Oklahoma is found at **Drysdale's**, 3220 South Memorial. If they don't have the Western wear you're looking for, it probably doesn't exist. There are 100,000 pairs of jeans and 20,000 pairs of boots in the store, plus a huge selection of hats, shirts and Native American jewelry. Call the store at ☎ 918-644-6481.

■ Where to Stay

Hotels

 The Doubletree at Warren Place is so lovely and well managed, it rates four diamonds from the AAA excellence watchdogs. There's a fitness center, indoor pool and sauna, lighted jogging path, and a private lounge for guests on the executive floor. Basic rates are about $150 for a double room, but ask about the special deals at almost half-price, if they are available. Phone for reservations and information at ☎ 918-495-1000. Take the Yale exit off I-44 and drive south to the hotel at 6110 South Yale. Another top-notch Doubletree is downtown at 616 West 7th Street, ☎ 918-587-8000. Both hotels can be booked at ☎ 800-222-8733.

Adams Mark is next to the Tulsa performing Arts Center downtown at 100 East 2nd Street. The amenities are great: indoor-outdoor pool, fitness center, shuttle service to Utica Square, and a ritzy restaurant. Call ☎ 918-582-9000 or 800-444-ADAM for reservations. Rates are in the $125 range, but ask about the weekend specials.

Chain Hotels

Better-than-average chain hotels in the Tulsa area include $$ **The Best Western Trade Winds Central Inn**, ☎ 918-749-5581, $$$ **Sheraton Tulsa**, ☎ 918-627-5000, and the $$ **Holiday Inn East Airport**, ☎ 918-437-7660. $ **La Quinta** has three pleasant hotels at various locations around the city, all in the $50-or-less range, ☎ 800-531-5900.

Bed & Breakfasts

The Lantern Inn, 1348 East 35th Street, is registered with the Oklahoma Bed and Breakfast Association, but it is actually more like an English-style cottage – and no breakfast is served. Whatever you choose to call it – cottage or B&B – it's a delightful little house set on a lovely lawn near a variety of fine shops and restaurants. Guests sleep under handmade quilts, lounge in a claw-foot tub, relax in fluffy robes, and receive vouchers for meals at close-by restaurants. ☎ 918-743-8343 for reservations. $$

Tulsa's Tudor Treasure

The stately McBirney Mansion opened as a Bed and Breakfast/Showhouse in September 1997. Guests can stay overnight any day of the week or tour the 12,000-square-foot landmark on Saturdays from 2 until 4 pm. The Tudor-Gothic home is listed on the National Register of Historic Places and sits atop a hill on three acres of land overlooking the Arkansas River. Built in 1928 for banker James McBirney and his wife Vera, the three-story mansion has been remodeled to provide five luxury suites on the second floor. A 1,600-square-foot ballroom is down one level from the main floor and opens onto a terrace and garden.

Visit the mansion at 1414 S. Galveston or phone ☎ 918-585-3234 for information and reservations. Rates range from $69 to $225.

■ Where to Eat

 Tulsa offers all the typical dining choices of a cosmopolitan city, plus a mixed bag of unique alternatives. Two of the areas known for their hot new or long-time-favorite restaurants are 15th Street, along the stretch referred to as **Cherry Street**, and **Utica Square**. Outstanding menus are also offered at the city's top hotels. Other fine eateries are scattered about town, so you won't go hungry no matter where you find yourself at meal time. The following will give you some ideas.

Cherry Street is lined with restaurants offering a variety of menus and dining styles. Try $$ **Camerelli's**, 1536 East 15th, ☎ 918-582-8900, for

Italian; $$ **Bourbon Street Café**, 1542 East 15th, ☎ 918-583-5555, for New-Orleans-style Cajun; or $ **Big Al's**, 15th and Harvard, ☎ 918-744-5085, for healthy fruit smoothies, sandwiches, and vegetarian meals.

The park-like streets that make up **Utica Square** hold several surprises. $$/$$$ **Polo Grill**, 2038 Utica Square, ☎ 918-744-4280, has soups and salads for a light lunch and grilled seafood, followed by specialty desserts, for a hearty dinner. Try tiny $ **Felini's**,1742 Utica Square, for pasta salad, imaginative sandwiches, and fresh-baked goodies, or $ **Queenie's Plus**, 1834 South Utica Square, ☎ 918-749-3481, for hamburgers or quiche at an outdoor table. $$$ **Capistrano Café**, 1748 Utica Square, ☎ 918-747-2819, is a pleasant bistro with outdoor seating during nice weather.

For a memorable Sunday brunch or special dinner make reservations at $$$ **The Warren Duck Club** in the Doubletree Hotel at Yale and 61st Street. There's an appetizer bar for starters and a dessert bar for a perfect ending. Make reservations at ☎ 918-495-1000. $$$ **Bravo! Ristorante** in the Adams Mark Hotel serves up gourmet Italian food plus songs from famous musicals – both expertly presented by the talented waitstaff. Call for reservations, ☎ 918-582-9000.

■ Touring Nearby Areas

Jenks

 Jenks is only 10 miles south of downtown Tulsa, so it enjoys metropolitan amenities while holding onto its small-town charisma. The brochures claim the city is "Oklahoma's Original Antique Marketplace," a boast supported by a downtown full of craft, gift, and antique stores. Park in the lot at the corner of 2nd Street and A Street, then walk a block south to Main Street where you'll find specialty shops, charming tea rooms, and old-fashioned ice cream parlors. Stop at the Chamber of Commerce on the corner of Main and Elm for maps, brochures, and information, ☎ 918-299-5005.

Get in a round of golf at **South Lakes Golf Course**, an 18-hole championship course with seven lakes, 6,340 total yards, a par of 71, slope of 113 and USGA rating of 68.6. Green fees are $16.19 for 18 holes walking and $19.93 for 18 holes with a cart. Tee times can be made through the Tulsa automated system, ☎ 918-582-6000, or the pro shop at ☎ 918-746-3760.

Extend your stay at $$/**Five Oaks Ranch**, 528 East 121st Street, a large retreat with a big log cabin, a private pond full of fish, and 185 acres of wooded ranch land. The cabin rents for $140 per couple on the weekend, $95 during the week, and breakfast is included. Call for directions and reservations, ☎ 918-298-6405.

Sapulpa

Sapulpa is the Route 66 town famous for **Frankoma Pottery**. Located about 10 minutes by car from downtown Tulsa, the factory is at 2400 Frankoma Road, ☎ 918-224-5511. Visitors are welcome to tour the factory on weekdays from 9:30 am to 2 pm and shop the gift store Monday through Saturday from 9 am to 5 pm or Sunday from 1 pm to 5 pm. During the tour, you'll see oven/dishwasher-proof pottery handcrafted from Oklahoma red clay, then be able to buy the various Western-decorated pieces from the store. Good buys are available on "seconds" as well.

An historic walking tour of the town has been mapped out by the **Chamber of Commerce**, 101 East Dewy, ☎ 918-224-0170. Pick up a map then stroll and browse. If you visit in June, the **Route 66 Blowout** is a must. Classic cars, live music, and a juried art show create an old-fashioned street party downtown. Stay overnight at $$ **The McManor Bed and Breakfast**, 706 South Poplar Street, ☎ 918-224-4665, a two-bedroom/two-bath apartment adjacent to the 1920s Tudor house.

Golfers can play a challenging round at **Sapulpa Golf Course**, located on Route 66 just west of town, ☎ 918-224-0237. The par-70 course has a USGA rating of 71.3, a slope of 123, 6,565 total yards, and water hazards on every hole. Green fees are $12 weekdays and $14 weekends.

Sand Springs

The best outdoor adventure in Sand Springs is a performance of the musical *Oklahoma*. Ten miles west of Tulsa, the little town puts all its talent into producing an outstanding evening, starting with a barbecue dinner in **Discoveryland's** Circle-D Ranch Barn. Pre-show events include snooping through little gift stores for souvenirs, listening to Western music, and watching energetic dancers. Then the outdoor stage comes to life with horses, actors, dancers, and singers, and the night boot-scoots to the sound of Rodgers and Hammerstein. Call ☎ 918-245-6552 for ticket information. The show runs from mid-June to mid-August with dinner from 5:30 pm to 7:30 pm and the main performance beginning at 8 pm. The third Saturday in April **An Herbal Affair** moves into downtown. This is a welcome-back-spring festival featuring almost 100 vendors selling, discussing, and teaching about all things herbal. Check with the Chamber of Commerce for exact dates and information, ☎ 918-246-2560.

Tribal Trivia

- *Cherokee Advocate* was the first Native American newspaper. The inaugural issue was printed in 1828 in both Cherokee and English.
- The Choctaw financed their own removal from Mississippi to Indian Territory in 1831 by selling their farms.
- The Johnston County Courthouse in Tishomingo was originally the capital of the Chickasaw Nation.
- The Kiowa native dress is most often used to represent Native American attire: buckskin clothes, feathered headdress, and beaded moccasins.
- 39 federally recognized tribes are registered in Oklahoma.
- The Osage Reservation is now the only official Indian Reservation in the state.
- Tahlequah has been the Cherokee capital since 1839.
- Sam Houston, the Father of Texas, was an adopted son of the Cherokee Nation in Oklahoma.
- The Kiowa have a reputation for being overly generous, great horsemen, avid hunters, as well as talented artisans and musicians. However, they were once known as the tribe that killed more white men than any other.
- The Cherokee removal from Georgia and North Carolina to Oklahoma required seven different Trails of Tears – all tragic.
- Nomadic tribes, such as the Comanche, Kiowa and Apache, lived in the southwestern part of the state before The Five Civilized Tribes arrived in the early 1800s.
- In 1847, only 16 years after they were forcefully removed from their own farmlands, the Choctaw raised money to aid Irish farmers during the potato famine.
- During the Civil War, the Choctaws and Chickasaws supported the South. The Cherokee, Creeks, and Seminoles divided their allegiance between the North and South.

Tulsa

Northeast Oklahoma

I t's almost impossible to find an uninteresting road in the countryside outside Tulsa. Oil money built glorious treasures in and near the state's second largest city, and nature supplied the rest. There are fertile rolling hills and gleaming lakes, flowering azaleas and towering pines. Legendary Native Americans, Wild-West showmen, oil barons, and pioneers all added to the rich culture and left the area with fabulous mementos.

West of Bartlesville, some eco-scientists are returning wheat farms to original prairie grass and allowing wild native animals to roam where stock cattle recently grazed. This **Tallgrass Prairie Preserve** is a fascinating place simply because it is almost as it was before man tried to improve on nature. Frank Phillips' rural retreat at **Woolaroc** and Will Rogers' boyhood home at **Dog Iron Ranch** give vastly different perspectives on the lifestyles of famous Oklahomans. Seven state parks offer lodging and recreation on the shores of scenic **Grand Lake o' the Cherokees**, and all types of activities take place on and along the **Illinois River**.

■ Touring

Tulsa to Bartlesville/Woolaroc

Approximately 48 miles one-way

 Peoria Avenue in Tulsa is also SH-11, a nice non-highway north through **Skiatook** and **Barnsdall** to **Bartlesville** and the **Woolaroc Wildlife Preserve, Mansion, and Museum**. Skiatook is a tiny town, not quite rural, not quite suburbs, with an enjoyable group of antique shops, Indian galleries, and cafés. Farther north, the state highway takes you into Osage country where oil made this Native American tribe the wealthiest in the land. You can still see the first oil well – in fact, you can't miss it since it sits in the middle of Main Street in the small town of Barnsdall. In 1914, when the well came in, the pumping jack was fenced off and a sign erected to proclaim "America's Only Main Street Oil Well." The claim has since been upheld by *Ripley's Believe It Or Not*.

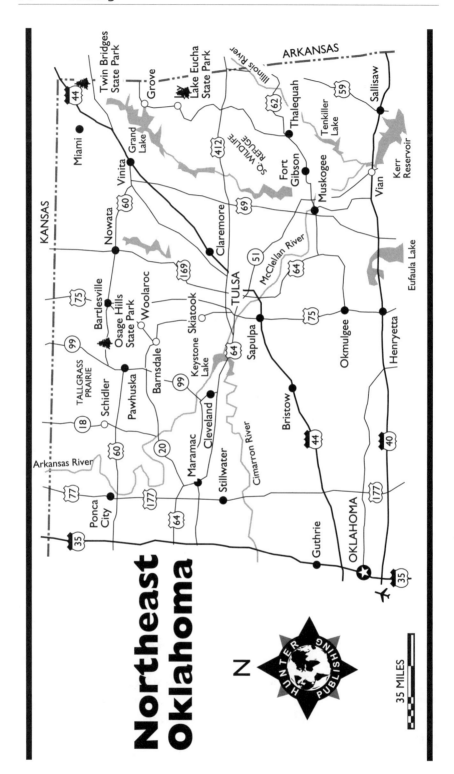

Northeast Oklahoma

35 MILES

The Buffalo Hunt *by Charles M. Russell, Woolaroc Museum.*

After Barnsdall, take SH-123 north. About 12 miles before you reach Bartlesville, **Woolaroc** will be on your left (west), ☎ 918-336-0307 or 800-636-0307. This terrific compound deserves at least a full day of exploration, but if you're "just taking a drive," it's still worth the $4 admission fee to park and take a short stroll through the grounds. You will see exotic animals such as emu and white elk on the two-mile drive through the woods from the entrance gate to the museum. Continue by driving the five-mile **North Road Tour** that begins east of Elk Lake.

The word "Woolaroc" is made up from the words WOOds, LAakes, and ROCks. There are 3,500 acres of the three on the compound, which was owned by Frank Phillips, founder of Phillips Petroleum. This retreat in the Osage Hills was once used by Frank and his wife, Jane, to entertain some of the most influential politicians, entertainers, and businessmen in the country. Today, the public can roam through the oil man's lodge and stroll the gorgeous grounds.

Phillips was an honorary member of the Osage Indian Tribe, and had a lifelong interest in Native Americans and the Old West. His lodge was built to resemble the El Tovar Lodge at the Grand Canyon. A building behind the lodge was originally constructed as a small museum to house an airplane (also named Woolaroc) that won a contest in 1927 when it became the first plane to fly nonstop from California to Hawaii. This

Buffalo on the grounds of the Woolaroc Museum.

monoplane was sponsored by Phillips, and the $35,000 prize was given by James Dole, the pineapple millionaire.

The original single-purpose museum has been enlarged over the years and now houses exhibits depicting events in the development of civilization in North America. Original art by Remington is on display, along with thousands of artifacts from prehistoric civilizations and ancient Native American tribes.

Woolaroc is open daily during the summer from 10 am to 8 pm. Between Labor Day and Memorial Day, visitors may tour the buildings and grounds from 10 am to 5 pm, Tuesday through Sunday.

Twelve miles north on SH-123 is Bartlesville. Stretch your legs on the 13-mile trail that begins in downtown Johnstone Park and follows Caney River. Then drive by **Price Tower** at the corner of Sixth Street and Dewey, designed by Frank Lloyd Wright and built in 1956. Architects and architecture fans from all over the world admire the 19-story glass structure, the tallest building ever designed by Wright. Those with a real interest can tour the building on Thursday. ☎ 918-336-8707 for times and ticket information.

Another architectural treasure is **Shin'enKan**, "home of the faraway heart," at 2919 Price Road just west of US-75, ☎ 918-333-3275. Tours are only on Thursday and the second Saturday of each month, but you can drive up the narrow road that leads to the house for a view of the exterior. Bruce Goff, the internationally renowned architect, built Shin'enKan over a 23-year period then donated it to the University of Oklahoma for use as a conference center. If you go on a tour, your favorite part will probably be hunting for hidden doors.

Two more *little* houses are worth a drive-by or tour depending on your interest and time limits. **LaQuinta** is a 32-room Spanish-style home built in 1930 on the Bartlesville Wesleyan College campus at 2201 Silverlake Road. Call ☎ 918-335-6234 for information about free tours. **Frank Phillips'** home was built in the Greek Revival style in 1908. The 26-room mansion is open for tours Wednesday through Sunday at 1107 South Cherokee. Call ☎ 918-336-2491 for hours and information.

Jacob Bartles, the man responsible for founding Bartlesville, also founded the town of **Dewey**. When the railroad laid track through what is now Bartlesville on a tract of land surveyed and suggested by Bartles, the nearby town of Silver Lake, where Bartles owned a trading post, was deserted. Since he had technically run himself out of business, Bartles loaded his store onto log rollers and dragged it with oxen up the muddy banks of the Caney River. He never closed during the months-long move, opening the store each day that it was "on the road." After he settled his little trading post about five miles north of his namesake town, Bartles started construction on a Victorian-style home which became a hotel. Both the hotel and town are named Dewey in honor of Admiral George Dewey.

The **Dewey Hotel** is open during the summer, but there is no air conditioning, so you'll want to visit early in the day. Tours start at 10 am, Tuesday through Saturday, and at 1pm Sunday. From US-75, drive west on Don Tyler Boulevard to the intersection of Delaware. The hotel is on the northwest corner at 801 North Delaware, ☎ 918-534-9978.

Across the street at 721 North Delaware, a museum is dedicated to Tom Mix, the cowboy movie star known as "the good guy in the white hat." Inside the **Tom Mix Museum** you'll see memorabilia from Mix's exciting life as marshal of Dewey, stuntman in the Miller Brothers 101 Ranch Wild West Show, a Rough Rider during the Spanish-American War, and an actor in more than 300 movies with Tony the Wonder Horse. ☎ 918-534-1555 for hours and information.

Prairie Song, **I.T.** (Indian Territory) is a village depicting life in the 1800s. It's about five miles east of town at the Moore Ranch on Durham

Road – turn in at the longhorn sign on the south side of the road. As you drive up, notice the mound on the left side; it was once a popular lookout-point for outlaws watching for lawmen. Prairie Song started in 1983 with a reconstructed log cabin on the 1,400-acre ranch and now includes a school, chapel, general store, post office, and dance hall. The public is invited to tour Monday, Wednesday, and Friday at 10 am and 2 pm. Call ☎ 918-534-2662 for information on tours or RV camping.

Osage Hills to Ponca City

Approximately 56 miles

West of Bartlesville, US-60 leads to **Osage Hills State Park**, about 11 miles away. This is a pretty drive, especially in the fall when the deeply wooded hills turn earthy red and gold. A stone lookout offering a fabulous view of the countryside is near the tent camping area. Find the structure by turning north (right) off the main park road and driving up a steep paved road. Stop a park officer on patrol or call the park office for maps and information, ☎ 918-336-4141.

From Osage Hills, continue west on US-60 to **The Tallgrass Prairie Preserve**, 36,000 acres of pristine land owned by The Nature Conservancy. Native grasses and plants grow wild here in their most natural state, and buffalo roam freely much as they did 100 years ago – and thousands of years before that. The Conservancy's goal is to restore the fragile ecosystem that once supported herds of buffalo, antelope, and elk on miles and miles of unbroken prairie.

It's an amazing sight: nothing but grass – some of it as tall as a man – meeting the sky at the edge of the earth. At different times of the year there are magnificent wildflowers, and an occasional tree can be seen standing alone in the distance. And, of course, there are **buffalo**. About 500 roam 7,000 acres now, and plans call for 2,000 to wander freely on every part of the preserve some day soon. In early summer, watch for the newest of that number running and romping with their mothers. The small-only-by-comparison calves have light brown hide and adorable faces – which you should view only through binoculars.

There are scenic turnouts along the 50-mile road running through the preserve, so you have many opportunities to get out of your car – or turn around if you don't want to drive the entire distance. Just remember, this is not a national park or a petting zoo and the tallgrass hides all manner of stinging, biting, tromping wildlife. Don't stray too far from the safety of your automobile, and never assume that those amazing buffalos welcome your presence. For information, stop at Headquarters 17 miles north of town on Tallgrass Drive. The office/gift shop is the renovated bunkhouse of old Chapman-Barnard Ranch, once the home of actor Ben Johnson, ☎ 918-287-4803.

The town of **Pawhuska** lists 86 buildings on the National Historic Register, including City Hall, built by the Osage tribe in 1894 for Council meetings. The tribe now runs a museum and a gift shop in a 1920s sandstone structure at 600 North Grandview Avenue, ☎ 918-287-2495. Other interesting mementos from Osage oil-boom days, when mineral rights made them a mega-rich tribe, are kept at **The Osage County Historical Museum** at 700 North Lynn in the old Santa Fe depot, ☎ 918-287-9924. Ask at the desk for keys to the one-room school house and railroad cars located outside.

Don't leave town without seeing the unusual windows at **Cathedral of the Osage** (Immaculate Conception Catholic Church) at 1314 North Lynn. At first glance, these are simply beautiful stained glass, but look closely at the window on the south side and you will see Christopher Columbus and native Indians instead of traditional religious figures. Another window shows actual members of the Osage tribe with a Jesuit priest. Call the rectory if you would like more information or wish to take a guided tour of the church, ☎ 918-287-1414.

Back on US-60, take a nine-mile detour to **Shidler**, north on SH-18. (If you drive through Tallgrass Prairie Preserve to the west exit, you'll be in Shidler.) Take a slow-speed cruise down Broadway to see the jail built in the 1920s to cage those led astray by oil money (or the lust for oil money). Then catch a glimpse of the Heritage Mural created by nationally-recognized local artist Joe Perales at Broadway and Cosden.

Head west one-quarter mile on SH-11 to **Bivin Garden**. If the Tallgrass Prairie is nature in the raw, this is nature well-done. Ray and Mollie Bivin live on the six-acre prairie oasis, but they allow guests to enjoy their creation on weekends or by appointment during the week. In 1981 they brought in 21 dump trucks of top soil and set to work. Today there are flower beds, rock gardens, ornamental ponds, an aviary, and hundreds of trees and shrubs. This is a home as well as a showplace, and a number of pets are in residence. In addition, you'll see pheasants, peacocks, parakeets – maybe a steer or two. A $2 admission fee is charged, and this little wonderland is well worth the ticket price and the road-trip detour. Call ☎ 918-793-4011 for information.

Northeast Oklahoma

From Bivins Garden, continue west about 25 miles to **Ponca City**. State Highway 11 goes across Kaw Lake and enters the town from the North; US-60 enters from the South. Ponca City is the answer to any questions about the impact of black gold on the prairie.

First the land belonged to the Ponca Tribe. It was deeded to them by the US government, and the tribe was rather forcefully *persuaded* to move onto it in 1876 from their native land in Nebraska. Then, in 1893, a fellow named B.S. Barnes (perhaps you'll see the irony in his initials) sold $2 certificates to 2,300 people who wished to participate in a drawing for homesites near the Ponca railway station. The homesites just happened to be on Ponca land, but Barnes overlooked this and successfully sold all his lottery tickets. The main attraction was underground water.

Several years later, soon after Oklahoma became a state, the land's true value became apparent when oil was discovered. Once the "Ponca Pool" began putting out an impressive amount of oil, wildcatters arrived, followed by extravagance, decadence, and wild excess. The leader of this untethered pack was a man named E.W. Marland. The company he founded is called the Conoco Refinery Corporation now, but back then it was Marland Oil, and its profits helped build Ponca City. Start your tour at Marland's first house, built in 1914, at 1000 East Grand Avenue at 10th Street.

The home is now **Ponca City Cultural Center and Indian Museum**, ☎ 580-767-0427, exhibiting Native American artifacts, and a large collection of memorabilia from the 101 Ranch. When Marland lived there, the house's 22 rooms were air-conditioned (remember this was the early 1900s), cleaned by a central vacuum system, and included an indoor swimming pool. Admission is $1, and the center is open from 10 am to 5 pm on Monday, the same hours Wednesday through Saturday, and from 1 pm to 5 pm on Sunday.

In 1925, Marland built and moved to a 55-room mansion at 901 Monument Road. Find it by driving north on 14th Street (US-77) to Lake Road. Turn right (east) and go around a 17-foot bronze statue of a pioneer woman to Monument Road. At press time the **Pioneer Woman Museum** adjacent to the statue was closed for expansion. Call ahead to see if it has reopened, ☎ 580-765-6108.

Marland Mansion, ☎ 580-767-0420 or 800-532-7559, was built in Italian Renaissance style to resemble the Davanzati Palace in Florence at a cost of $5½ million in the 1920s. Marland lived there with his first wife,

Mary Virginia Collins, her niece, Lydie, and her nephew, George, who were adopted by the Marlands when they were young children. Mary died in 1926, and Marland appalled polite society by *unadopting* his daughter and marrying her. Yes, these were wild and decadent days, indeed. Ask the guides to give you all the gossip when you tour the mansion Monday through Friday at 1:30 pm or Saturday and Sunday at 1:30 pm and 2:30 pm. There's no charge to visit the grounds and museum, but admission to the mansion is $4 for adults. Self-guided tours are possible during the summer from 9 am to 5 pm, Monday through Saturday, and noon to 4 pm every Sunday. Winter hours are from noon to 4 pm daily.

Sallisaw to Tahlequah

Approximately 58 miles one-way

This drive takes you along the southwestern edge of the Ozark Mountains, beginning in the Arkansas River Valley and ending in the center of the Cherokee Nation. The Arkansas river flows into **Robert S. Kerr Lake** about eight miles south of Sallisaw off US-59. The lake is a fine spot to begin a drive, especially in the spring when wildflowers bloom and in the fall when the hickory and oak leaves are changing. In winter, drive to the area below the dam to view bald eagles. In summer, swim at **Kerr Beach**, the largest sand beach in the state. When you're ready to hit the road, drive north on US-59 through Sallisaw, where John Steinbeck begins his novel, *The Grapes of Wrath*, about "Okies" fleeing to California. Of course, Sallisaw is several hundred miles east of the legendary Dust Bowl, but that's how "literary license" works.

One of the most interesting sites in this area is **Sequoyah's Cabin**, where the half-Cherokee, half-white silversmith lived during the 1820s. Sequoyah invented the Cherokee alphabet and made that tribe the only one with a written language. At first, his fellow tribesmen were not pleased with his literary talents, and one legend says he was brought to court and charged with possessing mysterious evil spirits. However, during the trial, Sequoyah taught the jury how to read and write, so they had no choice but to acquit him. The cabin he built in Indian Territory in 1828 is now protected by a sandstone building built by public workers during the 1930s. There are also walking paths, picnic areas, and a visitor's center/gift shop. You can tour the log structure and its artifacts at no charge Tuesday through Friday from 9 am to 5 pm and on weekends from 2 pm to 5 pm. Find the cabin by driving north on US-59 to SH-101.

Turn east and go about seven miles to the home site. The phone number is ☎ 918-775-2413.

Sequoyah, aka George Guess

His history is unclear and speculative, but historians agree that a baby boy named Sogwali was born sometime during the American Revolution to a Cherokee woman and a white man in the village of Tuskegee on the Little Tennessee River.

Some say his father was a German or Dutch trader named Gist, but there are no official records of such a man. There are, however, documents showing that General George Washington sent Nathaniel Gist to conduct a peace council with the Cherokees in the spring of 1777. Corn Tassel, the Cherokee chief who became Gist's friend, had a sister named Wurteh who bore a white man's child. It is also known that Gist left the Cherokees to fight in the American Revolution and never returned to Tennessee. So it is possible, even probable, that he fathered a Cherokee son named Sogwali, whom Christian missionaries called Sequoyah and the world knew as George Guess.

Throughout his life, Sequoyah was distrustful, even disparaging, of "the white man." He dressed as a Cherokee, never learned to read or speak English, and followed native religious beliefs taught him by his mother. But Sequoyah recognized the importance of the white man's ability to write and read English, and he became convinced it was necessary for Cherokees to learn to communicate in writing among themselves in their own language. Since no Native American language had a written alphabet, Sequoyah set out to put Cherokee words onto paper.

It is unclear exactly when Sequoyah finished his 85-character Cherokee alphabet, but by 1822 he had taught many Indians to read and write their native language. People from all parts of the world were amazed that an uneducated Indian could achieve such a feat, and his fame spread quickly. In 1828, when Sequoyah was in Washington as part of an Indian delegation attempting to clarify the tribe's land holdings, the first issue of the weekly newspaper, *Cherokee Advocate,* was printed in both English and Cherokee.

Sequoyah's invention was invaluable to all Native Americans because it proved to the white population that Indians are as intelligent as any other race. It also united the Cherokee Nation and made them leaders among other tribes.

In August 1843, Sequoyah, the famous Cherokee known to many as George Guess, died in San Fernando, Mexico after a long illness. His grave has never been positively located, so there is no tombstone to mark his final resting place. However, a statue of him stands in the US Capitol's Hall of Statuary.

On the way to Sequoyah's cabin, you'll pass a small cemetery on the south side of the highway. This is where Charles "Pretty Boy" Floyd, the sagebrush Robin Hood, is buried. Due to his friendly generosity to the poor, 20,000 people turned out for his funeral in Sallisaw in 1934 – in spite of the fact that he had robbed more than a dozen small banks, including the Sallisaw State Bank. Don't be surprised if you find flowers at the grave.

Drive back to Sallisaw and take US-64 west to Vian. If you have time, take the six-mile auto tour through the woods and marshes in **Sequoyah National Wildlife Refuge**, 3½ miles south of town off SH-82. It's beautiful, the birds and wildlife are abundant, and there's a half-mile trail on which to stretch your legs. Another route is west on US-64 over the Illinois River to the town of Gore, which calls itself the "Trout Capitol of Oklahoma" because the river here maintains a temperature of 48°, which the fish find perfectly romantic and ideal for raising their young. From here, you can drive north on the especially scenic SH-100 for six miles to **Lake Tenkiller**.

A shortcut is SH-82 north out of Vian, which will get you to Lake Tenkiller without doing the SH-100 half-loop. The two state highways intersect near the lake, and from there, you'll be on the main road leading to Tahlequah through the **Cookson Hills**. This stretch of highway covers rough terrain with steep hills, deep forests, sandstone cliffs, and clear creeks. It's obvious why outlaws often hid here earlier in the century.

Lake Tenkiller is a popular lake, with all the facilities of a state park. This is an ideal place to drive aimlessly, or walk along the shore, but if you're destination-minded, continue North to Murrell Road, just before the intersection of US-62. Turn east (right) and follow the road about a mile to **Murrell Home**, an antebellum structure built in the mid-1800s by George Murrell for his Cherokee wife, Minerva Ross, niece of Chief John Ross. The white, two-story house is furnished in mahogany and brocade, and will give you a sharp picture of gracious living in Indian Territory before the Civil War. Outside, there are 38 acres of land, picnic tables, a one-mile walking trail, and a bird sanctuary. Admission is free and the home is open during the summer on Wednesday through Saturday from 10 am to 5 pm and Sunday from 1 pm to 5 pm. Days and hours of operation are different during the winter, so call ahead, ☎ 918-456-2751, to check.

Nearby, on Willis Road off US-62, **The Cherokee Heritage Center** includes the **Tsa-La-Gi Ancient Village**, the **Cherokee National Museum/Adams Corner**, and **The Trail of Tears Outdoor Drama**. This fascinating compound is engrossing, heartbreaking, and entertaining. The story is well known, but the actuality of it becomes real when you tour the exhibits. In 1838, a group of men representing a minority of the Cherokees signed the Treaty of New Echota giving up their lands in Georgia for land west in Indian Territory. Soon after, 7,000 United States troops marched onto Cherokee land, burned their homes, and forced them to walk westward toward a strange wilderness that would be their new home. Four thousand of the original 16,000 Indians who started the march died from hunger, exposure, and illness.

The Tsa-La-Gi (the native word for Cherokee) Ancient Village is a replica of a 16th-century walled village that recreates the lifestyle of the Cherokees before European contact. Native Americans in costume guide visitors through the exhibits, which include basket-weaving, pottery making, and meal preparation. In the National Museum, the history of the Cherokee is presented from the beginning of their tribe in North America to modern day. Adams Corner represents a rural village from 1875 to 1890 during the final years of the old Cherokee Nation. Demonstrations of soap making, quilting, and weaving give visitors a look at Indian ingenuity and skill at living with nature. A two-hour play called *The Trail of Tears Drama* tells the story of the Cherokees being driven from their homes.

The Cherokee National Museum is open Tuesday through Saturday from 10 am to 5 pm and Sunday from 1 pm to 5 pm. Tsa-La-Gi and Adams Corner are open Tuesday through Saturday from 10 am to 5 pm with the last tour beginning at 3:30 pm. The grounds are closed from January through March. *The Trail of Tears Outdoor Drama* is presented from mid-June to mid-August at 8 pm Monday through Saturday. Admission to the Heritage Center and Villages is $5 for adults and $3 for children. Show tickets are $9 for adults and $4.50 for children on weekdays, $10 for adults and $5 for children on Saturday. For reservations and additional information, call ☎ 918-456-6007.

From the Cherokee Heritage Center, it's a two-mile drive on SH-82 to **Tahlequah**, home of Northeastern State University and the 150-year-old capital of the Cherokee Nation. Street signs are written in English and Cherokee, and the 1869 Capitol is still the center of town. Stop at the Chamber of Commerce, 123 Delaware Street, ☎ 918-456-3742, for a walking tour map.

Tahlequah to Miami

Approximately 85 miles one-way

East of Tahlequah, SH-10 follows the twists and falls of the Illinois River through the Ozarks to **Jay**, Huckleberry Capital of the World. Along the way, you will pass tall oak and hickory forests, sandstone bluffs, rolling foothills, and deep-green river banks. Stop often simply to look around, sniff the fresh air, and enjoy this gorgeous part of the state.

You will find huckleberries during the growing season in Huckleberry Canyon Park, one block east of the courthouse in downtown Jay. Follow a trail behind the Delaware County Bank to the shady park, and bring a picnic. During the 4th of July weekend each year, the town holds the Huckleberry Festival with a parade, arts and crafts show, and, of course, huckleberries – bushels and bushels of them served free over ice cream. Call the Chamber of Commerce at ☎ 918-253-8698 for details.

Approximately 10 miles north of Jay, SH-10 crosses the Honey Creek arm of **Grand Lake o' the Cherokees**. In fall, watch for flocks of American white pelicans on their annual migration. The town of Grove is across the lake, and **The Cherokee Queen** offers paddlewheel cruises from the dock near Honey Creek Bridge. Call ☎ 918-786-4272 for reservations.

Nearby, take a self-guided walk through dozens of turn-of-the-century buildings stuffed with wonderful antique furniture and artifacts at **Har-Ber Village**, ☎ 918-786-6446. Find the huge outdoor village 3½ miles west of downtown Grove on Har-Ber Road, south of Main Street. Pick up a walking-tour map at the entrance and follow it through the village, which includes a courthouse, post office, drug store, school, and chapel. There are over a hundred buildings here, and you probably can't see everything on one visit. However, admission is free so you can return as often as you like. Har-Ber Village is open from March 1 to November 30 Monday through Saturday from 9 am to 6 pm and Sunday from 11 am to 6 pm.

Northeast Oklahoma

Grove has two botanical gardens, **LenDonwood** and **Satsuki**. Len-Donwood is the larger, with waterfalls, azaleas, and a large collection of rhododendrons. Satsuki is more intimate, with stunning Oriental designs. ☎ 918-786-2938 for information on the gardens, and ☎ 918-786-9079 to request maps and general information from the Chamber of Commerce, at 104-B West Third Street.

Follow SH-10 North as it parallels Grand Lake to **Twin Bridges State Park**, where the Neosho and Spring rivers converge. This pretty park is an excellent spot for a car-break to watch American white pelicans on their spring and fall migrations. Find a terrific viewing point by driving to the campgrounds on a 200-foot bluff overlooking the rivers; go west on US-60, off SH-10 near the town of Wyandotte, to SH-137. Turn north and look for entrance roads on each side of the highway.

In the town of **Miami**, on the Neosho River after SH-10 turns west and crosses SH-137, drive by **The Coleman Theatre**, a Spanish-Mission-style landmark on Historic Route 66. Will Rogers and other vaudeville stars appeared here when "The Mother Road" was America's main highway. You can still drive along a 13-mile stretch of the original nine-foot-wide pavement near the theater.

An Oklahoma Welcome Center is east of town on I-44. Stop in for a cup of coffee, good information about any attraction in the state, and as many maps and brochures as you care to carry away. For more specific information on Miami and the local area, stop by the Chamber of Commerce at 111 North Main, ☎ 918-542-4481.

Spring River State Park is a most enjoyable spot in the northeast corner of the state, near the point where Oklahoma meets Kansas and Missouri. Just sit, or paddle a canoe through the tree-tunnel that shades the river. Either way, it's a great way to spend time. If you don't have a canoe or raft, call or drop by **Spring River Canoe Trails**, six miles east of town on SH-10, ☎ 918-540-2545.

Hunting the Uncommon

The following deserve a detour from the above tours.

Claremore

This little town is best known as the place Will Rogers called home. It's 30 miles northeast of Tulsa on Historic Route 66. Take I-44 until it becomes Will Rogers Turnpike. At the point where the *Mother Road* joins the turnpike just outside Catoosa go northeast to Claremore.

The **Will Rogers Memorial** is here, and his statue sits on a park bench in front of the *Claremore Daily Progress* newspaper office downtown.

Another not-to-be-missed attraction is the **J.M. Davis Historical Arms Museum**, 313 West Lynn Riggs Boulevard on Historic Route 66, ☎ 918-341-5707, free admission Monday through Saturday from 8:30 am to 5 pm and Sunday from 1 pm to 5 pm. This state-run museum is one man's lifetime collection of guns and related articles – more than 200,000 total.

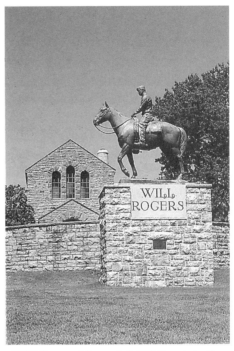

Will Rogers Memorial, "Riding into the Sunset" by Electra Waggoner. (Fred W. Marvel)

Will Rogers

Born November 4, 1879 in Indian Territory that would become Oklahoma, William Penn Adair Rogers was known as "The Indian Cowboy" from the Cherokee Nation. He performed in Wild West shows and vaudeville acts around the world, and was the most loved entertainer of his time.

- "My ancestors didn't come over on the *Mayflower*, but they met 'em at the boat."
- "I am just an old country boy in a big town trying to get along. I have been eating pretty regular and the reason I have been is because I have stayed an old country boy."
- "I never met a man I didn't like."
- "Comedians haven't improved. Nothing has improved but taxes."

When sound came to the cinema, Rogers starred in many movies and was voted the most popular male actor in Hollywood.

■ "Everybody is ignorant. Only on different subjects."

■ "All I know is what I read in the papers."

■ "Live your life so that whenever you lose, you are ahead."

■ "Nowadays it is about as big a crime to be dumb as it is to be dishonest."

His political remarks were applauded by all America, but he refused the nomination to become governor of Oklahoma. However, Rogers was elected mayor of Beverly Hills and played a major role in the election of President Franklin Roosevelt in 1932.

■ "This country is not where it is today on account of any one man. It is here on account of the real common sense of the Big Normal Majority."

■ "We will never have true civilization until we have learned to recognize the rights of others."

He died in a plane crash in 1935 near Point Barrow, Alaska with his good friend, aviation legend Wiley Post.

■ "You can be killed just as dead in an unjustified war as you can in one protecting your own home."

■ "No man is great if he thinks he is."

■ "It's great to be great, but it's greater to be human."

Muskogee

This is a pleasant town near the meeting of the Verdigris, Grand Neosho, and Arkansas rivers. It is about 50 miles southeast of Tulsa on the Muskogee Turnpike (US-51 out of Tulsa). See the Five Civilized Tribes Museum and Honor Heights Park on Agency Hill. Another interesting stop is the Ataloa Art Lodge.

Five Civilized Tribes Museum, ☎ 918-683-1701, on Agency Hill off 48th Street and Honor Heights Drive, maintains one of the finest Native American art collections in the world. Plans are underway to move the museum from its present home in the historic 1875 Union Agency Building to a new 45,000-square-foot facility on 38 acres at the intersection of US-69 and US-62, but the move will be several years in the future. Currently, hours are Monday through Saturday from 10 am to 5 pm and

Sunday from 1 pm to 5 pm. Admission is $2 for adults, $1.75 for senior citizens, and $1 for students.

Ataloa Art Lodge, 2299 Bacone Road, on the Bacone College campus near the junction of SH-16 and US-62, ☎ 918-683-4581, $2 admission. Constructed of native sandstone, this small museum holds rare antique Native American treasures representing tribes from all of North America. Perhaps the single most touching item is the beaded baby bonnet belonging to six-month-old Lost Bird, the lone survivor of the Battle of Wounded Knee in December, 1890.

■ Adventures

On Foot

Hiking

 Some of Oklahoma's best and longest hiking trails run through spectacular scenery in the northeastern part of the state. Sixty-mile **Jean-Pierre Chouteau Trail**, 18-mile **Greenleaf Trail**, 14-mile **Whispering Pines Trail**, and 18-mile **Will Rogers Country Centennial Trail** all meander along lovely lakes or rivers, through dense forests and open meadows in this lush region. In addition, there are nature paths and shorter hiking trails in most of the state parks that cluster along the eastern border.

❏ Jean-Pierre Chouteau Trail

You can pick up the trail in several places because it runs for 60 miles from just east of Tulsa to just east of Muskogee. Recent reports from seasoned hikers say the trail needs work in several spots, so you may want to reconnoiter by car or check with nearby state parks for trail conditions before you set out with a backpack. Maps and information can be obtained by calling **Webbers Falls Lake Office**, ☎ 918-489-5541, **Chouteau Compound**, ☎ 918-687-6091, or the **Tulsa District Corps of Engineers**, ☎ 918-581-7351.

Jean-Pierre Chouteau starts at **Rogers Point** across US-66 from the Port of Catoosa on the Verdigris River. A dirt access road leads to the parking lot and the trailhead. This first section is about six miles long and ends at Dog Creek. There is no bridge over Dog Creek or the next

Northeast Oklahoma
- Adventures -

1. Eagle's Nest Trail
2. Will Rogers Country Centennial Trail
3. Jean-Pierre Chouteau Trail
4. Whispering Pines Trail
5. Short Mountain Trail

N

35 MILES

creek crossing, Cat Creek, so be prepared to wade across a shallow stream. Turn around at Dog Creek for a 12-mile hike.

The trailhead to the second section is on the east side of Cat Creek. This 13-mile stretch ends at Newt Graham Lock and Dam #18 near a visitor's center, which is open daily from 8 am until dark. Consider beginning at the visitor's center, seven miles south of the town of Inola, and hiking back toward Cat Creek so that you can pick up maps and current information on trail conditions before you start.

The third and longest section of trail begins on the south side of Bull Creek and follows the river for about 31 miles to Fort Gibson Park, five miles southwest of the junction of SH-80 and SH-51. A visitor's center with maps and brochures is located upriver from Fort Gibson Park near Chouteau Lock and Dam #17 in Pecan Park. Find the center off US-62 about four miles from the town of Okay – hours of operation are daily from 8 am to dark.

Campgrounds and public day-use areas are at regular intervals along the trail, and most have water and restrooms. If you plan to camp outside one of these areas, a Primitive Camping Permit will be required from the Webbers Falls Lake Office in Gore, ☎ 918-489-5541. **Afton Landing** is the only camp with hot showers. It's on flat ground above the north bank of the river about five miles west of Wagoner, and makes a good starting/stopping point or midway campground.

Most segments of this trail are on level, open grasslands with great views of the river. The bottom lands are dense with oak, hickory, pecan, and sycamore trees which are fresh green in spring and a blaze of rust and gold in fall. Both bikes and horses are allowed on the trail, so prepared to meet one of them as you trek along. However, check with the visitor's centers or Webbers Falls Lake Office for tips on when and where you might expect the most solitude. Certain parts of the trail are not accessible to horses because the water crossings are not horse-friendly, and you shouldn't have equines in the public use areas since they are restricted to primitive camping.

❒ Greenleaf Lake Trail

Greenleaf Lake is small, only 930 acres, and this 18-mile primitive trail double-loops around it. Until recently, parts of the trail have been closed, in seemingly random order, by the military command at Camp Gruber. This procedure was frustrating to hikers who never knew when they would be allowed access. However, the problems appear to be resolved, and **Greenleaf Lake Trail** now will be closed for military maneuvers on only five weekends each year. Get a list of those closings by contacting the park office at ☎ 918-487-5196. Hikers are also prohibited from using the trail through the Gruber State Game Management Area during the fall hunting season.

Oklahoma Ankle Express, a hardworking and dedicated backpacking club, built and maintains the trail in **Greenleaf State Park**, ☎ 918-487-5622. Recently, the group constructed a handicapped-accessible cabin overlooking the lake, which offers specially designed features and a walkway to an accessible nature trail. Because of this personal hands-on attention and the varied terrain in the park, Greenleaf is one of the most popular trails in the state.

Find the trailhead at the campground located between the Ranger Office/Information Center (turn east into the park off SH-10) and the lake. Blue paint marks trees on the main trail, and white-paint blazes indicate the connecting trail at Mary's Cove. From the park office trailhead, the course heads south past the "cabin on the lake" to the dam. You must cross a highway bridge, then pick up the trail again as it moves south along the lake. It is possible to begin your hike at a trailhead south of the dam, if you object to crossing on the highway.

When you cross another bridge at the far tip of the lake, you enter the State Game Management Area. Here the trail splits, creating a long narrow loop that makes it possible to hike out along one leg and return on the other. A half-mile crossover connects the two legs of the loop at Mary's Cove, about four miles from the bridge. Day-trippers can cut off here to head back to the trailhead – or set up camp and head back the next day. Long-distance hikers will want to continue to campsites at the end of the loop – another three miles. The design of Greenleaf, with connecting trails and campsites, allows hikers to plan trips of different lengths.

 Check your skin for ticks after a summer hike.

Allow about three hours to hike four miles from the parking lot south of the dam to the crossover trail at Mary's Cove. It will take another couple of hours to hike to the point where the trail ends and curves back to form the northern loop. Even seasoned hikers may find the entire distance too long to travel in one day, since there are stretches of rugged terrain and some medium-steep grades that can slow you down and drain your energy.

❏ Whispering Pines Trail

Sequoyah State Park, eight miles east of Wagoner off SH-51, sits on a peninsula that juts out into **Fort Gibson Lake**. Several types of trails twist over the peninsula between Park Headquarters at the northern entrance and Western Hills Guest Ranch at the southern tip. The longest is **Whispering Pines Trail**, a 14-mile hiking/biking path with four connecting sections. Shorter interpretive, nature, and fitness trails also cut through groves of dense trees and open, grassy meadows, so stop at the Nature Center near the lodge for a map and information to prevent getting lost in the jumble. ☎ 918-772-2545.

You'll be sharing the sand/rock/gravel trails with bikers, but much of the path is wide enough to accommodate both activities without crowding or danger. The Blue Section leading from the lodge to the swimming beach is a 1¼-mile paved loop.

❏ Eagle's Nest Trail

Kaw Lake east of Ponca City has 168 miles of shoreline open for public use, so you can park anywhere and hike along the lake. The best spot is the **Eagle's Nest Trail** that follows the lake from **Osage Cove** to **Burbank Landing**, 12 miles away. Osage Cove is on a steep slope on the southeast shore about three miles down a paved park road off US-60 adjacent to Sandy Park. Pick up the trail here and hike east through prairie land and stands of oak trees around two water inlets to Burbank Landing. From November until March, watch for bald eagles who like to spend the winter here.

Day-trippers will want to turn around and retrace their path when they've hiked half the time or distance allotted for the trip. If you plan to camp, reverse the route and begin at Burbank Landing, three miles north on a gravel road 3½ miles east of the Sandy Park road off US-60. Backpack the 12 miles to Osage Cove and set up camp beside the lake or on the heavily-treed slope above the shore. Phone the project manager for maps and information, ☎ 580-762-5611.

Northeast Oklahoma

❏ Short Mountain Trail

Eight miles south of Sallisaw, on **Robert S. Kerr Lake**, a 5½-mile trail takes hearty hikers to the top of Short Mountain. It's a steep climb, but the view from the summit of **Short Mountain** is worth the effort. The trailhead is located off US-59 at the South Dam Site. From here the trail passes a rock quarry, then follows the shore to the mountain. Once you reach the top, the trail winds along the top, and you get great views of the lake and locks. For maps and information, contact the Robert S. Kerr Project Office at ☎ 918-775-4474.

❏ Miscellaneous Hikes

A terrific view of **Tenkiller Lake** is the prize for anyone who hikes two-mile **Island View Nature Trail** from the dam (six miles north of Gore on SH-100) along the shore to Strayhorn Landing. The trail gets narrow and rough after the first half-mile or so, but it's doable, so hang in there. Strayhorn Landing is on the forested ridge of a peninsula overlooking the clear blue lake.

At **Keystone Lake**, try one of these three trails: one-mile **Whispering Hills Trail**, which makes a lazy loop along the shore in Keystone State Park off SH-51 near Sand Springs; the 1¼-mile fitness trail in Campground Area 1; **Washington Irving Cove South Nature Trail** on the north side of US-64, which runs along one of the most beautiful sections of the lake.

Golfing

❏ Bartlesville

 Adams Municipal Golf Course, 6001 East Tuxedo, ☎ 918-337-5313. This popular 18-hole, par-72 course has 6,800 total yards, a USGA rating of 72, and a slope of 119. Fees are $15, and carts rent for $16.

❏ Fort Gibson

Sequoyah Golf Course, ☎ 918-772-2297, is near Western Hills Guest Ranch in the foothills of the Ozark Plateau. Eighteen holes cover a short course with a par of 70. Large oak and pecan trees line the fairways, white-tail deer roam near the course, and every tee box has a view of **Fort Gibson Lake**. The most demanding hole is a 395-yard par-four with an uphill approach to an elevated green. Five of the holes have water play.

Green fees are $10.50 for 18 holes and $8 for nine holes on weekends, $8 for either 18 or nine holes on weekdays. Gas carts are available for $16 (18 holes) and $9 (nine holes). Pull-carts rent for $2. Clubs are available, but caddies are not.

Take SH-51 east from Tulsa about 40 miles, then begin looking for signs for Sequoyah State Park. The golf course is about three miles from the park's entrance. Tee-time reservations are accepted up to a year in advance, beginning as early as 6:30 am. **Western Hills Guest Ranch** is a state-run resort eight miles east of Wagoner on Fort Gibson Lake, ☎ 918-772-2545 or 800-654-8240.

❑ Grand Lake Area

Shangri-La Golf Courses, ☎ 918-257-4204 or 800-331-4060, include a Blue Course and a Gold Course. Both have wonderful views of Grand Lake and offer challenging features. Blue Course has 18 holes, 7,012 total yards and a par of 72. Gold Course is 18 holes, 5,932 yards with a par of 70. Golfers may play either course daily from 6:30 am until dark during the summer, and from 8 am to 5 pm every day during the winter.

Green fees are $39 with cart on either course during winter. Summer fees are $75 including cart on the Gold Course, and $480 with cart on the Blue Course. Guests at the resort can make tee-time reservations anytime during their visit. Public reservations are accepted up to two weeks in advance.

❑ Muskogee

Eagle Crest Golf Course, 40th Street and Border, ☎ 918-682-0866. A wooded 18-hole, par-72, 6,269-yard course with several water hazards. Green fees are $12 on weekends and $10 on weekdays for all-day play.

On Wheels

Biking

A wealth of trails and roads in the northeast section of Oklahoma offer wonderful biking opportunities. **Sequoyah State Park** on **Fort Gibson Lake** opened the first official state biking trail several years ago, and since then other parks have constructed new trails and opened existing hiking trails to bikers. Now, all state park trails are open to bikers unless posted otherwise, and the north-eastern trails are particularly long and scenic.

In addition, The Department of Wildlife Conservation allows mountain bikes access through the **Cookson Hills** and **Sparrow Hawk** areas, and the US Army Corps of Engineers maintains long trails around **Kaw Lake** and **Oologah Lake**. The 60-mile **Jean-Pierre Chouteau Trail** offers a scenic ride along the **Verdigris River** from Tulsa to Fort Gibson.

☐ The I-44/Arkansas River Triangle

When you look at a map of Oklahoma you'll see a perfect triangle formed by the Arkansas/Missouri border, I-44, and the Arkansas River. Within this perfect triangle is the perfect back-roads biking experience – parks, lakes, rivers, and small towns connected by lightly traveled rural roads.

In the far southeast corner of this triangle, SH-101 travels about 19 miles from **Sallisaw** to the state line through the **Cookson Hills**. Pick up this route about three miles north of town at the junction with US-59, then travel east for seven miles to **Sequoyah's Cabin**, a one-room home where the inventor of the Cherokee alphabet lived with his family. Turn around here for a 14-mile round-trip.

At **Robert S. Kerr Lake**, eight miles south of Sallisaw off US-59, moun-tain bikers may use the 5½-mile **Short Mountain Trail**. The trail begins at the south end of the dam, passes a rock quarry and climbs rather steeply to the top of Short Mountain. Views of the lake from the top are worth the effort – and you can always walk your bike over the tougher parts.

Several scenic roads go all directions from **Tahlequah**, but SH-10 north along the **Illinois River** is outstanding. Don't try this road during the summer when traffic is heavy, but consider an off-season ride as far north as you can manage.

South of town, you can connect several rides to make a loop past three beautiful lakes, each offering campsites at state parks. The following itinerary – with loosely estimated mileage – will give you some ideas. US-62, SH-82, and SH-10 leave Tahlequah as one road (Muskogee Ave-nue). At the south edge of town turn east onto Willis Road at the signs for Park Hill. This road leads to the Cherokee Heritage Center and the Murrell Home, and you may prefer to begin your bike tour from one of these parking lots.

Soon after you leave the Murrell Home going south, the road turns east and winds along the Illinois River headwaters of **Tenkiller Lake** passing Horseshoe Bend and Carters Landing, then finally connecting to SH-82, just before the bridge over the river at the upper lake – a distance of about 13 miles. On the west side of the bridge, a paved access road goes south to **Cherokee Landing State Park**. East of the bridge, SH-82 joins SH-100 and continues south as one highway paralleling Tenkiller Lake. **Tenkiller State Park**, 13 miles south of the bridge, is an excellent spot to camp overnight – you can pick up snacks and drinks at **Cookson** (five miles from the bridge) or at stores along the highway.

Tenkiller State Park, near Vian. (Fred W. Marvel)

At the south end of Tenkiller State Park, there's a dam and overlook. Here, you can pick up SH-10A west to **Greenleaf Lake and State Park** – about 10 miles. From Greenleaf Lake, SH-10 goes north about 15 miles to the junction of US-62 at Fort Gibson east of Muskogee. At this point you have some options. One is to turn east on SH-10 and return to your starting point south of Tahlequah – about 17 miles.

Another choice is to pick up SH-80 and ride north to **Fort Gibson Lake**. About nine miles from town, SH-80 follows the **Grand Neosho River** past the **Canyon Road** day-use recreation area to the dam at the southern end of the lake. A turn to the west at the dam will take you to **Sequoyah Bay State Park** and the state waterfowl refuge. If you continue up the east side of the lake, you will come to SH-51 at the town of Hulbert. A turn to the west will take you six miles to the peninsula site of **Sequoyah State Park** and **Western Hills Guest Ranch**. A turn to the east will take you 17 miles back to Tahlequah.

Northeast Oklahoma

Sequoyah State Park's **Whispering Pines Trail** is a 14-mile multi-use path open to mountain bikers. Pick up a map at the Nature Center, north of the lodge at the southern end of the peninsula. The easy-to-ride Green Section is a double track that runs from the Nature Center, north for about two miles. Near the Visitor Center, south of SH-51, the sandy-surfaced Red Section runs about 2½ miles to a small airport. The Yellow Section is more narrow and runs about two miles from the pro shop at the golf course across some active roadways to the north end of the Green trail. A paved Blue Trail runs from the lodge to a loop at the swimming beach.

The 60-mile **Jean Pierre Chouteau Trail** runs from the west side of Fort Gibson along the McClellan-Kerr Navigation System to the **Port of Catoosa** east of Tulsa. Most of the trail is flat and traverses grasslands and deep oak and hickory woods. If you plan to ride the entire trail over several days, apply for a permit for primitive camping from the **Webbers Falls Project Office**, ☎ 918-489-5541.

Near the town of **Grove**, you'll find plenty of scenic roads – including another section of SH-10. Depending on traffic, the trip up SH-10 from **Jay** to **Wyandotte** is a nice ride with stops at the Honey Creek and Cowskin (Elk River) arms of **Grand Lake o' the Cherokees**. Park and county roads around the lake are lovely and often uncrowded. However, much of the shoreline is privately owned, so beware of trespassing.

Off SH-10, about five miles north of Jay, turn west onto SH-127 and peddle to **Zena**, where unsurfaced roads lead to the Summerfield Hollow area of the lake. Five miles farther north, a turn to the west off SH-10 onto a park road will take you to **Honey Creek State Park**, a particularly beautiful area.

A relatively short loop is created at the south end of Grand Lake by SH-20 (west of Jay), SH-28 (which crosses Pensacola Dam and passes by **Disney** and **Little Blue State Parks**), and SH-82 (which intersects SH-28 in the town of **Langley**). The entire loop is about 30 miles with convenient resting spots all along the way.

❒ The Northeastern Corner

The roads in this region, just south of the Kansas border, are some of the most scenic in the state. **Spring River** and **Twin Bridges State Parks** provide gorgeous viewing spots on both the Spring and Grand Neosho Rivers, so put a camera in your backpack. From Wyandotte, take SH-60 west about two miles to SH-137. Turn north to find the entrances to Twin Bridges campgrounds on both sides of the road. Bike around this wooded bluff stopping in various areas to look out over the two rivers. Continue up SH-137 to the town of Quapaw, about 12 miles, turn east on 1st Street, and peddle almost four miles to Spring River State Park. The wide, slow Spring River is popular with canoers, and its banks are ideal for shady naps.

❑ Osage Hills & Kaw Lake

The land around **Kaw**, **Hulah**, and **Copan Lakes** is operated by the Corps of Engineers and open to mountain bikers. Road trips are possible from Kaw along SH-11 to **Bivin Garden** near **Shidler**, and along SH-10, SH-99, to **Osage Hills** and **Wha-Sha-She State Parks**. Use one of the lakes or parks as a base camp and take long rides along these roads, or connect them into a multi-day loop trip that includes **Marland Mansion** in Ponca City and **Woolaroc** near Bartlesville.

From Sarge Creek Cove at the east end of the SH-11 bridge over Kaw Lake, bike east through rolling plains about eight miles to Bivin Garden. This colorful oasis has flower gardens, ponds, and aviaries to visit. After a stop here, go another fourth-mile into Shidler for a snack. You can return by the same route or turn south on SH-11 and pick up US-60, about eight miles away. US-60 will take you back to the south end of Kaw Lake, and an unpaved road west of McFadden Cove connects to SH-11. This route will add over 20 miles to your trip, so be sure you have the time and stamina to finish before you take that southern turn in Shidler.

Many paved and gravel roads surrounding Kaw Lake provide good biking opportunities. One possibility is the 12-mile **Eagle View Trail** from Osage Cove to Burbank Landing. From US-60, turn north onto a paved local road leading to the dam. At the dam turn right onto another paved road and follow it east and north for two miles, then turn left and go just over half a mile to the Osage Cove campground entrance booth. Ask at the booth for directions to the trail that hugs the shoreline.

Osage Hills State Park is on 1,199 acres in wooded hills 11 miles west of Bartlesville with a 1¾-mile multi-use trail and scenic winding roads. From the park, cycle US-60 toward Bartlesville, then turn south on SH-123 to visit Woolaroc, a unique 3,600-acre museum/wildlife preserve/cultural center – total distance about 23 miles. Loop back to Osage Hills by going south on SH-123 to Barnsdall, then turning west on SH-

11 to SH-99, which leads back north to US-60. This route is especially recommended in the spring and fall.

Another loop from Osage Hills takes you to **Hulah** and **Copan Lakes**. Travel west on US-60 to SH-99, turn north and connect with SH-10, which leads to Wah-Sha-She State Park on the south shore of Hulah Lake. Ten miles farther east, SH-10 comes to Post Oak Park on the south shore of Copan Lake. Paved and gravel roads around both lakes are open to bikers. From Copan you can take US-75 south to Dewey, then west on US-60 to Osage Hills. A worthwhile side-trip is the four-mile detour east of US-75 between Dewey and Bartlesville on Durham Road, which takes you to the historic buildings at **Prairie Song**.

❒ Oologah Lake

Will Rogers' Country Centennial Trail was built for horses, but the Corps of Engineers welcomes hikers and bikers on this 18-mile path at the south end of **Oologah Lake**. Take SH-88 east from US-169 near the town of Oologah to a parking area on the east side of the spillway. Pick up the trail near the spillway and bike north along the lake 1.7 miles to **Kite Hill**, where rugged trails wind and climb to the top and your efforts are rewarded with an outstanding view. You can skip Kite Hill and continue along the east side of the lake to Blue Creek Park on a slope above a bay. If you bypass the hill, the trail measures 12½ miles. Parking is also available at Blue Creek, so you can begin and finish at either end.

Dog Iron Ranch, Rogers' birthplace, is at the southwestern shore of the lake on Country Road-East-West 38 about two miles north of SH-88. You can bike from the ranch to the **Will Rogers Memorial** in **Claremore** by taking the paved connector road from CR-38 to SH-88, then riding east and south – a route that is especially colorful in the fall – for about 12 miles. Take Will Rogers Boulevard off SH-88 in Claremore and go up the hill to the 20-acre site where Rogers, his wife, and two children are buried near the Memorial.

Motorcycles & Off-Road Vehicles

❒ Kaw Lake

 A section of the Sarge Creek Cove area is open to motorcycles and ORVs. From SH-11, on the east side of the lake, turn north onto a paved park road leading to the restrooms. (The campgrounds are to the south.) You may ride in the designated area north of SH-11all the way to the fence. For maps and information, call the park office, ☎ 580-762-5611.

☐ Keystone Lake

The White Water Park area, on the southeastern shore of **Keystone Lake** off SH-151 south of US-64 just past the dam, has a designated riding area for motorcycles and ORVs. Call the Corps of Engineers' project office, ☎ 918-865-2621, for maps and information.

On Horseback

☐ Will Rogers Country Centennial Trail

 The famous cowboy philosopher Will Rogers was born and lived most of his life in Indian Territory near what is now **Oologah Lake**. So it is fitting that a trail open to horseback riders on the southeast shore of this lake is named for him.

The Will Rogers Country Centennial Trail is 18 miles long and runs through public hunting grounds, so riding is not allowed during deer season. At other times, riders may follow the trail from the Spillway Area at the south end of the lake to Blue Creek Park on the eastern shore. A five-mile stretch of trail leads up Kite Hill and offers riders wonderful views.

Check with the **Corps of Engineer Project Office** near the dam, ☎ 918-443-2250, for maps and information. Equestrian camping is allowed in designated areas.

☐ Jean-Pierre Chouteau Trail

This 60-mile trail was constructed for hiking, but three sections are open for horseback riders. Other areas aren't suitable for equestrian use because bridges are not horse-proof, and riders can't cross the creeks on horseback because of deep water and steep banks.

The Jean-Pierre Chouteau Trail follows the McClellan-Kerr Arkansas River Navigational System from Fort Gibson almost to Port Catoosa near Tulsa. Terrain along the river varies from open prairie to thick woods, with abundant wildlife. Five public parks along the trail have camping and public use areas, but horses are not allowed at any of them.

If you want to camp out with your horse, contact the **Corps of Engineers**, **Tulsa District**, ☎ 918-581-6510, for a special permit. No rental stables are located along the trail, so you must have your own horse. Maps and additional information can be obtained from the Lockmaster at Chouteau Lock, southeast of Wagoner, or the Webbers Falls Project Office, ☎ 918-489-5541.

❏ Monkey Island

The best way to see **Grand Lake** is from the back of a horse. **Monkey Island Trail and Hay Rides**, ☎ 918-257-5186, offers horseback riding adventures for every level of skill. Thirty-minute guided rides are priced at $10, and one-hour rides are $20 per person, with a limit of 10 riders per group.

Monkey Island is a 100-acre ranch with varied terrain; rides cross through woods and along the lake shore. Find the stables on SH-125 less than one mile south of SH-85A. Reservations are not necessary, but call ahead to guarantee that horses will be available when you arrive. Trail rides are given from 10 am to dusk every day except Tuesday.

❏ Sequoyah State Park

Western Hills Guest Ranch, ☎ 918-772-2046, offers trail rides and hay rides. Call ahead for reservations if you're not staying at the ranch. Consider the "Cowboy Adventure Package," which includes horseback riding, if you plan to stay overnight.

On Water

 A vast portion of northeast Oklahoma is covered by water. Fun-to-run rivers and fish-filled reservoirs spread across the plains and hills, so you're never far from a flowing stream or sparkling lake. The largest and most developed bodies of water offer specialty adventures in addition to outstanding fishing and boating. Lesser lakes and rivers provide a variety of recreation opportunities, usually at a calmer pace with more solitude – and, for some, there is no better way to pass a day.

Oologah Lake, parallel to US-169 north of Tulsa, is a favorite for sailing. **Tenkiller Lake**, deep in Cherokee territory near the little town of Gore, caters to scuba enthusiasts. **Grand Lake o' the Cherokees**, in the far northeast corner of the state, is home to **The Cherokee Queen II**, a Mississippi-style paddleboat offering sightseeing and dinner cruises. A scenic peninsula on **Fort Gibson Lake** is one of the state's most popular vacation areas, **Western Hills Guest Ranch**. The scenic **Illinois River**, rolling in from Arkansas, draws crowds of canoe and raft enthusiasts.

☐ The Illinois River

Almost 200,000 people float a 70-mile stretch of the Illinois River each year from early May to late October. Rated Class II, the scenic stream gives a safely thrilling ride at an average fall of eight feet to the mile, with easy-to-maneuver channels and gentle rapids. Outfitters line SH-10 north of Tahlequah providing canoes, inner tubes, rafts, and kayaks for self-guided float trips – running from three hours to several days.

The average price for a five-mile, three-hour canoe trip is $10 per person, including shuttle service, life preservers, and insurance. Full-day canoe rentals are about $15 per person, and raft or kayak rates are slightly higher. Since prices, equipment, and services vary somewhat from one outfitter to another, call around before you decide where to rent. Some suppliers offer trip packages and group rates. You'll want to bring your own cooler full of snacks and drinks – no glass or Styrofoam containers are allowed – and wear shoes, since the river bottom is rocky.

The Illinois pours into Oklahoma from the dam at Lake Frances on the Arkansas border with the first public access area off SH-59 north of the town of Watts. From here the clean, clear stream twists through sandstone bluffs past towering oak trees and rolling Ozark hills. The first chance to take out is the low-water bridge 7½ miles down river. Below Chewey Bridge, at the 21.7-mile point, there are unlimited access areas.

This upper portion of the river is not always a floater's dream. Water levels can get very low during dry summer months, and you may do more dragging than floating. On the other hand, after heavy rains, water depth and speed increase sharply, and you could find yourself faced with more river than you're prepared to handle. But, for the most part, this stretch of water offers a fine ride, especially if you have your own equipment and are willing to take whatever conditions you find.

The lower part of the Illinois runs for just over 21 miles from Hanging Rock Camp, 8.8 miles downstream from Chewey Bridge, to Riverside Park near Tahlequah. This stretch is comparable to the upper section, but the river becomes deeper and wider as it moves toward Tenkiller Lake. Water flow is slower and more adequate year-round in the lower river, and there are numerous access points for launching and taking out.

Equipment, shuttle service, campsites and lodging are provided along a scenic 20-mile stretch of SH-10 north of Tahlequah. Check with the following for reservations and river conditions:

- **Falcon Floats** (☎ 918-456-8058 or 800-OK-FLOAT)
- **Sparrow Hawk Camp** (☎ 918-456-8371 or 800-722-9635)
- **Diamondhead Resort** (☎ 918-456-4545 or 800-722-2411)
- **War Eagle Recreation** (☎ 918-456-6272 or 800-722-3834)
- **Peyton's Place** (☎ 918-456-3847 or 800-359-0866)
- **Eagle Bluff Resorts** (☎ 918-456-3031 or 800-366-3031)
- **Thunderbird Resort** (☎ 918-456-4747 or 800-749-4700)
- **Hanging Rock Camp** (☎ 918-456-3088 or 800-375-3088)
- **Arrowhead Camp** (☎ 918-456-1140 or 800-749-1140)
- **Riverside Camp** (☎ 918-456-4787 or 800-749-CAMP)

There are no overnight accommodations at **Green River**, ☎ 918-456-4867, but this SH-10 outfitter rents canoes and rafts and provides shuttle service. **Spencer Ridge Resort**, right on a blacktop road at the end of the scenic Cherokee Turnpike east of the junction with US-69, offers camping, cabins, canoes, and shuttle service, ☎ 918-597-2269. **Cedar Valley Camp**, on the second blacktop road off US-62 east of SH-10, has campsites, canoes, and shuttle service, ☎ 918-456-2484.

Barren Fork Creek originates in Arkansas, crosses the border south of Westville, and parallels US-62 until it joins the Illinois about seven miles below Riverside Park. Some outfitters on SH-10 may be willing to shuttle you to the less popular Barren Fork in high season, but there are no suppliers specifically set up for this area – with good reason. Water in this creek is often too low for enjoyable floating. However, if you prefer nature far from the clamorous crowd, try this stream. You can always walk the dry spots or simply sit on the bank and fish. After the Barren Fork joins the Illinois, it flows another six miles to Carter's Landing at the headwaters of Tenkiller Lake.

There's plenty of fishing action on all sections of the Illinois. Anglers will want to try the faster currents for smallmouth bass using soft-shell crayfish or minnows for bait. These feisty little fellows thrive in cool, clear, rocky-bottomed streams, and the Illinois is one of the few rivers in the state with these exact conditions. Sixty-eight other species of fish live in these waters, most notably largemouth bass and rainbow trout. Trout, like smallmouth, favor fast-moving currents, while the largemouth lolls in deeper, calmer areas.

Below Tenkiller Dam at the south end of the lake, the Illinois continues for 10 miles through gorgeous Ozark-like hills. Flow on this portion of the river is controlled by releases from the dam, and the Corps of Engineers decided several years ago to stop providing release schedules to outfitters. Tragically, this put most suppliers out of business, and canoe rentals are not available. However, if you have your own equipment and don't mind waiting for ample water to pour from the dam, this is an excellent trip.

Since the water is cold year-round, trout thrive in the river below the dam and several rustic resorts cater to fishermen and summer vacationers. **Fin and Feather Resort**, ☎ 918-487-5148, and **MarVal Resort**, ☎ 918-489-2295, both off SH-100 north of I-40, offer everything you need for a day or week of river play. Both resorts send newsletters and brochures, so call and ask to be added to the mailing lists.

❐ Tenkiller Lake

This sparkling lake stretches 34 miles through the Cookson Hills offering outdoor folk more than 130 miles of shoreline, 10 marinas and 14 parks. Because of good underwater visibility, the lake is popular with scuba divers. After a rainy period, visibility usually is down to about five feet. However, by the first part of June when drier weather sets in, divers can expect 15- to 20-foot visibility. By late summer, the water temperature warms to an average 80°. Even in winter, Tenkiller is almost as warm as Broken Bow in the summer – about 65°.

Gene's Acqua Pro Shop at Strayhorn Landing off SH-10A at the south end of the lake runs a three-day training course for beginners. Certified divers can play in the underwater aqua park – which contains a submerged swing set, school bus, boat, and other toys – or explore natural caves, hunt for turtles, and race the fish. Gene's provides PADI instruction, rental equipment, and dive trips. The shop is directly across the lake from Pine Cove Marina. Hours are 9 am to 6 pm daily. Call ahead for weather and lake conditions. For information on scuba school or dive adventures, call Gene's at ☎ 918-487-5221 or 800-932-2755.

Above water, the lake is a favorite with sailors, water skiers, swimmers, and fishermen. Year-round fishing is good, and there are five heated docks for winter crappie fishing. Several other species of fish are abundant in the lake, including both black and white bass, catfish, perch, and walleye. Rainbow trout are stocked below the dam. The trout fishery here is a major attraction, and serious anglers congregate during the summer hoping to hook one of the huge stripers that feed on the trout.

Tenkiller is operated by the Tulsa District Corps of Engineers, and maps are available at the project office near the dam on the south end of the lake off SH-100, ☎ 918-487-5252. A vacation guide is available from the **Lake Tenkiller Association**, ☎ 918-457-4403.

The *Cherokee Princess*, a good-sized cruiser, can be chartered for group lake tours leaving from **Burnt Cabin Marina**, ☎ 918-457-5421. A taped commentary plays during the 1½-hour tour, which costs about $7 per person for groups of at least 15 adults. Burnt Cabin Marina is on the west side of the lake off Indian Road.

Other popular facilities on the lake include:

- **Tenkiller State Park** (southeast side), ☎ 918-457-4403
- **Cookson Bend** (east side), ☎ 918-487-5252
- **Pettit Bay** (west side), ☎ 918-487-5252
- **Snake Creek Cove** (east side), ☎ 918-487-5252
- **Sixshooter** (east side), ☎ 918-457-5152
- **Elk Creek** (northeast side), ☎ 918-457-5142.

All of these facilities have boat ramps and marinas. Snake Creek, Sixshooter, and Burnt Cabin also have heated fishing docks.

Several islands dot the lake, and they are popular spots for picnics and lake gazing. From Tenkiller State Park you can see **Goat Island** rising 30 feet to the northwest. **Big Island** is the largest, at the southern tip. All the islands are undeveloped and make perfect hideaways – but you're on your own if you run into trouble.

❏ Oologah Lake

Oklahomans love to sail, and one of their favorite glides is through the blue-green water of **Oologah Lake**. The wind is often just right here, and the active **Spindrift Sailing Club** (☎ 918-582-1171) keeps the lake busy and beautifully decorated with colorful, billowing sails. Several spots along the lake offer wonderful views, including Dog Iron Ranch, Will Roger's birthplace, which sits on a hill above the west side two miles east of US-169. Another great vista is from the dam/overlook on SH-88 at the southern end of the lake. Check with the sailing club for a schedule of events and races – or information on classes.

Fishermen, skiers, and swimmers also find plenty to do at Oologah. With almost 30,000 acres of water, Oologah is the fifth largest lake in the state and second largest in the northeastern region. Best bets for fishermen are sand bass, hybrid-striped bass, crappie and walleye. Boat ramps are located in several areas around the lake with the most facilities at **Hawthorn Bluff** near the dam, ☎ 918-443-2250.

Other Corps of Engineer developments include:

- **Big Creek** (far north end on US-60), ☎ 918-273-3538
- **Spencer Creek Cove** (east side), ☎ 918-443-2250
- **Blue Creek** (southeast side), ☎ 918-443-2250
- **Double Creek Cove** (northwest side), ☎ 918-273-3538.
- **Winganon**, on the east side, across the water from Spencer Creek Cove, is a primitive area with a boat ramp, ☎ 918-587-7927.

❏ Grand Lake o' the Cherokees

This huge 59,200-acre lake is the third largest in the state with well over a thousand miles of shoreline. The majestic **Cherokee Queen II**, a three-deck paddlewheeler, is the most entertaining way to tour the Grand. During the summer visitors can take a two-hour sightseeing cruise at 2 pm, Wednesday through Sunday, or a two-hour dinner cruise at 6:30 pm on Saturday. A dance is held on the boat following dinner on Saturday from 9 pm to 11:15 pm. Tickets for the sightseeing tour are $8.50 for adults, $7 for senior citizens, and $5 for children. Dinner, which includes barbecue ribs and baked chicken, costs $19.50 for adults and $10.50 for children. Only adults may come aboard for dancing on

Northeast Oklahoma

Saturday nights – tickets are $6. Call the office on SH-59 near Sailboat Bridge, ☎ 918-786-4272, for information and dinner reservations. A highlight of the tour is seeing the luxurious houses that line the shore.

Grand Lake is one of the state's best reservoirs for largemouth bass and is home to a large paddlefish population. The ancient paddlefish, also known as the spoonbill, is found mostly below the dams in the Arkansas and Neosho rivers. This unique fish can grow to over 100 pounds, and a record-setting 134-pounder was pulled from Grand in 1992. Crappie and catfish are also plentiful in these waters.

Many facilities here are private, but there are several state parks and numerous public boat ramps. **Cherokee II State Park**, on the east side of the lake near the town of Disney on SH-28, has multiple facilities, ☎ 918-435-8066. **Bernice State Park** (west side), and **Honey Creek State Park**, (east side), both reached at ☎ 918-786-9447, have boat ramps, showers, and other facilities. The largest resort on the lake is **Shangri-La**, ☎ 918-257-4204 or 800-331-4060. Built as a fishing lodge, the resort is well known for its outstanding amenities, including two beautiful golf courses.

A schedule of sailing events can be obtained from **Grand Catalina 22 Fleet**, ☎ 918-743-5965, or the **Grand Lake Sailing Club**, ☎ 918-747-3750.

❏ Fort Gibson Lake

Western Hills Guest Ranch (☎ 918-772-2046), in Sequoyah State Park, juts out into 19,100-acre Fort Gibson Lake just an hour's drive from Tulsa and minutes from Muskogee. This popular retreat, nestled between the rugged Boston Mountain Range and the forested Cookson Hills, draws return vacationers year after year because of its beautiful location and the variety of nearby activities. The lake itself produces an abundant supply of several species of fish, and there are facilities for both power and sail boats.

Two islands visible in the lake from Taylor Ferry near SH-51 are actually ancient Indian grounds known as the **Norman Mounds**. All treasures are protected by federal antiquities laws, so don't try to dig up anything. However, you're welcome to picnic or fish on the islands. The mounds were probably temples or burial grounds built about 1250 AD by a tribe related to the Wichita Indians. A third mound, east of Western Hills Guest Ranch, is thought to be the major political and religious center for all Indians in the Arkansas Basin from about 900 A.D. until approximately 1100 A.D. If you don't have your own boat, rent a pontoon from one of the marinas. The islands slope gently down to the water making access fairly easy.

Sequoyah Bay State Park, ☎ 918-772-2545, is across the lake from the peninsula location of Sequoyah State Park, ☎ 918-772-2046, at the southern end of the reservoir. Both parks have boat ramps and swimming beaches. Other developed areas with launch sites and access points are operated by the Corps of Engineers, ☎ 918-687-2167. They include **Flat Rock Creek**, **Rocky Point**, and **Blue Bill Point**, separated by water mid-lake off US-69 on the west side; **Taylor Ferry North** and **Taylor Ferry South**, separated by an inlet farther south on the west side offSH-51; **Jackson Bay**, near the waterfowl refuge off SH-16; **Wahoo Bay**, a day-use area on the southern end west of the dam; and both **Hulbert Landing** and **Wildwood**, on the southeast side. **Canyon Road** is a day-use facility below the dam on the Grand Neosho River.

Chouteau Bend on SH-33 on the far northwest arm of the lake offers boat rental and showers, ☎ 918-476-6422. **Mazie Landing** on SH-69 south of Chouteau Bend has a marina and cabins, ☎ 918-476-8965. For maps and general information on the lake area, phone the Fort Gibson Lake Office, ☎ 918-485-4623. Contact **Tsa-La-Gi Yacht Club** for sailing information and a schedule of events, ☎ 918-357-3384.

❏ Kaw Lake

This pretty reservoir, about the size of Fort Gibson Lake, wraps around Kaw City northeast of Ponca City, just far enough east of I-35 to be called a northeastern lake. Deep blue cool water, rocky banks, and abundant mud flats make Kaw one of the best catfish lakes in the state. There are two swimming beaches, several access points for boaters, and plenty of suppliers. A steady breeze attracts sailing fans in the summer (call **Indian Nation Sailing Club**, ☎ 580-762-3589, for information), and the abundance of fish attracts migrating bald eagles in the winter (contact the **Wildlife Department**, ☎ 405-521-4616, for a viewing brochure).

Contact the **Kaw Lake Association** on West Doolin Street in the town of Blackwell, ☎ 580-353-1260, for maps, brochures, and a schedule of events. The biggest celebration of the year takes place on the south end of the lake the second weekend of June. There's a couple of bass tournaments, a sailboat regatta, and a timed boat rally. Activities at the north end of the lake center on Native American powwows, which are open to the public. Contact the **Kaw Nation of Oklahoma** for dates and information, ☎ 580-269-2552.

The Corps of Engineers operates public use facilities at **Bear Creek Cove**, **Washunga Bay**, and **Sarge Creek Cove** – all on the east side. South shore facilities include **Osage Cove**, **Sandy Park**, and **McFadden Cove**. **Coon Creek** is on SH-11 on the west side, and **Trader's Bend** is farther north on the west side. Information on all these developments is available from the project office at ☎ 580-762-5611. Details on Pioneer Beach are available from the office on SH-11 at Kaw City, ☎ 580-269-2575.

☐ Lesser Lakes & Rivers Worth a Try

Several smaller Oklahoma rivers are part of the canoe-trails system overseen by the **Scenic River Commission**, ☎ 918-456-3251 or 800-299-3251. Unlike the Illinois, these lesser rivers tend to dry up quickly in the summer. But if you have your own equipment and transportation, you will find a bit of solitude and some gorgeous scenery. After spring and autumn the following are usually fine for fishing and floating: **Lee Creek**, off SH-101 west of the town of Short; **Barren Fork**, running parallel to US-62 west of the town of Westville; **Flint Creek**, flowing over the Arkansas border north ofUS-412 above Fiddlers Bend where it joins the Illinois. The **Spring River** feeds Grand Lake and originates in the far northeastern corner of the state near the town of Miami. The best access point is in Spring River State Park on SH-10 near Quapaw. Get directions and information by calling ☎ 918-542-4481 or 918-540-2545.

Both **Skiatook Lake** and **Keystone Lake** are popular with Tulsa residents for weekend escapes and day outings. Skiatook covers 10,500 acres northwest of the city on SH-20, and its meandering shoreline is dotted with pretty bluffs overlooking low rolling hills and flat tall grass prairie. Public-use areas are maintained by the Corps of Engineers and provide access to the lake for fishing (largemouth bass and channel catfish are plentiful) and boating. Maps and information are available at the project office near the west end of the dam, ☎ 918-396-3138.

Keystone spreads across 26,000 acres west of Tulsa and neighboring Sand Springs off US-412 parallels US-64 and SH-51. Fishing is popular at this sprawling lake, with stripers, walleye, and catfish in abundant supply. White sandy beaches appeal to swimmers and boaters, and both the state and Corps of Engineers maintain boat ramps, campgrounds, and parks around the lake. Maps, information, and reservations are available at the state park office off SH-51 at the south end of the dam, ☎ 918-865-4991, or at the project office off US-64 at the north end of the dam, ☎ 918-865-2621.

❑ Locks, Dams & Waterways

The **McClellan-Kerr Waterway** was created to facilitate industrial shipping on the Arkansas River as it flows through Oklahoma from its origin in Colorado to its termination at the Mississippi in Arkansas. Portions of the waterway are open to recreational use, and private boats can navigate the system, which links Tulsa to Little Rock, Arkansas. For maps and regulations, contact the **Tulsa District**, **Corps of Engineers**, ☎ 918-581-7666 or the **McClellan-Kerr Waterway Association**, ☎ 918-682-9131.

■ Where to Stay

Hotels, Resorts & B&Bs

Afton/Monkey Island

Shangri-La Resort, ☎ 800-331-4060, www.shangrilaresort. com, on Grand Lake's Monkey Island off SH-125, is a major facility with golf, indoor/outdoor tennis, and health-spa services. Basic rooms are in the $80 range, the suites and package-vacations are in the $200 range.

Bartlesville

Hotel Phillips, 821 Johnstone, ☎ 918-336-5600 or 800-331-0706, fax 918-336-0350. Owned by Marriott, but more like a fine independent establishment, this 164-room hotel has all the amenities, including bathrobes, newspapers, and a chocolate on the pillow each night. Ask about weekend bed & breakfast packages. Rooms are $65 to $125.

Jarrett Farm Country Inn, US-75 in Ramona 13 miles south of Bartlesville, ☎ 918-371-9868. This is an impressive, award-winning inn set on 230 acres atop a hill between Tulsa and Bartlesville. Gourmet dinner is served Thursday at 5:30 pm and 8 pm seatings, Friday and Saturday at 6 pm and 8 pm seatings. Overnight guests stay in three-room suites in duplex guesthouses near the heated pool. A full gourmet breakfast is served in the solarium each morning. Suites are $135 to $195, and dinner is about $65 per couple. The inn is closed on Sunday and Monday nights, and reservations should be made well in advance.

Billings

25 miles southwest of Ponca City

The Homestead Bed and Breakfast, SH-15 and US-77 east of town at the GT Ranch, ☎ 580-725-3400. This is a new log cabin built to be a bed & breakfast on a working cattle ranch. A Western theme is used in the rooms; each has a private bath. There is plenty to do nearby, but most guests feel so pampered and at ease, they never leave the ranch. Rates are $65 to $100.

Checotah

South of Muskogee, east of US-69

Sharpe House, 301 Northwest 2nd Street, ☎ 918-473-2832, was once a rooming house for school teachers. It's not unusual for breakfast to include Mexican omelets or *huevos rancheros*. Room rates are $35 to $50.

Chandler

Read Ranch, ☎ 405-258-2999, on Historic Route 66, 25 miles east of Oklahoma City and five miles west of Chandler, has RV hookups, campsites, and mini-bunkhouses. The big feature here is all the Western activities to keep groups and families busy. Ask about the *City Slicker Specials*, which include two-day campouts. Call for rates on the activities or accommodations that appeal to you.

Claremore

Carriage House Bed and Breakfast Inn, 109 East 4th Street, ☎ 918-342-2693, is a restored home built in 1906. The house is decorated with antiques and features hardwood floors and original fireplaces. Rooms are in the main house or carriage house (which is sometimes called the honeymoon cottage because of the two-person Jacuzzi). Full breakfast and bedtime snacks are served. Rates are $50-$75.

Country Inn Bed and Breakfast, Route 3 northeast of town, ☎ 918-342-1894, is a secluded barn-style building on five acres of land adjacent to the main house. Breakfast is served at your convenience, and guests may use the pool and borrow bikes for a ride in the country. Prices range from $37 to $64.

Fairland

Six miles from Grand Lake o' the Cherokees on US-60

J-M's Country Bed and Breakfast, 56900 East 210 Road, ☎ 918-676-3881, fax 918-676-5228, is a baby dude ranch with all the modern amenities – even a pool. Continental or full breakfast is available, and rates are between $45 and $75.

Gore

MarVal Resort, ☎ 918-489-2295, Gore Landing Road off I-40 at the 287 exit or off the Muskogee Turnpike at exit 55, is an upscale campground located on 105 acres near the Illinois River. There are a variety of overnight options ranging in price from $12 for a tent site to $75 for a cabin that will sleep four. Day-use is also available.

Grove

Candlewyck Bed and Breakfast Inn, 59600 East 307 Lane, ☎ 918-786-3636, is right on Grand Lake o' the Cherokees, surrounded by trees. Breakfast is served in a dining room overlooking a wooded cove, and a private boat dock is available for guests. Suites at this elegant B&B run from $99 to $225.

Oak Tree Bed and Breakfast, 1007 South Main Street, ☎ 918-786-9119, is a traditional home within walking distance of downtown. Rooms are priced from $50 to $60.

Red Port 11, 1½ miles northeast of Sailboat Bridge on Grand Lake, ☎ 918-786-2362, offers lakeside motel-style units and cabins with kitchenettes. This basic family resort has all the amenities for a fishing and boating vacation. Motel units rent for $38 and cabins range from $42 to $47.

Blue Bluff Harbor Resort, ☎ 800-891-5531 or 918-786-5531, 63251 East 256 Road, has modern cottages, a heated fishing dock, and a café.

Northeast Oklahoma

Call for seasonal rates on the cabins, which accommodate four to six people.

Hills Resort, ☎ 918-786-5109, near Honey Creek bridge off US-59 on Lake Road #3, has 17 cottages, which accommodate one to 12 in one to five bedrooms. Rates begin at $34 and go to $120.

Henryetta

Guesthouse Inn & Dome, ☎ 918-652-2581 or 800-515-3663, at US-75 and I-40, has a dome-covered indoor pool and recreational facility featuring a big screen TV and pool table. Big John's Restaurant is adjacent with daily specials and buffets. Call for exact rates, which range from $40 to $60.

Mannford

Near Keystone Lake west of Tulsa

Chateau in the Woods Bed and Breakfast, 4½ miles north of town, ☎ 918-865-7979. This waterfront B&B is surrounded by trees on Keystone Lake. Breakfast is served outdoors on a wrap-around deck. Rooms rent for $95 to $165.

Muskogee

Graham-Carroll House, 501 North 16th Street, ☎ 918-683-0100 or 800-878-0167, offers lovely suites in a renovated Victorian mansion built with oil money. Features include gardens, fountains, a conservatory, whirlpool tubs, and fireplaces. Breakfast is served in a formal dining room with an elegant chandelier. Rates are $80-$95.

Miss Addie's Tea Room and Bed and Breakfast, 821 West Broadway, ☎ 918-682-1506. As the name would suggest, this restored turn-of-the-century drugstore is part tea room and part B&B. Lunch is open to the public downstairs between 11 am and 2 pm. Upstairs, there are rooms with private baths. A full breakfast is served to overnight guests on weekends. Rooms rent for $45 to $65.

Pawhuska

The Inn at Woodyard Farms, on Lynn Avenue off US-60, ☎ 918-287-2699, is on the rolling prairie of Osage County. Featuring king-size and queen-size beds, this country farmhouse retreat serves a large breakfast with homemade biscuits. All rooms have private baths and rent for $60 to $65.

Ponca City

Rose Stone Inn, 120 South Third, ☎ 580-765-5699 or 800-763-9922, fax 580-762-0240. This 25-room inn is a luxury downtown accommodation serving evening snacks and a full breakfast buffet. You can request limousine service and guest privileges at the YMCA gym. Room rates run from $49 to $89.

Marland Estate Conference Center and Hotel, 901 Monument, ☎ 580-767-0422 or 800-532-7559, fax 580-762-8182. Thirty-five rooms and two suites were built at the Marland Mansion when the estate was used as a school run by nuns. The rooms are basic, but nicely decorated and peaceful. A pool, restaurant, and meeting rooms are on the grounds. Room rates are $40 to $45, the suites rent for $90, and the gatehouse cottage is $125 per night.

Davarnathey Bed and Breakfast Inn, 1001 West Grand, ☎ 580-765-9922, was built in 1906, and is operated by the same husband and wife who run Rose Stone Inn. There are three rooms with private baths, and guests are served a continental breakfast. Rooms are $60 to $70.

Salina

The Plum Tree Inn, two miles south of town on SH-82, ☎ 918-434-6000 or 800-285-6911. This inn sits on 23 acres overlooking Lake Hudson. Four of the five rooms – all with private bath – have lake views. Rates are $55-$85.

Stillwater

Friend House Bed and Breakfast, 404 South Knoblock, ☎ 405-372-1982, is two blocks from Oklahoma State University. The house was built in 1912 and has three rooms with private baths. Guests have their choice of full or continental breakfast. Room rates begin at $60.

Thomasville, 4115 North Denver, ☎ 405-372-1203, was the home of the town's first mayor. Guests are welcome on weekends by referral and with a reservation. Rates begin at $60.

Northeast Oklahoma

Stroud

Stroud House Bed and Breakfast, 110 East Second Street, ☎ 918-968-2978 or 800-259-2978, fax 918-968-2978. This home was built in 1900 and renovated in 1992. Each of the four rooms has a private bath, and guests are welcomed with a homemade cookie. Rooms are priced from $65 to $100.

Tahlequah

Fin and Feather Resort, ☎ 918-487-5148, SH-10A at the south end of Tenkiller Lake, has 82 units ranging from one-bedroom cabins to five-bedroom houses. There is an indoor pool, tennis courts, and a game room. Buffet meals are served in the large dining room. The **Annual Fall Festival**, with quality arts and crafts, is held the last weekend in September. Accommodations range from $56 to $285 per night.

Bed and Breakfast of Tahlequah, ☎ 918-456-1309, 215 West Morgan Street, is actually a garage apartment with a small kitchen. Breakfast is brought to the door each morning. Rates are in the $40 range.

Glenn's Bed and Breakfast, ☎ 918-456-4451, 340 Bailey Boulevard north of town near the Illinois River, has two rooms with private baths. In the $40 range.

Lord and Taylor's Bed and Breakfast, ☎ 918-457-4756, near Tenkiller Lake, has four rooms, two with private bath. Rooms rates are $40 to $60 and include a large continental breakfast.

Oak Hill, ☎ 918-458-1200, fax 918-458-1101, 2600 South Muskogee Avenue, has 35 rooms, one luxury suite, and a complimentary breakfast bar. Rooms are in the $50 range.

Wagoner

Western Hills Guest Ranch, ☎ 918-772-2545 or 800-654-8240, is a state-run resort on SH-51 in Sequoyah State Park on Fort Gibson Lake. This Western style lodge has 101 rooms and suites renting from $40 in the winter to $175 in the summer. There are also 54 cottages that range from a low of $45 off-season to $98 during peak-season. Ask about the *Cowboy Adventure Package*.

Camping

Reservations for camping at any state park can be made through the central reservation system, ☎ 800-654-8240, or call one of these campgrounds noted for their scenery or outstanding facilities.

Osage Hills State Park, ☎ 918-336-4141, off US-60 between Bartlesville and Pawhuska, has eight native stone cabins, as well as campsites. Cabin rates range from $53 to $68. Campsites are $6 to $17.

Western Hills Guest Ranch, ☎ 918-772-2545, on SH-51 on Fort Gibson Lake at Sequoyah State Park, has 54 cottages and 321 campsites. Cottages rent from a low of $45 for one room off-season to a high of $105 for a two-bedroom during prime season. Rates for RV and tent camping range from $6 to $17.

Greenleaf State Park, ☎ 918-487-5196, three miles south of Braggs on SH-10A, has 14 cabins and 139 campsites. The handicapped-accessible cabin is $45 to $75 for disabled persons. Other cabins rent for $53 and $58. Campsites are $6 to $17.

Keystone State Park, ☎ 918-865-4991, 10 miles west of Sand Springs on US-412 to the Dam Road turnoff, has 21 cabins and 143 campsites. Cabins rent for $58 for the one-bedroom, $85 for the two-bedroom, and $150 for the three-bedroom. Campsites are $6 to $17.

Tenkiller State Park, ☎ 918-489-5641, 10 miles north of the Vian exit on SH-82, has 40 cabins, 10 cabanas, and 221 campsites. The cabanas rent for $33, the one-bedroom cabins for $48, and the two-bedroom cabins for $68. Campsites range from $6 to $17.

■ Where to Eat

Afton/Monkey Island

$$/$$$ **Roadhouse**, ☎ 918-257-8185, SH-125 south, serves fresh seafood and steaks topped with whiskey-pepper sauce. Open 5 pm to 10 pm every evening from early spring until late fall. In the winter, the restaurant is open the same hours Wednesday through Sunday.

Bartlesville

$$ Murphy's Steak House, 1625 South West Frank Phillips Boulevard off US-75, ☎ 918-336-4789, open Tuesday through Sunday from 11 am to 11:30 pm. Arrive early to avoid the crowd that always lines up here on weekend nights. The specialty is steak, of course, but the open-face hamburger topped with gravy is a local favorite.

$$ Villa Italia, 821 Johnstone inside Hotel Phillips, ☎ 918-336-5600, open for breakfast from 6:30am to 10 am, Monday through Friday, and from 7 am to 11 am, Saturday and Sunday; dinner is served from 5 pm to 10 pm, Monday through Thursday, and from 5 pm to 11 pm, Friday through Sunday. This is a small, casual restaurant with a romantic atmosphere. The menu includes Italian cuisine and steaks.

$ Dink's Pit Bar-B-Que, 2929 South East Frank Phillips Boulevard, ☎ 918-335-0606, open Sunday through Thursday from 11 am to 8 pm and Friday and Saturday from 11 am to 9 pm. This is a local favorite, serving dependably delicious barbecued meats with all the traditional side dishes.

Oologah

$ Goodies, 155 Cooweescoowee, ☎ 918-443-2323, serves breakfast and lunch from 7 am to 2 pm, Monday through Saturday. Baked goods are the drawing card here – cinnamon rolls in the morning and sandwiches on homemade bread for lunch.

Claremore

$/$$ Hammett House, 1616 West Will Rogers Boulevard, ☎ 918-341-7333, down the hill from the Will Rogers Memorial, is open Tuesday through Saturday from 11 am to 9 pm. This popular restaurant has been in business for more than 30 years under two husband-and-wife owners. Loyal patrons return again and again for moderately priced home-style meals and outstanding homemade pies.

$ The Pink House, 210 West 4th, ☎ 918-342-2544, serves lunch from 11 am to 3 pm Tuesday through Saturday. This fancy tea room is housed in a Victorian home built in 1902. The menu includes sandwiches, soups, casseroles, and a variety of desserts.

Grove

$/$$ **Rheingarten Restaurant**, 911 South Main Street, ☎ 918-786-8737, serves dinner Monday through Thursday from 4 pm to 8 pm, Friday and Saturday from 4 pm to 9 pm, and opens for Sunday lunch from 11:30 am to 3 pm. The aroma of German food lures diners to this remodeled home decorated with beer steins.

Muskogee

Don't bother to ask residents where to find the best barbecue in town. Everyone has their favorite "pit," and you'll just have to try a few to discover the one that suits you best.

$ **Slick's Barbecue**, 2329 West Shawnee, ☎ 918-687-9215, open 11 am to 8 pm every day except Wednesday, when it closes at 2 pm, and Sunday, when it doesn't open at all. Slick's been turning out barbecue for more than 35 years on hickory pits behind this just-the-basics café. Wear your grubbies; meals are served on butcher paper.

$ **Al's Barbecue**, 1306 South 32nd Street, ☎ 918-683-0910, open 11 am to 8 pm every day except Sunday. Convenient to several motels and attractions along US-69. Prices are inexpensive.

$ **Cowboys Barbecue**, 401 North York, ☎ 918-682-0651, open from 10:30 am to 9 pm, Monday through Saturday, closed Sunday. Loyal customers wouldn't go any place else.

$ **My Place Bar-B-Q West**, 4322 West Okmulgee, ☎ 918-683-5202, open Monday through Saturday from 10 am to 9 pm. Serves traditional barbecue meals with all the trimmings.

$/$$ **Little Italy**, 2432 North 32nd, ☎ 918-687-5699, open for lunch Tuesday through Friday and Sunday from 11 am to 2 pm; dinner served Tuesday through Thursday and Sunday from 5 pm to 9 pm, Friday and Saturday from 5 pm to 10 pm. This is one of the most popular restaurants in town because of the low lights, comfortable atmosphere, and delicious Italian food.

$ **Miss Addie's Tea Room**, 821 West Broadway, ☎ 918-682-1506, open daily for lunch 11 am to 2 pm; an English tea is served from 2 pm to 4 pm, and breakfast is from 8 am to 11 am on Saturday and Sunday. This little tea room is furnished with antiques and serves light homemade lunches and desserts.

$ Harmony House Eatery and Bakery, 208 South 7th Street, ☎ 918-687-8653, open from 7 am to 3 pm, Monday through Friday. The trademark here is cookies – made from scratch in many varieties. Lunch is sandwiches or a more filling daily special.

When you can't decide what you're hungry for, try one of these two casual restaurants that serve "a little bit of everything."

$/$$ Okie's, 219 South 32nd Street, ☎ 918-683-1056, open Monday through Saturday from 11 am to 10 pm.

$/$$ Jasper's, 1702 West Okmulgee, ☎ 918-682-7867, open Monday through Wednesday from 11 am to 10 pm, Thursday through Saturday from 11 am to 11 pm.

Sallisaw

$ Wild Horse Mountain Barbecue, ☎ 918-775-9960, US-59 south of town, is a rustic café with a barbecue pit out back. The quality is so good, customers drive out of their way to eat here.

Tahlequah

$/$$ Jasper's, ☎ 918-456-0100, 2600 South Muskogee Avenue, serves everything from sandwiches to lobsters. Open Monday through Saturday, 11 am to 10 pm.

$/$$ The Peppermill, ☎ 918-456-3200, on 4th Street at the Bertha Parker Bypass, is a Western restaurant serving everything from a breakfast buffet to steak dinners. Hours are Sunday through Thursday from 6:30 am to 9 pm and Friday and Saturday from 6:30 am to 10 pm.

■ Where to Shop

Bartlesville

 Keepsake Candles, two miles west of town on SH-60, ☎ 918-336-0351, open Monday through Friday from 9 am to 5:30 pm, Saturday from 10 am to 5 pm, and Sunday from 1 pm to 5 pm. Tours are held at 11 am, 1 pm, and 3 pm Monday through Friday. Stop by early when the factory and display rooms are less crowded. Keepsake candles are made from molds of antique glassware, which creates a unique wax work of art. Call about special fall and Christmas events.

The Antiques and Collectibles Association lists 10 malls, 20 antique shops, and 10 specialty stores as members in the Bartlesville area. Call the Chamber of Commerce, ☎ 800-364-8708 or 918-336-8708 and ask for the pink map of merchants who fly the pink "ANTIQUES" flag at their store. **ITIO Trading Post**, 101 East Frank Phillips Boulevard, ☎ 918-337-9292, open Monday through Saturday from 10 am to 5:30 pm. The initials stand for Indian Territory Illuminating Oil, an old company that once used the Trading Post building. Actually a mini-mall of shops, the Trading Post offers fine shoes and clothing, antiques, gifts, and a coffee bar/chocolate shop.

Yocham's, east on US-60, ☎ 918-335-2277, open Monday through Friday from 9 am to 5:30 pm and Saturday from 9 am to 4 pm. Custom saddles with starting prices over $1,000 are the specialty here, but you can also buy other leather items and Western jewelry, accessories, and furniture.

Claremore

The Claremore Guild, 714 West Will Rogers Boulevard, ☎ 918-341-7878, is a 450-member organization that represents fine antique and craft stores, bed & breakfast accommodations, and quality apparel shops. Call or stop by for a map and list of members' locations.

The Belvedere, 121 North Chickasaw, ☎ 918-342-1127, is open from mid-October through mid-December, Thursday through Saturday from 10 am to 5 pm and Sunday from 1 pm to 5 pm. This restored mansion owned by the Rogers County Historical Society is used throughout the year for special events. Each fall, the mansion opens for two months to sell antique and handmade gifts for Christmas. Call for exact dates.

Grove

The Old Homestead, ☎ 918-786-8668, 6 West 3rd Street, features country treasures including Lang & Wise Villages, Redware by Greg Shooner, Old World Pewter, and Yankee Candles. Open Monday through Saturday from 10 am to 5 pm.

Muskogee

Beaver Antiques, 540 Court, ☎ 918-682-5503, open Monday through Saturday from 10 am to 5 pm, buys and sells individual pieces and entire estates. Featured items include toys, collectibles, furniture, and primitives.

Main Street USA, 2426 North 32nd Street (US-69), ☎ 918-687-5517, fax 918-687-6188, open from 9 am to 6 pm daily. Over 200 dealers have booths in this huge complex.

Old America Antique Mall, US-69 South, ☎ 918-687-8600, and at 24th Street and Shawnee, ☎ 918-686-8600, both open daily from 10 am to 6 pm. Over 200 dealers offer antiques and collectibles.

Arrowhead Mall, 501 North Main Street, ☎ 918-683-4100, open 10 am to 9 pm, Monday through Saturday, and Sunday from noon to 6 pm. The major department stores in this 65-merchant mall include Dillard's, Penney's and Sears. Several types of fast food are served in the food court. Luby's Cafeteria and Garfield's Restaurant also are inside the mall.

Tahlequah

Cherokee Nation Gift Shop, inside the Cherokee Tribal Complex, 3½ miles south of town on US-62, ☎ 918-456-2793 or 800-256-2123. Call before you visit to check on the hours of operation. You'll find handmade Native American items such as baskets, beadwork, and art.

Satanta – The Orator of the Plains

Satanta, or White Bear, was chief of the Kiowas when he earned the title of "Orator of the Plains."

In a speech delivered to high-ranking US officials on Medicine Lodge Creek in 1867 he said:

"All the land south of the Arkansas belongs to the Kiowas and Comanches, and I don't want to give away any of it. I love the land and the buffalo and will not part with it.

I want you to understand well what I say. Write it on paper....

I have heard that you intend to settle us on a reservation near the mountains. I don't want to settle. I love to roam over the prairies. There I feel free and happy, but when we settle down we grow pale and die....

A long time ago this land belonged to our fathers; but when I go up to the river I see camps of soldiers on its banks. These soldiers cut down my timber; they kill my buffalo; and when I see that my heart feels like bursting; I feel sorry.

I have spoken."

Satanta's fine speech failed and The Medicine Lodge Treaty put an end to the Great Plains as one big Indian reservation.

Azalea Festival, Honor Heights Park, Muscogee. (Fred W. Marvel)

■ Powwows, Festivals, Arts & Crafts Fairs

April

 Muskogee, **Azalea Festival**, Honor Heights Park at 48th Street on Agency Hill, ☎ 918-684-6302. More than 60 varieties of azaleas bloom in this 40-acre park during the annual spring festival, which includes a garden show, bike tour, and a barbecue/chili cookoff.

Muskogee, **Grand Moccasin Festival**, Bacone College, ☎ 918-682-2586. The sky fills with color during the hot air balloon race at this Native American celebration held each April.

May

Muskogee Renaissance Faire, ☎ 918-687-3625, takes place two weekend in May with medieval entertainers and craft demonstrations.

Summer

Tahlequah's Outdoor Drama at Tsa-La-Gi tells the story of *The Trail of Tears* from the end of June until mid-August each year; Cherokee Heritage Center, ☎ 918-456-6007. This amphitheater performance dramatizes the history of the Cherokee people, including the tribe's forced move from Georgia to Oklahoma's Indian Territory. The drama is presented at 8 pm every day except Sunday, and a Cherokee dinner is served before the play from 5 pm to 7:30 pm. Tickets for the show are $9 for adults and $4.50 for children. Dinner is priced at $8 for adults and $5 for children.

Pawnee Bill's Wild West Show, ☎ 918-762-2108, is a re-enactment of the Western show that was once famous all over the US and Europe. The show is presented each Saturday from late June until early August at the Pawnee Bill Ranch on the west side of Pawnee off US-64. Dinner is served at 6:30 – $6 for adults and $3 for children. The show begins at 7 pm and is $8 for adults and $2 for children.

June

Bartlesville OK Mozart Festival, at the Community Center on Adams Boulevard and Cherokee; ticket office, ☎ 918-336-9800; events office, ☎ 918-336-9900. This nine-day musical event is held in mid-June to celebrate the music of many composers, including Mozart. World famous guest artists play in the 1,700-seat center designed by the Frank Lloyd Wright Foundation, and festival cafés and shops sell food and unique gifts. More than 80 events take place during the festival, including firework displays, equestrian performances, and children's programs. Call for exact dates, a schedule of events, and ticket prices. Many concerts and activities sell out quickly, so contact the Festival office early in the year for information.

July

Pawnee Indian Powwow, ☎ 918-762-2108, is held in and near Pawnee on Fourth of July weekend and is one of the largest free powwows. Hundreds of dancers from several tribes compete in native dance contests.

Sac & Fox National Powwow, ☎ 918-968-3526, is a tribal homecoming held in Stroud each July with dancing, crafts show, and Native American food.

August

Cherokee National Holiday, ☎ 918-456-0671, takes place in Tahlequah each summer. The celebration includes a state of the nation address by the Cherokee chief, arts-and-crafts market, cultural workshops, and a rodeo.

November/December

Muskogee Garden of Lights, Honor Heights Park at 48th Street on Agency Hill, ☎ 918-684-6302. More than a million lights decorate the park from the day after Thanksgiving through December 31st, beginning at 5:30 each evening.

Northeast Oklahoma

Southeast Oklahoma

The Southeast quarter of Oklahoma is an excellent region to explore. There are breathtaking drives along the **Talimena Scenic Byway**, challenging bike rides down old logging paths in the **Ouachita** (WASH-i-taw) **National Forest**, and exceptional fishing at **Lake Texoma**. At night, you can tuck into a cozy bed at **Tatonka Cabin** deep in the pine woods near **Beavers Bend** or camp under the stars in the **Arbuckle Mountains**. Unpretentious cafés along two-lane back roads serve family-style meals featuring catfish, barbecue, and cowboy-sized steaks. Add a touch of panache with a glass of Oklahoma-grown-and-bottled wine from **Cimarron Valley Winery** south of Atoka.

Antique lovers and craft collectors will want to stop in the small towns to snoop among the shops, and history buffs can spend many hours exploring deserted log cabins and last-century's cemeteries.

The Choctaw Nation was the first native tribe to be moved to Oklahoma's Indian Territory in the early 1830s, and many place names in southeast Oklahoma are Choctaw words. One promise of The Treaty of Dancing Rabbit Creek, which forced the Indians out of Mississippi, was money from the white man's government to erect a new council house in their new assigned territory. The tribe built their capitol about a mile

Retreats such as Tatonka Cabin near Beavers Bend are common in the southeastern part of the state. (Paul Beardon)

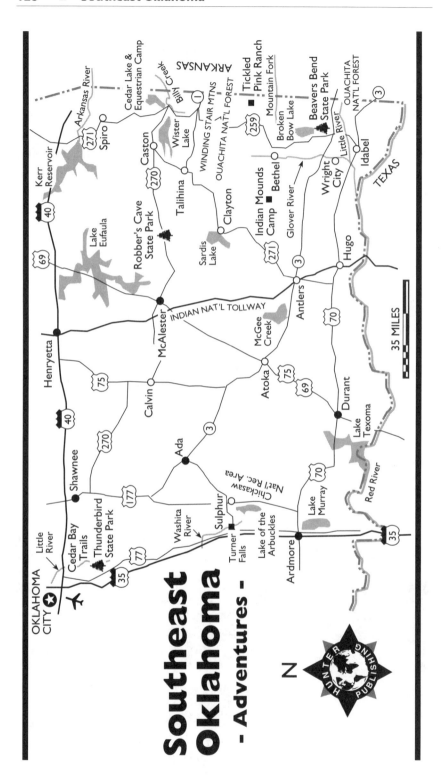

and a half northwest of what is now the town of Tuskahoma, and their museum and courtrooms still are active today. Every Labor Day, the Choctaw celebrate their National Holiday at the Council House, and the area erupts into festivities.

Nearby, the **Ouachita National Forest** spills over the Arkansas border onto 200,000 acres of forest-covered mountain wilderness. Nine recreation areas offer camping, hiking, mountain biking, horse trails, hunting, and fishing. **Talimena Scenic Byway** twists for 54 miles through these mountains offering photographers and sightseers many turnouts with great vistas.

Southeastern Oklahoma offers endless possibilities for adventure. Hike through dense forests, canoe white water rivers, fish well-stocked lakes, bike mountain paths, ride horseback across open valleys, and rappel down sandstone cliffs.

This section will guide you to isolated wilderness and jam-packed swimming holes, breathtaking forested mountains and boggy hollows, historical inns and all-you-can-eat catfish buffets. Start on any of the suggested road trips, stop to see the sights that interest you, and check out the details on outdoor activities for each area.

■ Touring

Talimena Scenic Byway & the Ouachita Forest

45 miles (Talihina to Arkansas border)

Begin this drive north of **Talihina** at the intersection of US Highway 271 and State Highway 1. Take two-lane SH-1 east toward Arkansas into the forested mountains. This route, named The Talimena Byway, has steep grades and sharp turns with marked lookout points along the way. Inspiring wild flowers and dogwood trees burst out in a vivid splash of color over the Winding Stair and Rich Mountains, the highest points between the Appalachians and Rockies. During the fall, changing leaves paint the east-west mountain ridge vibrant shades of amber, gold, and rust. Deer, bear, and a variety of smaller wildlife often wander near the road, so keep your camera available for sudden photo opportunities.

Ouachita National Forest

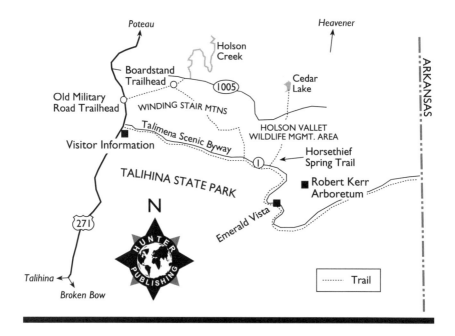

The highway was built solely for its scenic value and winds for 54 miles deep into Arkansas. You may be lured into following one panoramic view after another until you have traveled the entire distance, but if you want to limit your drive to the Oklahoma side, turn around at the border and start back west. **Queen Wilhelmina State Park**, a short distance from the border on the Arkansas side, is a logical turnaround stop. Built on one of the highest elevations in the Rich Mountains, the views from here are magnificent, there is no admission fee, and you can picnic or shake off road fatigue before you head back west to Oklahoma.

North-South through Ouachita National Forest

122 miles

This tour begins on Highway 59, northeast of Spiro, where archaeologists have uncovered burial and ceremonial mounds of 60 Indian tribes who lived in the area between 600 AD and 1450 AD. Explore **Spiro**

Mounds Archaeological Park's 11 ceremonial mounds, then drive south through Choctaw country until you come to the world's tallest hill. **Cavanal Hill** stretches 1,999 feet above the surrounding area, and thus misses the British Geological Society definition of a mountain by one foot. Witteville Road, on the north side of the town of Poteau, leads from US-59 for 4½ miles to the top of "The Hill," where you get a grand view of Sugar Loaf and the Ouachita Mountains.

Seven miles farther south on US-59, the unusual **Heavener-Runestone State Park** is built around a 10-foot-wide slab of sandstone carved with eight runic letters, each six to nine inches high. Find it by following the signs south of Poteau, which lead you east up the side of a mountain – or maybe it's a hill. If you're reasonably fit, climb the sandstone steps up to the nature trail that cuts into the forest and winds along a scenic cliff. Enjoy the view from the picnic tables, then drive south again on US-59/270 to the **restored home of Peter Conser**. You'll be fascinated by the story of this Choctaw lawman who held the powers of judge, jury, and executioner during the territorial days of the 19th century.

Soon after you leave the Conser house, near Hodgen, US-59/270 begins to curve east, then intersects with SH-1, The Talimena Scenic Byway. Take US-259 south of SH-1. This is a gentle roller-coaster ride through the Winding Stair Mountains with a required stop at the epitome of tourist traps, **Babcock's Store**. Bill and Joan Babcock are aware that their shop, at the intersection of US-259 and Octavia Road, is so tacky it's chic. You can buy a coonskin cap if you want to, and don't pass up a treat from the old-fashioned soda fountain. A sign outside the front door proclaims, "Store Ours – Closed When Gate Is." But, mostly the store is open every day except during the cold of January. Call ☎ 580-244-3827 if you want to match your scheduled stop to store "ours."

The drive south to **Hochatown/Beavers Bend** is gorgeous, especially in the spring when the dogwood and wildflowers are in bloom and again in the fall when the trees turn a dozen shades of red and gold. The paved roads that lead east from US-259 toward Broken Bow Reservoir in the Beavers Bend Resort Park offer short, lovely drives that end at **Cedar Creek Golf Course**, **Lake View Lodge**, or **The Forest Heritage Center**. If you have time, drive slowly down one or all these shady roads, stop for a cold drink, watch fishermen reel in fish from Mountain Fork River, and try to spot an eagle soaring overhead.

From here, follow the highway south to **Idabel** and the small but nationally acclaimed **Museum of the Red River** at the intersection of US-259 and US-70. The town calls itself "The Dogwood Capital of Oklahoma" because SH-3 from Idabel east to Haworth is an officially designated dogwood trail. An additional trail is identified along several town's streets, and the **Dogwood Days Festival** is held every year in early April. Maps and festival information are available at the Chamber of Commerce office at 13 N. Central in Idabel, ☎ 405-286-3305.

The Red River Valley

65 miles

History buffs will like this drive west from **Fort Towson** along US-70 to **Lake Texoma State Resort Park**. In 1832, the Choctaw Indian Tribes were forced from their land in Alabama and Mississippi and moved to Indian Territory along the north bank of the Red River, where they became one of the Five Civilized Tribes. Traditionally farmers, they quickly cultivated the land and built productive plantations. Later, many Indians worked for the railroad and the overland mail service. Some operated toll gates and bridges; others became lumberjacks. A few became bootleggers. When the Civil War broke out, tribe members put on uniforms and became Confederate soldiers.

Today, you can scout out traces of this diverse and bizarre history as you travel US-70 west from **Fort Towson** to **Lake Texoma State Resort Park**. Drive around **Hugo Lake**, a 13,500-acre reservoir about seven miles east of the town of **Hugo**. If you're in this area near the fourth weekend in September, expect to see numerous vintage cars on the roads. Any pre-1960 vehicle can enter the **Hugo Lake Rod Run**, and owners proudly flaunt their "babies" throughout the weekend.

Kids – and most adults – will want to spend part of the day in Hugo, **Circus City**, **USA**. Tour the headquarters of Carson & Barnes and Kelly-Miller Brothers circuses, then stop at Mount Olivet Cemetery to see the monuments in "Showmen's Rest," a "tribute to all showmen under God's Big Top."

Under God's Big Top

The Showman's Rest area in Hugo's Mount Olivet Cemetery is the final resting place of fun-loving entertainers such as:

- John Carroll, the Elephant Man, who established a trust for the preservation of Showman's Rest in the 1960s.
- John Strong, the Tall Grass Snowman, whose nine-foot statue towers above a marker reading , "Peace Be With You Big John/The Man With More Friends Than Santa Claus."
- Freckles Brown, the famous rodeo clown.
- William Edmond Ansley, Buster Brown of Buster Brown Shoes.

Unusual grave markers abound, such as:

- The circus tent tombstone over Jack B. Moore's grave.
- A wagon wheel monument over the final resting place of Ted Bowman which reads, "There's Nothing Left But Empty Popcorn Sacks and Wagon Tracks. The Circus is Gone."
- Two horses standing watch over Harry Rooks, a well-known horse trainer.
- A whimsical marker at Peggy Fournier's site that reads, "I Would Rather Be In California."

As you pass through **Durant**, watch for signs pointing to "The World's Largest Peanut" which has been moved inside City Hall because of its frequent abductions by local teens. Your photo album won't be complete without a jumbo-size glossy of you and your travel companions beside this three-foot aluminum legume. Spend only a few minutes viewing the Opera House, unless turn-of-the-century architecture is one of your passions. Then settle in at the Palace on US-69 for a few games of Choctaw Indian **High Stakes Bingo**. You might win big – say $50,000 – but you may lose big, too. If you feel lucky, and can afford it, buy a bingo card package for two consecutive weekend days and your lodging will be complimentary. ☎ 800-788-2464 for all the details. Otherwise, set a time or dollar limit on your visit, then get back on the road.

If you didn't get enough history at Fort Towson, detour north of Durant about 14 miles to the junction of SH-78 and SH-199. On a hilltop three miles west of the junction, you'll find the remains of **Fort Washita** in a remote setting. The fort was built in 1842 by the federal government to protect Choctaw and Chickasaw tribes from raids by the Comanches

Southeast Oklahoma

and other Plains Indians who were terrorizing everyone who tried to settle in the valley. Indians never attacked the fort, and it became a well-known place for gold-seekers to rest up and prepare for the journey across the Texas desert on their way to California. Military re-enactments now take place in the fort during living history events. The largest is the **Fur Trader's Rendezvous** held in April, but some type of event takes place here almost every month. When you visit, ask at the visitors' center for directions to the nature trail that leads to an old cemetery.

Back on US-70, it's only a short distance to **Lake Texoma State Resort Park** and southeast Oklahoma's Lake Country.

Three Lakes and a Waterfall

60 miles

Water is everywhere in south-central Oklahoma. Lakes, streams, springs, rivers, and waterfalls cover an L-shaped area from Durant to Ardmore to Davis so compactly that you can see it all in one day. Begin at one of the three major lakes – Texoma, Murray, or Arbuckle – pick a back road, and start exploring. You can't make a wrong turn, and getting lost is the adventure of this trip.

If you insist on a plan, the following is as good as any:

Leave from **The Resort at Texoma**. It's at the end of the Roosevelt Bridge, on the west side of the lake, coming from Durant on US-70. A friendly ranger will help you sort through the various brochures and maps available from the Park Office in the same parking area as the Lodge, across the road from the golf course pro shop (☎ 405-564-2566). Then head west on US-70 about 10 miles to Kingston. Here the highway turns north to Madill then back east again for about 20 miles to **Lake Murray**.

You're now in the foothills of the **Arbuckle Mountains**, a spot so picturesque it was developed by the Civilian Conservation Corps during the Depression solely for recreational use. You can get a panoramic view of the area from **Tucker Tower**, a rock castle built of limestone quarried from the surrounding hills. The structure was probably intended as a medieval-style summer retreat for Oklahoma governors, but now looms over the lake as a geological museum and nature center. Hours are 9 am to 7 pm every day during the summer and 9 am to 5 pm Wednesday through Saturday the rest of the year, except in December and January when the center is closed. ☎ 580-233-2109 for more information.

The tower is located on the east side of the lake on State Route 77S, which loops around Lake Murray and intersects with US-70 on both ends. Follow the loop, turn off on any narrow road or path that looks interesting, and enjoy the scenery. When you come to US-70 again, go east to US-77 and turn north to **Ardmore**. The downtown area has been renovated with brick-paved sidewalks and electric "gaslights," and the people at the Chamber of Commerce on Main Street hope you will stop by for a walking-tour map of the historic district.

If you prefer to stay in the great outdoors, you can take US-77 up into the **Arbuckle Mountains Area**, but US-177, a few miles to the east, is prettier and farther away from the traffic of Interstate-35. **Chickasaw National Recreation Area**, the only National Park in Oklahoma, encompasses **Lake of the Arbuckles**, **Veterans Lake**, and several creeks and springs near the towns of **Sulphur** and **Davis**.

A short distance after you pass the tiny towns of Nebo and Drake, turn off US-177 onto Buckhorn Road. Drive down to the lake, and stroll the trail that begins at the first (most eastern) picnic area and ends at campground D. This path follows the shoreline for almost a mile, and you probably won't want to walk the entire distance since there are even more delightful spots to explore farther north. Just for a change, look for Cedar Blue Road on the left as you drive back toward US-177. This curvy road rejoins US-177, which will take you to the **Travertine District**, a bit north of Buckhorn Road.

Visitors have come to this scenic area since the 1800s to "take the waters," which flow from the ground loaded with sulphur, bromine, and other minerals. You can gulp a medicinal dose from the fountain at **Vendome Well** in **Flower Park** west of the junction of US-177 and SH-7. Fresh water flows from Antelope Springs and Buffalo Springs near the **Travertine Nature Center** east of US-177. A cautious sniff will tell you whether water from a particular source is mineral or fresh. A tiny sip will confirm any olfactory analysis.

Stop at the Nature Center, which is built, bridge-like, across Travertine Creek, to pick up information about all types of activities in the Chickasaw Recreation Area. A ranger leads nature walks from the center at 9:30 am year-round on weekends, and the interpretive area is open from 8am to 5pm every day except Christmas and New Years. Dur-

Turner Falls, near Davis – a 77-foot waterfall on Honey Creek in the Arbuckle Mountains (Fred W. Marvel)

ing the summer, the center stays open later, and rangers lead campfire talks and night hikes. (☎ 405-622-3165 for information.) Inside the Nature Center, a one-winged barred owl is protected in a large wire cage beside the information desk, and various snakes and turtles are housed in glass enclosures. There's also a selection of regional history and guide books in the gift shop.

Back on the loop road that winds through the Travertine District north and east of **Veterans Lake**, watch for **Little Niagara**, **Travertine Island**, and the viewpoint for **Bison Pasture**. All of this is seen best from a hiking trail, but it's possible to get within view of most areas by car. Two ecosystems overlap in the park where mixed-grass prairie meets deciduous forest, which creates a unique environment for birds, animals, and wildflower.

Leave the Travertine District through the Broadway Avenue entrance that leads into the town of Sulphur. This is SH-7, which passes north of Lake of the Arbuckles to the town of **Davis**, home of 77-foot **Turner Falls**. Take US-77 south of town to the entrance of **Turner Falls Park**. From Spring Break in March until Labor Day in September, the park is crowded with swimmers, campers, and fishermen. Families have held their reunions here for three and four generations; drawn back year after year by the clean facilities, endless activities, and wholesome atmosphere.

Cedarvale Botanical Gardens and Restaurant is just north of the falls on SH-77. The attractions here are 30 acres of flowers, a suspended bridge across Honey Creek, and a walking path through tall, dense trees. Plan your driving trip so that you can enjoy lunch or dinner at the restaurant, where fresh trout is cooked any way you want it. Call ☎ 580-369-3224 to check off-season hours, but meals are usually served every day during the summer from 11 am to 8 pm.

US-69 from Lake Eufaula to Krebs

30 miles

The town of Eufaula is nearly surrounded by **Lake Eufaula**, which was created in 1964 by construction of a dam on the Canadian River. Brick sidewalks downtown connect Victorian-era buildings, which are almost lake-side property. Both **Fountainhead State Park**, ☎ 918-689-5311, and **Arrowhead State Park**, ☎ 918-339-2204, sit along the lake's 600-mile shoreline. Fountainhead is north of Eufaula on SR-150 off US-69. Arrowhead is south of Eufaula, four miles east of the town of Canadian off US-69. Both parks offer boating, golf, trails, and camping, but Arrowhead also has a 90-room resort lodge and a swimming beach.

The resort at Arrowhead State Park is built on hilly terrain out of native stone and rough timber and offers a gaming center, deluxe suites, cottages with small kitchens, and a swimming pool. Golfers often come in by small planes at the park's airstrip to play 18 holes on the rugged, challenging course.

From the lodge, take State Park Road west to US-69 and turn south toward **McAlester** for a short, lovely drive to **Krebs** near the junction of US-270. This little town was settled by Italian immigrant coal miners, who arrived on the Katy railroad a couple of decades before and after 1900. Since Krebs was governed by both Choctaw law and US courts, the immigrants found some loopholes in the confusing rules about manufacturing and selling alcoholic beverages and soon became well known for producing "Choc beer" – a rather odd mix of hops, barley, and tobacco.

Now the town is known for its abundant and delicious Italian food. For over 50 years, **Lovera's Famous Grocery and Meat Market** has been making and selling spicy sausages and Italian-style cheese. They also import a large quantity of food specialties from Italy and will ship

Southeast Oklahoma

orders anywhere in the US. From SH-31/Washington Street, turn onto West 6th Street, then follow the crowd and the aroma to a two-story stone building. Out back, homemade sausage is smoking. Inside, homemade cheese is hanging over the deli counter. You probably won't be able to order prudently, so consider taking an ice chest. It's just too tempting to stock up on salami, prosciutto, homemade butter, and spaghetti sauce. Call ☎ 800-854-1317 to place an order or ☎ 918-423-2842 for store hours and information. Ask if they will be making sausage and cheese on the day you want to visit.

Roseanna's, at 205 East Washington, has been owned and operated by the same Italian family for over 20 years. Tables are grouped in individual rooms, and the menu includes the traditional pasta with red sauce and salad with vinaigrette dressing. Be sure to have the ravioli appetizer. Call ☎ 918-423-2055 for hours and information, but usually the restaurant is closed Sunday and Monday and open from lunch through dinner on other days.

Dinner at **Pete's Place** or **Isle of Capri** has been a tradition for generations. Pete's was started in 1925 when Poppa Pete began serving Italian specialties in his home. His grandson runs the business now, but the location's the same, and the food is still dependably delicious. Open every evening for dinner and Sunday for lunch and dinner. Pete's is at the corner of 8th Street and Monroe. Call ☎ 918-423-2042 for more information.

Isle of Capri has been operated by the same Italian family since 1950. Like Pete's, the menu is traditional steak-and-spaghetti and the portions are huge. Closed Sunday, the restaurant is open at 150 Southwest 7th Street for dinner Monday through Saturday. Call ☎ 918-423-3062 for information.

If you're in the area during Memorial Day or Labor Day weekend, plan to attend one of the annual two-day festivals. In May, the **Italian Festival** takes place at the Pittsburgh County Fairgrounds, west of McAlester on US-270. Admission is free, and you pay only for food and games. Besides the outstanding home made feasts, there are arts and crafts sales, folk music concerts, and bocce ball tournaments. You can get a brochure and more information by phoning ☎ 918-426-2055. On Labor Day Weekend in September, the **Ethnic Festival** is held in Krebs, and the food, entertainment, and art include traditional German, Greek, and Mexican fare, as well as Italian. Again, there is no fee for admission, and you pay as you go for food and games. Call ☎ 918-423-2842 for details.

US-271 from Talihina to Antlers

62 miles

Talihina is called "the village between the mountains" because it sits in a valley formed by the **Winding Stair Mountains** and the **Kiamichi Mountains**. Although it is best known as the starting point for the **Talimena Scenic Byway**, the town is also the perfect beginning for a drive along US-271, southwest through the heavily wooded **Potato Hills**. You may spot hang-gliders above the western horizon, and if you're interested, take a two-mile detour to an access road at the junction of SH-1 and SH-63, which leads to the Buffalo Mountain launch site.

Then, load your camera and start along scenic US-271 toward **Albion**. Watch for a herd of emus and rheas strutting about the fields of Perdido Robar Ranch, just five miles down the road. These ostrich-like birds from Australia are big-bucks-valuable, and they behave as if they know it. For your own safety, keep your distance, but take a few minutes to watch or photograph these haughty creatures.

The timber industry preserves the native beauty of this stretch of highway between **Sardis Lake** and the town of **Antlers** by replanting what

Ouachita National Forest, Talimena Scenic Drive. (Fred W. Marvel)

they harvest. Small ranches and tiny communities are spread sparsely along this route, and fishermen, campers, and horsemen congregate in the area year-round. On Thanksgiving weekend, about 200 four-wheel-drive vehicles show up for the annual Turkey Day Run over logging trails near **Clayton Lake State Park**.

Less than two miles south of Clayton, you'll see a stone-and-wood inn built as a hunting lodge and now catering to tourists. This is a fine place to overnight or have dinner. The kitchen turns out fresh catfish platters and soon-to-be-famous homemade cake. (Clayton Country Inn, ☎ 918-569-4165). Horseback riders will like Indian Mounds Camp, a bit south of the inn, where they can camp out with their horses and ride 100 miles of marked trails. ☎ 918-569-4761 for directions and information.

SH-2 runs almost parallel to US-251 south of Clayton. Both are pretty drives to Antlers, and it's difficult to decide, which route to take. If you have time, drive south on one then turn around in Antlers and drive north on the other. About the only site to see in Antlers is the historic **Frisco Train Depot**, which is open Tuesday mornings for tours. The Heritage Train from Hugo pulls in here on some weekends, but otherwise, the town is known as a rendezvous point for outdoor sportsmen who come to Pushmataha County for uncrowded recreation.

It is interesting that the town got its name from the Indian custom of attaching deer antlers to trees to mark water sources. Hunters and traders stopped at the town's spring to water their horses long before the railroad came through in 1887. During spring and fall, the trees in this area are dazzling.

If you're interested in wine and vineyards, take a slightly-out-of-the-way drive to **Cimarron Cellars**. From Antlers, the fastest route is SH-3 to Atoka, about 30 miles, then south on US-69/75 for about 12 miles to the winery's road. Watch for the tasting room and shop as you approach the winery road. It will be on the left as you travel south, ☎ 580-889-5997. About a half-mile past the store, a sign on the highway directs you east on a dirt road to the vineyard and winery. Call ahead for an appointment to tour, ☎ 580-889-6312.

■ Adventures

On Foot

Hiking

The system of hiking trails in Southeastern Oklahoma is quite extensive and offers every type of experience for both back-packers and day trippers. More than 500 miles of trails twist through the mountainous **Ouachita National Forest** alone. Another 24-mile trail cuts through **Beavers Bend State Park**, a 13-mile stretch parallels Travertine Creek in the **Chickasaw National Recreation Area**, and a combination of trails runs nine miles over or around the huge rocks at **Robbers Cave**. Most lakes and parks have at least a short nature path for strolling and watching the wildlife. **Lake Wister** features a 6.2-mile hike near the **Winding Stair Mountains**, and **McGee Creek** has 11 trails, which are 1.2 to 4.8 miles long. Check at the ranger station or park office for directions and maps – or just choose a scenic spot and start walking.

❒ Ouachita National Forest

This is hikers' heaven: tall trees, mist-covered mountains, sparkling springs, and secret spots. The best way to experience the forest is on foot, without a plan. There are 12 developed and countless undeveloped trail-heads within this area, and the main **Ouachita Trail** runs east-west for 192 miles from **Talimena State Park** to **Lake Sylvia**, near Little Rock, Arkansas.

If the Ouachita Trail is your goal, start at either Talimena Park or at the Old Military Road parking area, a couple of miles east of the Visitor Center on the **Talimena Scenic Byway**. The trail follows the Byway for several miles, and there are parking areas with access paths as you travel east toward Arkansas.

In addition to the main trail, there are many alternate routes through the forest. The following selection is a sample of the best Oklahoma has to offer. Some are in wilderness areas, but all have developed trailheads with parking areas, bulletin boards, and registration logs. For more information or maps of these trails, call the **Choctaw Ranger Station**

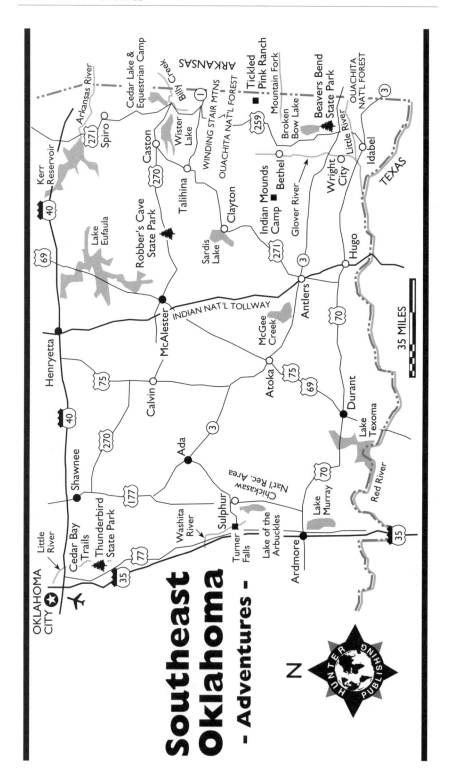

Southeast Oklahoma
- Adventures -

(two miles south of Heavener on SH-59) at ☎ 918-653-2991, or the **US Forest Service** in Hot Springs, Arkansas at ☎ 501-321-5202.

Cedar Lake

Cedar Lake Recreation Trail is a beautifully civilized walk – too comfortable to be a true hike, but worthy of mention due to its peaceful charm. The trail circles 90-acre Cedar Lake and follows the shoreline for 2.9 miles. The loop is unsurfaced, but easily hiked in about an hour, not counting stops to watch the birds and gaze at the tranquil water. This is a pedestrian-only trail accessible from any of the camping areas. Reach the lake, about two miles south of Heavener, by driving US-270/259 to Holson Valley Road. Turn west and go about three miles to Forest Road-269. The lake is about a mile north. The day-use fee is $2 per vehicle, and you can park on the left, near the start of **Old Pine Interpretive Trail**. Old Pine is less than half a mile long, has interpretive signs that identify the animals you might spot around the lake, and connects to the longer loop trail near the shoreline.

Old Military Road

Old Military Road is an unsurfaced trail with an interesting history. Back in 1832, a road was built between Fort Smith, Arkansas and Fort Towson, Oklahoma. Settlers and wagon trains, as well as the military, traveled this branch of the extensive Texas Road, and evidence of the original road is still in place. The southern trailhead is at Old Military Road Picnic Area, on the left about a mile east of the Visitor Center, at the junction of US-271 and SH-1. If you cross SH-1 and head south, you'll join the main Ouachita Trail in less than half a mile.

To hike the Old Military Road, go north. You're hiking toward the western end of the Holson Valley through the **Indian Nations National Scenic and Wildlife Area**. After approximately three miles, the trail curves to the right and heads southeast, then east for another three miles. Just before you reach Holson Valley Road (.6 mile farther east), you'll come to the junction with **Boardstand Trail**. You can turn around here, or continue on the Boardstand Trail for 7½ miles to where it intersects the Ouachita Trail and loops back to where you started – a total of 23.1 miles. This loop is rated moderately difficult, so be certain you have the stamina and experience to complete the trip before reaching the no-turning-back point. Overnight camping is permitted in developed and primitive areas along the route.

Southeast Oklahoma

Boardstand Trail

Part of the Old Military/Ouachita Loop, this unsurfaced trail starts .6 mile from a parking area at Deadman Vista, on the north side of SH-1 about a half-mile east of Forest Road 6010 (approximately eight miles east of US-271). The trail winds north, then west, then northwest until it crosses FR-6010 and Cedar Creek before joining the Old Military Trail (8.1 miles from the parking area). Another parking area is on Holson Valley Road .6 mile east of the trails' junction. If you can arrange to be dropped off at one parking area and picked up at the other, this is a great 8.6-mile day-hike through the Indian Nations National Scenic and Wildlife Area.

Refer to the description of the Old Military Trail, above, if you plan to do the entire 23.1-mile loop. Get a map at the **Choctaw Ranger Office** two miles south of Heavener on US-59, or call ☎ 918-653-2991 for information.

Billy Creek Trail

Billy Creek Trail is rough, but worth it. Start at Billy Creek Campground, which is six miles west of Big Cedar off SH-63. At the campground sign on the highway, turn north on Forest Road 22 and go three miles to the entrance. You'll share the trail with horses – watch your step – but the views and scenery are superb. Billy Creek flows through the 26,445-acre **Winding Stair National Recreation Area**, and the hiking trail curves down the south side of Winding Stair Mountain.

Allow a little more than two hours to travel the four miles between the campground and the intersection with Ouachita Trail, just north of the Talimena Scenic Byway. This used to be a logging trail, and the Civilian Conservation Corps used it during the construction of the Talimena. The hike climbs out of the valley to the mountain's ridge where you can either turn around and return to the campground, or continue on and join the Ouachita Trail.

Horsethief Spring Trail

Horsethief Spring Trail is about four miles long and connects Cedar Lake with the Ouachita Trail just west of the junction with Billy Creek Trail. When combined, Horsethief and Billy Creek connect the campgrounds at Cedar Lake and Billy Creek – about 8½-9½ miles total distance, which creates a nice two-day backpacking trip. Because of the mountains, allow more time than usual to travel the unsurfaced route – it gets steep and rocky near the top of Winding Stair Mountain.

☐ Beavers Bend State Park

Technically, when all the trails from **Broken Bow Lake** to the **Cedar Creek Area** are combined, they form the one-way 24-mile **David L. Boren Trail**. Actually, only about 12 miles is hikable at this time. North of the spillway, the trail has fallen into disuse and is visible only in erratic stretches between Stevens Gap and Cedar Creek. Adventurous experienced hikers can blaze their own trail with patience and good compass skills, but everyone else should stick to the southern 12-mile route. Backpackers will want to camp out at least one night, but there are several access points, so day trips are possible. In addition, there are four designated nature trails in the Beavers Bend Park.

Entering the park from the south entrance on US-259A off US-259 (259A loops and joins 259 again after it circles through the park), leave your car in the parking lot shared by the **Forest Heritage Center** and park office. A 1.1-mile loop takes you from the Heritage Center on an easy walk down to Beaver Creek and back. Signs along the way give information at key points. This loop crosses the DLB trail in two spots, and blue-on-white signs keep you on the right path. (The main trail is marked in all white.)

Just southeast of the Heritage Center, across from the tennis courts, **The Pine Ridge Nature Trail** forms a figure-eight loop through forest, up and down a couple of hills, and along the Beaver Creek bottom land. This trail is .75 mile long and easy going except for the slight rise and fall of the hills. As you walk along, keep turning right at every branch and you will return to your starting spot.

The Dogwood Nature Trail is called Big Oak Trail on older maps. It runs about a mile and gets rocky in places, but is generally an easy hike. The beginning of the trail follows Mountain Fork River (leave your car in the lot near the riding stables and train depot), then winds through a pine forest as it loops back to the parking area.

The David L. Boren Trail begins at the south end of Beavers Bend Park. It is actually several short, individually named paths that connect to form the DLB. This is a multi-use trail, so you may share it with mountain bikers and horses. However, traffic is light on most days, and hikers can count on some solitude, at least in the more remote areas.

South Park Trailhead, near the low-water dam, starts with a hilly one-mile stretch to Beavers Creek. From there, it splits. The right side follows the flat floodplain, which actually crosses the creek. The left joins Lookout Mountain Trail, which climbs to a scenic viewing point then joins Deer Crossing Trail – about 1½ miles away at highway 259A.

The Deer Crossing Trail leads north. This leg has some hills to climb, but it is not as steep as the Lookout Mountain Trail. After about two miles, it branches right and connects with the one-mile **Cedar Bluff Nature Trail**, a moderate trail with some gentle climbs. A turn to the left at the trail split will bypass most of Cedar Bluff and connect with Skyline Trail, a six-mile rugged path that should be attempted only by experienced hikers. Day hikers can call it quits here. Backpackers will enjoy the next challenge.

Skyline Trail has steep climbs and crosses the creek several times before it splits. A right turn joins the **Beaver Lodge Nature Trail**, which is a mile long and features two swinging bridges. A left turn goes toward the spillway. It is after this left turn that the trail becomes overgrown in most spots. It is possible to return to your starting point by road – a fairly easy three-mile hike. Campers can set up in any flat clearing without a permit. However, everyone is encouraged to register at the Nature Center (just so the staff knows who's out there), and open flames are strictly prohibited. Future plans include restoring the 12-mile trail north of Stevens Gap. Check at the Park Office or Nature Center for updates on any progress.

☐ McGee Creek Wildlife Management Area

Three types of trails run 34 miles through this 8,900-acre Natural Scenic Recreation Area adjacent to McGee Creek State Park – multi-use, hiking/biking, and hiking only. Each is designated with different colored signs. However, the only trail specifically restricted to hikers is the one-mile **Carnasaw Nature Trail**.

Take scenic SH-3 from Atoka east toward Antlers and the Kiamichi Mountains. Turn north at the town of Farris and go about three miles to the entrance of McGee Park. All visitors must stop at the ranger station for a permit, even if they plan to stay only a few hours. Since this area is a protected wilderness, permits are restricted to 40 non-reservable half-day passes per day. In addition, visitors may reserve a full-day permit or an overnight camping permit up to 90 days in advance. ☎ 580-

889-5822 for reservations or to see if any non-reserved space is available on a first-come basis.

Pick up a map while you're at the ranger station and ask which trails fit your purpose. There are at least 13 named trails, and most of them connect with others to make up anything from an easy walking loop to a multi-mile trek over rough terrain.

The Carnasaw Nature Trail is a one-mile loop beginning at the Overlook parking area. It connects with **Rocky Point Trail**, a hiking/biking path, which starts off north then curves back south for about a mile before it intersects with **Little Bugaboo Trail**. At this intersection, you have a choice. A right turn takes you onto Little Bugaboo, which parallels its namesake creek and leads to an equestrian campground and the trailhead of **Whiskey Flats**, a distance of about 1.4 miles. A left turn takes you onto the **West Branch Trail**, which leads to a backpacker camp on the **West Boundary Trail** 1.3 miles to the southwest. Other trails lead from both the backpacker camp and equestrian camp to the quiet water zone of McGee Creek, approximately 1.3 miles away.

Probably the most popular trail is the exciting **South Rim**, which winds over three miles from the park entrance around **Little Bugaboo Canyon** to the **North Rim Trail**, which is also a bit over three miles long. Both trails are multi-use and were once logging roads.

On the far east side of the Recreation Area, you'll find multi-use trails, which are often shared with bikers and horseback riders. They are accessible from the 4.8-mile **Boundary Trail**, which marks the park's border on three sides. **Hunter's Cabin Trail** runs 1.8 miles from the east boundary road to the junction of the South and North Rim Trails. **Hog Trail** branches off from Hunter .3 mile from the trailhead and heads south to an equestrian campground then on to the Southeast Boundary Trail – a total distance of 1.8 miles. **Coon's Way** branches off from Hunter about 1.3 miles from the trailhead and heads north to a junction with **Wolf Creek Trail** (.4 mile) and then on to the North Boundary Trail – a total of one mile. Wolf Creek is less than a mile long and leads to a backpacking camp .2 mile to the east and to the North Boundary, a half-mile to the west.

A good hike for "river rats" is the **Wildcat Trail**, which goes from Creekside Campground #2 through Wildcat Canyon, past Backpack Campground #3 to the North Rim – about 1.8 miles. The recreation area is huge, and parts of it are quite remote, so carry a compass when you start into the woods. Camping is permitted anywhere in the park, but the rangers encourage everyone, other than very experienced outdoorsmen, to stay within designated areas.

Deer, wild turkeys, river otters, and a few mountain lions are frequently spotted along the creeks and canyons within the wildlife management area. This is a beautiful section of the state – a must for all adventurers. Call McGee Creek State Park Office, ☎ 405-889-5822, for maps, reservations and information.

❏ Wister State Park

Wister State Park sits in the exquisite mountains of Kiamichi Country two miles south of the town of Wister on US-270, west of Heavener. A 6.2-mile unsurfaced trail begins near the swimming pool and cabins on the north side of 4,000-acre Lake Wister. Reach the trail head by turning west off US-270 into the park. This trail follows the northern shoreline and connects with .75-mile **Lonestar Nature Trail** near Wards Landing. Another .25 mile of paved trail is accessible by wheelchair.

Mountain bikes share the main trail, which is rated moderately difficult because of some challenging ridges and hills. Anyone in average good health can probably hike the entire distance in about three hours. But allow time for gawking. This area is gorgeous, especially in the spring when the dogwoods are in bloom, and again in the fall, when the foliage competes well with any other spot in the country. Information and maps are available by calling Wister State Park Office, ☎ 918-655-7756.

❏ Robbers Cave

Robbers Cave State Park is four miles north of Wilburton on SH-2. Stop at the new Nature Center, overlooking **Lake Carlton** (on the left soon after you enter the park), to sign up for a guided tour of Robbers Cave where notorious outlaws hid out during the 1800s. Several trails wind through the park, along the shore of four lakes, and across a couple of creeks. They can be combined to make an invigorating hike, and the legends that persist about this area make the trek that much more interesting. Maps and information are available at the Nature Center.

Mountain Trail is the longest (4.75 miles) and begins at the low-water dam near the park's entrance. It connects to **Cattailpond Trail** (2.25 miles) after it curves around the west side of **Wayne Wallace Lake** and heads northeast toward **Lost Lake**. **Rough Canyon Trail** (about a three-mile loop) circles Lost Lake and Robbers Cave and joins Cattailpond Trail at two spots. This entire hike is plus or minus 10 miles, one way, and you can get on and off the trail at several points. A natural stopping spot is one of the camping areas near Lost Lake or Robbers Cave. However, you can take Cattailpond Trail back to the junction with Mountain Trail and return to your original starting point.

Another 1½-mile trail makes a loop on the east side of SH-2, north of **Coon Creek Lake**. Mountain bikers and hikers share this trail, which begins between the cabin office and the cabins in Old Circle Campground. In addition, a short path runs from this campground to SH-2 and the Nature Center. From there, it is possible to cross the creek and pick up Mountain Trail again. Five camping areas and 117 campsites are scattered through the park, so you can schedule your hike for any distance and any amount of time.

The towering sandstone formations at Robbers Cave were a popular hideout for outlaws such as Belle Starr and the Dalton Gang in the 19th century. (Lynne M. Sullivan)

Near the cave, on the northern end of the park, you can hike – or climb – 100-foot sandstone cliffs. The easiest way to **Lookout Point** at the top is up the steps carved into the stone during a public-works project in 1935. It'is possible to explore parts of the caves, but some passageways have collapsed since Belle Starr, Jesse James, and various other outlaws made this their hideout. You can investigate on your own, but the guided tours are interesting, and help spark the imagination. Call ☎ 918-465-2565 for more information.

Southeast Oklahoma

❏ Lake Eufaula

Both **Fountainhead State Park** and **Arrowhead State Park** have short nature paths and longer day-hike trails on Lake Eufaula. At Fountainhead, **Indian Ridge Nature Trail** is a .75-mile loop near the campground in Area 4, south of SH-150 in the north end of the park. **Crazy Snake Trail** is also about .75 mile long and is located near the Nature Center on the Main Loop Road on the east side of the park. **Pickens Trail** is 2½ miles long and connects Area 3, near the Visitor Center, with Area 1, near the Resort Lodge.

Spring is lovely here. The dogwoods bloom late in March and the redbud trees extend the color until late April. The trail curves through dense trees and is unpaved but easy to hike one-way in a little over an hour. Call the Fountainhead State Park Office for more information, ☎ 918-689-5311.

At **Arrowhead**, 25 miles north of McAlester at the Canadian exit off SH-69, the **Outlaw Nature Trail** loops for a mile through hilly terrain near the Lodge. A three-mile trail provides a one-way link between the Park Office and Campgrounds 1 and 2. Both paths are unpaved, but the Outlaw is an easy stroll. The main trail winds down the side of a mountain and ends near the water. It will take most hikers 1½ hours to travel one-way over the rugged terrain either up or down the mountain, but allow extra time to observe the wildlife. For more information, phone the Park Office at ☎ 918-339-2204.

❏ Lake Texoma

Since Texoma sits on the Texas/Oklahoma border, the lake's three main hiking trails in both states will be covered here. More than 40 miles of trails surround the lake, including the 14-mile Cross Timbers Trail, the 15-mile Platter-Lakeside Trail, and the 15-mile Walnut/Brushy Creek Trail.

Cross Timbers starts in the **Juniper Point Recreation Area** off Highway 377 in Texas. The first part of the trail crosses rocky bluffs with terrific views of the lake to Cedar Bayou, a distance of 2½ miles. The mid-section passes through several elevation changes and heavily wooded areas on its way past Lost Loop Campground and **Eagle's Roost**. The last half of the trail flattens out, winds along **Paw Paw Creek** and comes out at **Rock Creek**. Most of the trail is moderately difficult, with several easy stretches. Call ☎ 214-465-4990 for details.

Platter-Lakeside is a multi-use trail for horseback riders and hikers. **Platter Flats** is on the lake, west of the town of Platter and north of Cartwright on the Oklahoma side. This 24-mile trail goes through heavily wooded areas then breaks out into open meadows before descending back into the trees again. Several spots offer wonderful views of the lake. **Lakeside Recreation Area**, at the end of the trail, is almost directly across the lake from Platter Flats, but 24-miles by land. Phone the **Texoma Project Office** at ☎ 214-465-4990 for more information.

Walnut/Brushy Creek is back on the Texas side in the Big Mineral arm of the lake. This 15-mile multi-use trail starts at Big Mineral Camp north of Gordonville on Highway 901 (☎ 903-523-4287 for information about the area). It ends at **Walnut Creek Resort** (☎ 903-523-4211), just to the northwest. Campsites, cabins, and other amenities are available at both ends of the trail.

Besides these longer trails, **Lake Texoma State Resort Park** has a two-mile trail that winds through Area 5 near the Rally Campground. The park is at the west end of the Roosevelt Bridge on US-70. Turn south at the Marina Mart and drive between the airstrip and the golf course across Yellow Bridge past the Rally area. Access to the trail is near RV camping and the picnic shelter, near the water in Area 5. Phone the park office at ☎ 580-564-2566 for more information.

☐ Lake Murray

Hiking is not top priority at Lake Murray, but there are a few places to stride out and see the scenery. Near the Park Office on SH-77S just south of US-70, the **Anadarche Trail** makes a 1½-mile loop. This easygoing walk follows a packed wood-chip path. Farther south, on the west side of the lake in the stables/scuba store/airstrip area, **Buckhorn Trail** connects the Lodge with **Tipps Point Campground**. This trail has a gentle slope, crosses two bridges, and offers an easy hike for nature-lovers who want to examine plants and watch for park animals. Again, the trail is packed wood chips. Check with the Park Office, ☎ 580-223-4044, for more information.

☐ Chickasaw National Recreation Area

About 20 miles of trails meander through prairie and forest in this immense region 75 miles south of Oklahoma City. The longest stretch connects several trails in the **Platt Historic Area**, near the city of Sulphur,

Southeast Oklahoma

which runs roughly from **Buffalo Springs** to **Veterans Lake**. Easy on-off points make these trails perfect for all-day roaming, with frequent refreshment breaks. Consider setting up in one of the picnic areas (**Travertine Island** is especially pleasant), then setting out in any direction to explore.

Antelope Trail and **Buffalo Springs Trail** are popular because they are an easy stroll through the trees, past a variety of plants and flowers, along **Travertine Creek**. Unless there has been an extended drought, about five million gallons of water flow from Antelope and Buffalo Springs each day.

Starting at the **Travertine Nature Center**, on the loop road off US-177, follow the signs east along the 1.2-mile main loop. Along the way, you will encounter three side trails: the **Prairie Loop**, approximately .6 mile across Travertine Creek, up a limestone slope; the **Tall Oaks Loop**, a half-mile across Travertine Creek, down to a stand of – you guessed it – tall oaks; and **Dry Creek Loop**, 1.8 miles across a rock bridge, through a forest of cedars and up a gentle limestone slope.

The **Travertine Creek Trail** begins at the Nature Center and goes west to **Little Niagara Waterfall**, which drops into a chilly swimming hole. Take the side trail to Travertine Island, where rock benches shaded by tall black walnut trees provide a perfect rest stop. Then continue on to **Pavilion Springs**, where you can turn around and return to the Nature Center or take **Veterans Center Trail** to the Oklahoma Veterans Center (about half a mile away).

Flower Park Trail also runs about half a mile from Pavilion Springs to **Vendome Well**. Back in the 1930s, "mud puppies" lolled along the banks of Vendome Stream. These pups were actually human visitors who covered themselves in mud from the mineral springs, then lay in the sun to bake away their arthritis and skin diseases. The easy stroll between Pavilion and Vendome is part concrete and part hard-packed gravel.

Bison Pasture Trail is 1.9 miles long and a bit more strenuous than the previous trails because of some rugged elevation changes. If you begin at the **Bison Viewpoint**, just south of Park Headquarters on US-177, you'll have a clear view of a herd of bison grazing in a fenced area below. The trail then loops through grasslands, crosses a stream bed, and enters a deciduous forest. The **Bromide Hill Trail** branches off and leads to a high vista called **Robber's Roost**, 140 feet above the main trail. A little farther west, there's a cutoff to Rock Creek Campground. You can turn around here or go on to the campground and pick up **Rock Creek Trail**, which parallels Bison Pasture Trail along Rock Creek to Hillside Springs, then back to Bison Viewpoint.

A dirt and worn-asphalt road leads to **Veterans Lake**, just south of **Bromide Hill**. Park at the dam and hike 1.4 miles along the shore to the parking area at the northeast corner of the lake. The trail winds through oaks and cedars to a prairie with tall grass and wildflowers. Try to be here at sunset when deer and armadillos may creep out of the woods to snack on open land. This is a one-way trail, so you'll have to return to your car along the same path, but the lake views are different in each direction.

☐ Lake of the Arbuckles

Lake of the Arbuckles is south on US-177. Take either Cedar Blue Road or Buckhorn Road west off the highway to the Buckhorn Campgrounds. The trail here is just under a mile long, one-way, and begins by the water's edge at the first picnic area off Buckhorn Road. Look for armadillos, or evidence of them, digging for an insect-and-earthworm dinner, as you walk along the shore toward Area D. Don't count on seeing many animals, but watch for wild turkeys and fox squirrels scampering through the underbrush and vultures circling overhead.

Two more trails are located at **The Point** on Point Road off SH-7 – west of the city of Sulphur and east of the Chickasaw Turnpike. **Fishing Rock Trail** follows the lake shore west of the road for about .8 mile through a hardwood forest and a grassy prairie. Carry your fishing pole. It offers the perfect excuse to stop and rest along the way. As long as you're holding the pole, no one will suspect that you're really napping, and you may catch a catfish to fry for supper. **Lakeview Trail** follows the lake shore east of the road for about half a mile. Wear your swimsuit on this easy walk and cool off in the water when you reach the pebbly beach.

Information about the **Chickasaw National Recreation Area** is available at ☎ 580-622-3163. The **Travertine Nature Center's** number is ☎ 580-622-3165.

❑ Little River/Thunderbird State Park

Hiking trails run through two areas of this park adjacent to **Lake Thunderbird** near **Norman**. Take SH-9 east off I-35 for about 13 miles, turn north to the **Clear Bay** Park Office, which is on the south side of the lake. All of the trails in this area twist along wooded gentle hills and offer terrific lake views.

Begin at Campground #1, where there are hiking-only and hiking/biking trails. The hiking trail follows the lake's shore and offers an alternate, parallel trail for the return trip. The multi-use trail leads to **Bobcat Loop**, a 1.1-mile stretch that shares a leg with the 1,3-mile **Coyote Loop**. Both trails come to a meeting with an access trail leading to the water's edge and a restaurant. This configuration allows hikers to go up Bobcat, break for lunch and return on Coyote.

The lower southeastern leg of Coyote also shares with 1.2-mile **Whitetail Loop**, which leads to a small pond where you can pick up a short unnamed trail to the restrooms at the south dam area. There is also a short nature trail loop between the restrooms and lake shore. In all, the three main trails and their entrance trails total over four miles. You can hike one loop, then pick up another until you've traveled whatever distance you want, then pick up another for the return trip. The possibilities are endless. Phone the park office at ☎ 405-360-3572 for maps and brochures.

Golfing

 Arrowhead Golf Course, ☎ 918-918-339-2769, is located in the rocky hills on the western shore of Eufaula Lake, northeast of McAlester. The Choctaw Nation owns the adjacent lodge, and there are plenty of non-golf activities to round out a full vacation. The 18-hole, par-72 course was redesigned and enlarged in 1981, with average-sized bent grass greens and some water play. Total yardage is 6,741, the USGA rating is 71.4, and the slope rating is 119.

Golfers often encounter wildlife on or near the course, which is located in a scenic area that offers wonderful views of the lake and Canadian River Valley. Hole #17, a 430-yard par-4, is considered the most demanding because of the long uphill tee shot to a narrow dogleg-to-the-left fairway and an elevated green. (This aggravation is what brings adventurous golfers back again and again.)

Green fees are: weekends, $13.06 for 18 holes and $7.84 for nine holes; weekdays, $10.97 for 18 holes and $7.84 for nine holes. Gas carts are available at $16.72 (18 holes) and $9.41 (nine holes). Pull carts rent for $2.09. (You'll need lots of pennies to pay these crazy fees.) There are no caddies, but rental clubs are available.

Tee-time reservations are accepted 21 days in advance at the pro shop beginning at 8 am. From McAlester, drive north on US-69 to Canadian. Turn east onto State Park Road and drive about four miles to the golf course.

Fountainhead Golf Course, ☎ 918-689-3209, is also on Lake Eufaula, and again, the lake views are spectacular. The front nine of this 72-par, 18-hole course is tight, with mature trees along the fairways. The back nine is wide open. Both are a challenge for any golfer. Total yardage is 6,919, the USGA rating is 71.3, and the slope is 116.

The most difficult hole is #2, a par-5 with a narrow, undulating, dogleg fairway. The reward comes on hole #3, a 200-yard, par-3 with a dazzling view of the lake. Finally, hole #18, a par-5, challenges a tired golfer with a pond just in front of the sloping green. Great fun, but enough frustration to convince a beginner to sell his clubs.

Fees are: weekends, $12.50 for 18 holes and $7.50 for nine holes; weekdays, $10.50 for 18 holes and $7.50 for nine holes. Gas carts rent for $16 (18 holes) and $9 (nine holes); pull carts rent for $2. There are no caddies, but a teaching pro is on site, and clubs may be rented. Fountainhead Resort is privately owned, and reservations can be made by calling ☎ 800-345-6343.

To reach the golf course, 14 miles southwest of Checotah, take US-69 south to SH-150. Go west about two miles to the pro shop, which opens at 7 am and begins taking tee-time reservations at 8:30am.

Lake Murray Golf Course, ☎ 580-223-6613, is a short, hilly, tree-lined course located in Oklahoma's largest state-owned resort park. The 6,200-yard course has a par of 70, a USGA rating of 71.6, and a slope of 127. Greens have bent grass, tees and fairways have Bermuda grass.

Long hitters have a challenge here because the tight fairways require more accuracy than distance. Hole #16, for example, is a 140-yard par-3 with a tricky shot over a 12-foot waterfall from the back tee and water hazards on three sides. While fishing your ball out of the water for the third time, remember the words of Ben Hogan: "Did you ever consider hitting it closer to the hole?" A golfer who misses the green is in trouble from the start on this one.

Green fees are: weekends, $12 for 18 holes and $7.50 for nine holes; weekdays, $10.50 for 18 holes and $7.50 for nine holes. Ther are chipping and putting greens, a driving range, and a pro on staff. Gas carts are available for $16 (18 holes) and $9 (nine holes), and pull carts rent for $2. Clubs can be rented, but there are no caddies.

Reservations are taken three days in advance beginning at 7 am when the pro shop opens. Call the lodge at ☎ 580-223-6600 for overnight reservations. Lake Murray is south of Oklahoma City off I-35 near Ardmore. Take exit #24 – Lake Murray Drive – and drive three miles east to the golf course.

Lake Texoma Golf Course, ☎ 580-564-3333, features seven ponds and a lake, which makes for water play on 12 of the 18 holes. Despite this challenge, or perhaps because of it, this is one of the busiest courses in the state park system. Total yardage is 6,128, the USGA rating is 67.8, and the slope is 112.

The front nine fairways are relatively flat and open. The back nine are more hilly and tight. All 18 greens have sand bunkers, and there are at least two bunkers along every fairway. If a golfer gets a good shot off the tee and stays out of the bunkers and ponds, he has a good chance of shooting a 71 par or better.

Green fees are: weekends, $12.50 for 18 holes, $7.50 for nine holes; weekdays, $10.50 for 18 holes and $7.50 for nine holes. The course has a lighted driving range, a putting green, a sand and chipping area, and a pro on site. Gas carts run $16 for 18 holes, $9 for nine holes, and pull carts rent for $3.50. Rental clubs are available but caddies are not. Tee times may be reserved four days in advance, beginning when the pro shop opens at 6 am.

From Durant, take US-70 west approximately 13 miles. Signs for the resort lodge and golf course direct visitors to turn off at the end of the bridge about six miles before reaching Kingston.

Cedar Creek Golf Course, ☎ 580-494-6456, recently went from nine holes to 18, and play became a bit tougher. This is one of the prettiest courses in the state, with 6,724 total yards, a par of 72, a USGA rating of 72.1, and a slope of 132.

Located in the foothills of the Kiamichi Mountains, this "Little Augusta" has rolling fairways lined on all sides by thick pine trees. Broken Bow

Lake provides the water – lots of water. Hole #14 demands a perfectly straight shot off the tee, but it's #16 that doglegs out into the lake so that the green is almost an island. Tough shots, but the scenery is so beautiful that golfers rarely seem ruffled.

Green fees are: weekends, $12 for 18 holes, $7 for nine holes; weekdays, $9.50 for 18 holes and $7 for nine holes. Rental gas carts are available at a cost of $16 for 18 holes and $9 for nine holes. Pull carts rent for $2 and clubs also may be rented. There are no caddies, but a pro is on site, and there is a driving range and a putting green.

The pro shop opens at 7 am and takes reservations up to a year in advance. A gorgeous new lodge overlooks Beavers Bend Lake, and reservations are taken at ☎ 800-654-8240. From McAlester, take the Indian Nation Turnpike south to the town of Antlers. Turn east on SH-3 to Broken Bow, then turn north on US-259. Cedar Creek Golf Course is 3½ miles east of the highway on Cedar Creek Road, about 12 miles from Broken Bow.

On Wheels

Biking

 Bikers will find plenty of interesting routes in this section of the state. The **Ouachita Mountain Area** alone has miles and miles of paved rural routes, endless logging roads, and an extensive network of recreational trails. Anyone with a multi-speed bike and average good health will enjoy the easy loop trail at **Robbers Cave State Park**. More determined riders will want to tackle the rugged terrain overlooking Broken Bow Reservoir at **Beavers Bend State Park**.

 Before you start, get a map and current trail information from a local source. Some trails are restricted to hikers or horseback riders, and some areas are off-limits or regulated by permits. It is especially important to be aware of hunting seasons. Nothing ruins a good bike trip faster than a hunter mistaking you for legal game. Be aware that you may be allowed to bike in an area open for hunting – it's up to you to know who's pursuing what where, and it never hurts to wear bright-colored clothing for extra visibility.

Southeast Oklahoma

☐ Winding Stair Mountains

The Winding Stair Mountains in the Ouachita National Forest provide the ultimate biking experience. Roadies can get to the mountaintops the hard way or the harder way. The hard way is up US-59/259 traveling north to south, or vice versa, between Heavener and Big Cedar. The highway crosses the Talimena Scenic Byway deep in the National Forest, two miles west of the Robert S. Kerr Memorial Arboretum.

The harder way is to take the Talimena Byway, SH-1, from the Talihina Visitor Information Center near the junction of US-271 to the Kerr Arboretum (about 15 miles) or the Queen Wilhelmina State Park near the Arkansas border (about 25 miles). This west-east route tests the mettle of even experienced bikers because of the unequivocally serious hills. Easier routes go around either side of the mountain – Valley Road to the north, and SH-63 to the south.

Mountain bikers can tackle about 90 miles of multi-use trails and hundreds of miles of ranch roads and logging paths within the forest, and some of the best routes are in the Winding Stair Recreation Area. This is definitely for experienced bikers only because the grades are steep, the trails are narrow, and spots near the top are rocky. For details about routes call the **Choctaw Ranger District** at ☎ 918-653-2991.

Old Military Road is actually a hiking trail, but bikers are allowed. Don't mistake this tolerance for a genuine welcome, and try to stay out of the hikers' way. That said, park at either the Holson Valley Road lot – about three miles east of US-271 on a gravel road off Holson Valley Road – or the Old Military Picnic Ground lot – about a mile from US-271 off SH-1. Consider the fact that Holson Valley is downhill from Old Military when you decide where to park. Unless you have a buddy who will drop you off at the top and pick you up at the bottom, you should probably do the uphill climb first so you can coast to the finish.

Horsethief Springs is a rough ride through unbelievable beauty. Start at Cedar Lake off Holson Valley Road about five miles from US-59. Signs for the lake are about two miles west on Holson Valley; turn right (north) and look for trailhead signs near the picnic area. Several trails start here, so follow the white paint blazes on the trees to Horsethief Springs picnic grounds. You ride up the mountain from the lake, so you are rewarded with a nice downhill ride back to your car. Another option is to work a deal with a friend who will drop you at Horsethief Springs and pick you up when you coast into the parking lot at Cedar Lake.

Oddly enough, horses are allowed on Horsethief Springs Trail, so watch out for them – and their generously shared droppings.

❏ Lake Wister

Lake Wister, ☎ 918-655-7756, just north of the National Forest boundary, has 6.2 miles of maintained multi-use trails and many miles of old farm roads. The trail links Wards Landing Campground, on a forested slope on the north shore, with the cabin area. Views are pleasant, the dogwood is beautiful in the spring, and the riding is mostly rated "Beginner," with a few hilly stretches that rate an "Intermediate" classification. Find Wards Landing off US-270 about half a mile north of the dam on a paved county road. Go west on the county road about three miles, then turn right at Wards Landing.

❏ Beavers Bend State Park

In Beavers Bend State Park, south of Ouachita Forest, about half of five-mile **Indian Nations Trail** is rated "Difficult" because of a 300-foot switchback climb. However, experienced trailheaders will consider the view from the top worth the struggle. The other half of the trail is rated "Intermediate," but even then, there's rugged terrain and taxing hills. Park at one of the campgrounds off US-259, north of **Broken Bow Lake**. Both Carson Creek and Stevens Gap Campgrounds are located in this area east of the highway, and you can pick up the trail at either. Ask a ranger for directions or ☎ 405-494-6556 for maps and information. The trail runs south from the campgrounds to the overlook at the spillway on US-259A.

South of Beaver's Bend, the **Tiak Ranger District** of the US Forest Service oversees almost 100 miles of forest roads near **Idabel**. These are not designated bike routes, but you can take long rides here without ever seeing another human. Call the office at ☎ 405-286-6564 for information and directions.

❏ McGee Creek Natural Scenic Recreation Area

More than 20 miles of multi-use trails wind through McGee Creek Natural Scenic Recreation Area 12 miles west of Antlers and 19 miles southeast of Atoka on SH-3. Because of the hills, most of the trails are rated "Intermediate," with a few rugged areas rated "Difficult." Only a certain number of permits are issued for the trails each day – and half of these may be reserved – so call the park office at ☎ 580-889-5822 to secure a pass.

Two-mile **Little Bugaboo Creek Trail** connects to 1½-mile **Whiskey Flats Trail** and descends into a valley that is a bugaboo to ride out of. Nonetheless, it should be done, because this is a wonderful ride. If you hurry, you (and anyone you bring with you) probably will be the only people on the trail, because this super-find has not been found by many – yet. Park at headquarters off SH-3 about nine miles north of Centerpoint Grocery Store, which is between Atoka and Antlers. A double-track trail is directly behind headquarters; it takes you to a single-track marked Little Bugaboo. Follow this up to Whiskey Flats, where you begin dropping fairly quickly down to the valley about 600 feet below. This is the fun part. Next is the bugaboo part. The only way out is the way you came in.

If you want an easier ride, ask at headquarters about the double-track trails and roads that lead to outstanding vistas in the recreation area. There are about 50 miles of trails here, so something should fit your experience, fitness, and energy levels. One easy trip is on South Rim Road from headquarters to the Bugaboo Canyon Overlook. Roundtrip is about five miles, and you can connect up to other trails if the scenery draws you farther.

❐ Clear Bay Trails

Little River State Park is now called **Thunderbird State Park**, but many maps and brochures still use the old name, so don't be confused. It's on the south side of Lake Thunderbird off SH-9, east of Norman. Four and one-half miles of hiking/biking paths, called the Clear Bay Trails, curve through the wooded park with side trails going down to the lake. Most of the hills are not steep, and there are frequent rest areas, so even beginners should find this an easy ride. However, the park is popular with residents from Norman and Oklahoma City, so you will not be alone here. In fact, the trail may be so crowded with hikers, you'll have to give up. Pick up the trail at the parking lot near the South Dam – bikes can't use the Clear Bay trailhead – about a mile past headquarters. A paved path leads down to the lake, then a dirt single-track begins off to the right. Follow it toward the trees and stay to the right every time you have to decide at a "Y" split. Eventually, you will either end where you started or connect with a paved road that will take you back to South Dam parking. Call ☎ 580-360-3572 for more information.

❑ Robber's Cave State Park

Another easy loop is found on top of the ridge overlooking Coon Creek Lake at Robbers Cave State Park. The trail is only 1½ miles long, but the scenery is so good, you won't mind going around several times. Find the trailhead near the Park Cabin Office/Store south of the Nature Center, which is off SH-2 about 5½ miles northwest of Wilburton. The park phone is ☎ 918-465-2565.

Motorcycling

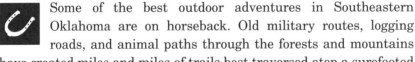

The Pear Orchard Motorcycle Use Area is on the eastern shore of Lake Murray on SH-77S about two miles south of US-70 between the Field Trial Area and Martins Landing. Stop at the park office on SH-77S soon after the turn off US-70 for maps and regulations, ☎ 580-223-6600.

Trains

The Hugo Heritage Railroad, ☎ 888-773-3768 or 405-326-6630, runs train trips through the pine woods of southeastern Oklahoma every Saturday from April through November. Passengers board the restored 1946 train pulled by a Kiamichi locomotive at the Frisco Depot and travel through scenic countryside to various destinations. Some trips include stops at special events such as Dogwood Days in Idabel. Others include dinner or special entertainment. Round-trip ticket prices range from $15 to $26 for adults. Departure times and routes vary, so call well in advance for a schedule.

On Horseback

Some of the best outdoor adventures in Southeastern Oklahoma are on horseback. Old military routes, logging roads, and animal paths through the forests and mountains have created miles and miles of trails best traversed atop a surefooted steed. There are several marked equestrian trails and a couple of overnight camping facilities for horses and riders. The main public trails are described here along with a few suggestions for guided rides and horse rentals.

Countless other horse trails are scattered throughout the region, and resource information is listed. Be sure to call ahead if you want to rent a horse. Some facilities are strictly BYOB (Bring Your Own Beast), but many state parks have riding stables.

 If you plan to ride independently through public land, contact the Department of Wildlife Conservation about permit requirements, ☎ 405-521-3851 – a $16-per-year license may be needed for some areas.

❒ Robbers Cave Equestrian Camp & Trails

This 50-mile horse trail follows old forest roads, pipeline right-of-ways, and creeks through rugged forest. **Robbers Cave Equestrian Campground** takes reservations up to a year in advance and offers restrooms, showers, and RV hookups. The grounds are on a flat stretch of grassy terrain with heavy woods. Campsites are level and well spaced for privacy, and the surrounding hills of the San Bois Mountains provide lovely scenery.

Anyone who doesn't want to spend hours in the saddle can map out routes that include one or more loops, which connect to create the total 50-mile trail. Caves, lakes, and canyons make the ride through old Indian Territory adventuresome, and it's easy to imagine outlaws hiding out here. Reservations, maps, and general information are available at the park office, ☎ 918-465-2565. From SH-2, four miles north of Wilburton, turn west and north and drive .75 mile to the equestrian area.

If you don't own a horse or you want to arrange a guided tour, call **Starr D Outfitters** (owned by the Dean family who run a large ranch south of Wilburton) on Ash Creek Road, ☎ 918-465-5200 or 918-465-2562. Guided trail rides are $8 to $28 per horse, depending on the length and distance ridden. One of the most popular trips is a three-hour $45 per-horse ride that includes time to explore the cave and a picnic lunch.

❒ Cedar Lake Equestrian Camp & Trails

About 12 miles south of Heavener, on Holson Valley Road west of SH-59, Cedar Lake Equestrian Campground marks the beginning of more than 70 miles of designated riding trails. A network of loops winds over the mountains and valleys to provide both short, gentle rides and tough, multi-day excursions. Cedar Lake is surrounded by the beauty of the Ouachita Mountains and is one of the best National Forest camps in the western part of the country. Access roads and parking pads are paved, and the lake side setting is unsurpassed. The campground itself has five handicapped-accessible sites, more than 100 primitive and developed sites, restrooms, showers, and horse wash racks.

Riders can travel unsurfaced trails from the campgrounds north to Blue Mountain or south across Tram Ridge to Emerald Vista near the Talimena Scenic Byway. One of the easiest rides is to Snake Mountain, just across Holson Road from the campground.

To reach the lake, take SH-59 to Holson Valley Road (Forest Road 5, a paved surface). Turn west and drive 2.8 miles to Forest Road 269. Turn north on this paved road and go about .75 mile to a "Y" where you turn left toward the equestrian camp. For maps, reservations, and information, contact the **Choctaw Ranger District** at ☎918-653-2991.

❏ Tickled Pink Ranch

You can bring your own or rent at this bed & ride ranch eight miles north of Smithville off US-259. A newly remodeled cabin sleeps six to 10 in two bedrooms, and horses are corralled out back. If you like it a bit more primitive, pitch a tent on the fenced grounds and tether your horse to a line. Either way, the scenery and riding are supreme. A hundred miles of marked trails are cut into the mountains, spring and fall color is lavish, and guests have access to 200,000 acres of public and private land. Call Sharon and Glen Gilstrap for reservations or information, ☎ 918-266-4138 in town, or 580-244-3729 at the ranch.

❏ Indian Mounds Camp

Near **Clayton Lake State Park** and **Sardis Lake**, just south of the town of Clayton on US-271, Indian Mounds Camp is built on the site of an ancient Indian village. The mounds that are seen throughout the complex are the ruins of lodges, which once housed these Native Americans. While the facilities are ideal for horse lovers, there are plenty of activities for guests with other interests.

Hiking and equestrian trails extend more than 100 miles over 983,000 acres, and Sardis Lake, Clayton Lake and the Kiamichi River are nearby.

If you don't own a horse, you can rent one for $10 per hour or $45 per day. All trails loop back to camp, and both novice and experienced riders will find a trail suitable for their skills. Twice a year, owner Jess Johnson plans a guided ride into the **Kiamichi Mountains** to view wildlife and

Southeast Oklahoma

Beavers Bend Resort Park, Near Broken Bow. (Fred W. Marvel)

outstanding scenery. A Spring Dogwood Ride is held the first weekend in May. The Fall Color Ride takes place the third weekend in October. Both include hot meals, a Western dance on Saturday night, and horseback church services on Sunday. Cost for the weekend is $75 per person.

At other times, the camp is open for camping and self-guided or guided rides. There are also a few camping trailers, and some tepees available for rent starting at $10 per night. Guest horses are always welcome for overnights.

Indian Mounds Camp is rustic, but the communications system is state-of-the-art. Contact Jess Johnson for reservations and information at ☎ 918-569-4761; fax 918-569-4567; www.indian-moundshorsecamp.com; e-mail trailleader@juno.com.

❏ McGee Creek Natural Scenic Recreation Area

Four horse camps and 50 miles of trails make McGee Creek Natural Scenic Recreation Area a favorite for horseback riders. A permit is required for both day and overnight use, and only a limited number are issued each day. However, half of each day's permits may be reserved – the other half are issued on a first-come basis. The 8,900-acre NSRA is adjacent to McGee Creek State Park on the far southwest edge of the Ouachita Mountain Range about 18 miles southeast of Atoka off SH-3. Horses are allowed on the multipurpose trails, which are old logging roads. The most popular are the **North Rim** and **South Rim Trails**, which overlook **Bugaboo Canyon**, and the **Boundary Trails**, which run along the NSRA east and south borders. ☎ 580-889-5822 for reservations or to see if all permits have been issued for the current day.

❏ Lake Murray

You'll need your own horse and a permit to ride on the 10-mile equestrian trail in the **Field Trail Area** on the north side of the lake off SH-70. But you can rent from the stables near the lodge if you want to take a guided ride over the wooded hills on the west side of the lake.

To reach the **Lake Murray Riding Stables**, take I-35 to exit 24, turn east and drive about two miles toward the Lake Murray State Resort Lodge. The stables are at the intersection of SH-77S and Lodge Road, across from Lake Side Grocery and Great Escape Dive Center. For more information, phone the park office at ☎ 580-223-4044.

On Water

 Southeastern Oklahoma is a watery place filled with some of the purest rivers and lakes in the country. Both the largest and second largest reservoirs in the state lie within the boundaries marked by I-40 to the north and I-35 to the west. Perpetual natural springs flow through the state's only National Park, and a magnificent waterfall tumbles into the state's most popular swimming hole. This chapter will lead you to well-stocked fishing sites, fast-running rivers, gentle streams, sandy beaches, and immense lakes. Whatever water adventure you seek, you can find in Southeastern Oklahoma.

Lake Broken Bow. (Fred W. Marvel)

Southeast Oklahoma

❑ Broken Bow Lake, Mountain Fork & Little River

Mountain Fork River originates in Oklahoma, flows east into Arkansas, then rolls back west into Oklahoma, where it turns south and spills into **Broken Bow Lake** before converging with **Little River**.

Upper Mountain Fork is fast and clear during the spring, which makes it a popular home for aggressive smallmouth bass, and the ideal launch site for rafts and canoes. Put in at the primitive campground under the crossing of SH-246 just west of Hatfield, Arkansas. You can float and fish (you'll need both an Arkansas and Oklahoma fishing license at this point) for several miles before you come to any significant rapids just past Low Creek.

If you're planning a one-day trip, stop at the 8.3-mile takeout point. For longer trips, you have two options: continue to the crossing at SH-4, another 11.3 miles; or go on to "The Narrows," near US-259 nine miles from SH-4 – making the trip a total of 28.6 miles. There are several hazardous rapids beginning about a quarter-mile below the SH-4 takeout. Scout before you continue into any questionable areas, and be aware that the river contains many deep holes.

This 28.6-mile journey can be broken into three parts and taken one section at a time, or traveled continuously during a three-day camp-out. Acceptable make-your-own-camp areas are all along the river, and there are primitive sites at the SH-246 crossing, the 8.3-mile takeout, and just below the SH-4 crossing. Cabins and inns listed under *Where to Stay* are one giant step up the creature-comfort ladder.

If you don't have your own canoe or raft, you can rent from **Mountain Fork Cabins & Canoes**, on the river one mile east of US-259 on SH-4 near Smithville, ☎ 580-244-3569; or try **Mountain Fork River Floats**, east off US-259 onto SH-4, then follow the signs, ☎ 580-244-3284.

When the Upper Mountain Fork dries up, as it tends to do during the summer, move down to the **Lower Mountain Fork** where water flow is determined by release from Broken Bow Lake. Finding your way around the unmarked roads is a bit tricky, but local residents and business owners are happy to give directions. This area is lovely year-round, but spring and fall are especially colorful.

Launch just below the regulation dam, which is off US-70 five miles east of the town of Broken Bow. Be cautious if the red beacon below the dam is on. This indicates that the generators are running, and the river should be considered dangerous. Never try to run the dam – there is an 18-foot drop, and a reverse surface current flows back toward the dam.

With these warnings in mind, this lower part of the river is generally tamer than the upper part, and adventurous beginners can manage without difficulty. Most of the roughest water will be in the first three miles, and you may want to take out at the parking area on the left near the US-70 crossing for a rest.

Below this spot, the water is mostly calm with occasional rapids and chutes and there are very few boulders to dodge. You can stop 3.2 miles downriver at a campground or continue five miles past the merge with Little River to the Ashalintubbi take out. After the merge, water-carved limestone formations will catch your attention along Little River. The entire trip from the dam to Ashalintubbi is 16.8 miles, and you can do it in one day if you have some experience and begin early. Plan to be on the river bank for sunrise, and launch by 8 am.

You won't find great fishing between the dam and the US-70 crossover because of the rough water, but below the 3.2-mile take out, you can catch smallmouth and largemouth bass, and – if you have the required stamp in addition to a license – rainbow trout. Brown trout are more strictly regulated, and at press time small ones must be released unharmed. Check current restrictions by calling the **Department of Wildlife Conservation**, ☎ 405-521-3721 or 800-ASK-FISH.

It can be difficult to fish from a fast-moving boat, so serious fishermen may prefer to wade into the river, and rainbow trout fishermen should use an ultra-light rod and reel and light tackle. Rainbow trout are not native to water east of the Continental Divide, but approximately 3,850 are stocked in the Lower Mountain Fork every two weeks, so you have a fair chance of catching one (the limit is six), especially if you concentrate your efforts near waterfalls and large boulders.

Canoes and shuttle service are provided at the following outfitters: **Beavers Bend River Floats**, in the State Resort Park, ☎ 405-494-6070; **WW Trading Post**, five miles east of Broken Bow on Mountain Fork Park Road between US-70 and the dam, ☎ 580-584-6856; **Goodwater Bait and Canoe**, east on SH-3 off US-70, ☎ 580-245-2383; and **Riverside Canoe Rental**, under the Mountain Fork River bridge on US-70, ☎ 580-835-7130. Some outfitters also supply fly-fishing equipment. If you've wanted to try this sport since seeing *A River Runs Through It*, call

Southeast Oklahoma

Oklahoma Parks & Resorts, ☎ 800-654-8240, for information about fly-fishing school.

Families enjoy the safe and easy float trip around 2½-mile "river bend" in **Beavers Bend State Park**. Two-man and three-man canoes can be rented for $15 and $20 for as long as it takes to make the trip. (You can do it in an hour, but the price is the same if it takes you all afternoon.) Giant 36-foot war canoes rent for $2 per person per hour and are popular with groups. The rental shack is on US-259A, which loops around the park, near Group Camp 2 and Camping Area D.

Broken Bow Lake is a 14,000-acre fisherman's paradise and a land-locked scuba diver's haven. Rocks and crystals are scattered thickly along the shore and around the lake's many islands and act as filters, which keep the water clear of sediment. Unless there has been a lot of rain, visibility is about 25 feet, and there are more islands to explore than in any other lake in Oklahoma. Divers usually wear wetsuits year-round because the mountain springs that feed the lake keep temperatures chilly, especially at the lower depths, even in the summer. (An early June average is about 67°.) Since the shore is rocky, booties are a good idea.

During the summer, **Broken Bow Scuba Services**, ☎ 580-584-9149, runs a water taxi out to the islands. Year-round, they also rent equipment, provide tank fills, give PADI certification classes, and offer inside information on where to find the best diving. Their prices on gear are advertised as "the lowest in the four state area," and they also plan trips to other dive destinations. Hours are 8 am to 5 pm Monday through Friday and 8 am to noon on Saturday. Air-fills-only are available on Sunday during the summer at 9 am. The shop is 10 miles south of the lake at 1000 South Park Drive in Broken Bow.

Beavers Bend Marina, at the end of Steven's Gap Road off US-259, ☎ 405-494-6455, sells everything for the fisherman and rents party barges, ski boats, and bass boats. This is also the place to pick up information on where the fish are biting.

Don't be confused by signs (or longtime residents) that call this area Hochatown (HOO-chee-town). The lake actually covers the original settlement known by that name, and, until recently, much of the area around the lake has been Hochatown State Park. Now, however, everything from the Cedar Creek Golf Course, north of the lake, to the Forest Heritage Center, south of the lake, has been combined into Beavers Bend Resort Park.

Wildlife – even deer seeking refuge from hunters – and many species of birds inhabit the large islands that dot the lake. If you have a boat, spend a few hours exploring what were the highest points in Hochatown before the dam was built. Camping is not allowed, but day hikers, bird watchers, and picnickers are welcome. Anyone without a boat can check with Broken Bow Scuba Service about catching a ride out to the islands, but it isn't necessary to set foot on them to appreciate their beauty. Good views are possible from shore, and the best is from the greatroom at **Beavers Bend Lakeview Lodge** (see page 177).

❏ Glover River

You'll need a good map to find the launch site, but this dramatic river trip is worth the trouble. Look for the point, north of Wright City, south of Bethel, and west of Broken Bow Lake, where the east and west forks of the Glover River meet and flow southward. Forest Road 56000 southwest of Bethel intersects an unnumbered forest company road that runs north from SH-3 to Battiest. Find FR-56000, then follow it to a low water bridge just below the confluence of the two river forks. Put in there at the bridge.

The first part of this trip is rocky, and you may have to walk around a few unnavigable spots, but you'll soon come to an amazingly scenic stretch. In the spring, the banks are in full bloom, and fall colors blaze in October and November. The bass and perch fishing is good, but you'll have to wade-fish the rougher areas. Stick with light tackle and small lures for the best results.

The first exit point from the river is at the 7.2-mile point. After that, you can use Camp Glover (10.3 miles) in an emergency, but the caretaker must be asked for permission to unlock the gate at the camp entrance. A better takeout is FR-53000/71400 crossing at the 16.3-mile point. Three exits are located farther down at: the 20.1-mile low water crossing; the 25-mile SH-3 bridge crossing; and the 27½-mile low water bridge about half a mile west of the town of Glover. The creek joins Little River a little farther down near Wright City.

Don't attempt the river when it's at high water levels unless you are experienced with heavy whitewater. Even when water levels are normal, there are many rocky outcroppings and small, but rapid falls, which make this an exciting, but challenging trip. Be especially cautious at Wold Falls (13.6-mile point) and Meat Hollow (15.0-mile point).

Much of the land along the river belongs to Weyerhaeuser Lumber Company and offers terrific natural camping. There are also primitive sites at Meat Hollow and the 16.3-mile crossing. The closest campgrounds with facilities are at **Pine Creek Lake**, six miles north of Valliant, ☎ 580-933-4239, and **Beavers Bend Resort Park**, off US-259 on the 259A loop, ☎ 405-494-6300.

There are no rental or shuttle services on the Glover River, but you can get information and water conditions from the **Oklahoma Scenic Rivers Commission**, ☎ 800-299-3251.

❐ Eagle Fork Creek

The scenery along this stream is spectacular due to its location between the Ouachita National Forest and the McCurtain County Wilderness Area. However, you will be walking instead of floating if there's been little rainfall. On the other hand, if there's been heavy rainfall, you'll be twisting and turning down the creek so fast, you'll need a lot of experience to stay upright.

 Judge the chances for a good trip by measuring the water depth at the low water bridge. One foot over the bridge almost guarantees an excellent experience. Two feet over is trouble. Wait until the water drops to a safe level before tackling the creek.

Find the first low water bridge about 1½ miles north of Octavia, west of US-259. If you put in there, be aware of strong currents below the two dams soon after the bridge. A better launch site is about 3½ miles down river at the second low water bridge. There's a waterfall just after the creek curves left and joins another fork of the creek on the right side. You won't be able to see what you're getting into until you're there, so portage on the left when you see what looks like a rapid about a mile past this second low water bridge. The fall is a four- or five-foot drop, so give it due respect.

If you don't want to challenge this rather serious waterfall, put in at the low water bridge about three miles farther down river. There's another fall after that, but it isn't as fierce. An old bridge about five miles from the third bridge is the last takeout point.

Fishermen can use lightweight gear and fly tackle to try for the bass, rainbow trout, and sunfish, which are abundant in these waters. A license is required for all fishing and a stamp is needed for trout.

❏ Lake Murray

This is one of the state's most popular lakes due to its clear water, abundant facilities, and location – midway between Oklahoma City and Dallas, Texas. Thanks to the economic depression in the early 1930s, federal relief programs were looking for ways to put people to work so they constructed a dam outside the town of Ardmore. It was named for "Alfalfa Bill" Murray, one of Oklahoma's more ostentatious governors. The Civilian Conservation Corps and Works Progress Administration paid workers $1.25 an hour to build the dam, a park, and several unique sandstone buildings. (The area was soon nicknamed "The Devils Kitchen" because of a proliferation of moonshine stills.)

This cheap labor resulted in a 6,500-acre lake, a 12,496-acre park (the largest in the state), and a scattering of cottages and shelters. Today, guests swim, boat, waterski, jet-ski, scuba dive, and fish on the lake. Land activities include hiking, biking, golf, tennis, horseback riding, and camping. Tucker Tower overlooks the entire area, offering good views of all the action.

SH-77S, off US-70, loops around the park and lake. From I-35, take exit 29 to US-70, then turn south onto SH-77S. Stop at the park office near this intersection for information and maps of the area, ☎ 580-233-4044.

A 50-room state-operated lodge is on the west side of the lake on Lodge Road, a left turn at the Lake Side Grocery/Great Escape Dive Center. Call **Lake Murray Resort Lodge**, ☎ 800-654-8240, for overnight reservations. Countless families return year after year to spend weekends or summer vacations at this homey lodge. Don't expect luxury, but you'll find everything you need and enough activities to keep the entire family busy for days.

Southeast Oklahoma

Lake Murray is a popular scuba site for residents of both Texas and Oklahoma. Water temperature here is cool, but by midsummer when the air temperature is over 90°, divers usually shed their wetsuits. Visibility is typically about 15 feet, depending on how much rain has fallen. Since this part of the state is known for dry, hot summers, divers can expect the best conditions from Memorial Day until late September.

The **Great Escape Dive Center**, ☎ 580-223-6494, is located on SH-77S and Lodge Road inside Lakeside Grocery on the west side of the lake. This full-service shop is open daily from 7 am to 11 pm and offers PADI certification, equipment rental, and tank fills. Their instruction decks at Marietta Landing provide easy access to the water, and submerged boats, cars, and motorcycles create a playground for divers to explore. Probably the most fun is feeding the fish. Bring a bag of peas or a can of Vienna sausage down with you; schools of catfish and perch will race to eat out of your hand.

Lake Murray Marina is on Boat Dock Drive, just south of the lodge, ☎ 580-223-9339. Turn left at a big, faded boat propeller sign to drive down to the water. Every type and all sized boats are docked there, and the marina rents boats, pontoons, and jet skis. Hours are usually 7 am to 9 pm daily, but vary off-season.

Both enclosed and open-air fishing docks are located near the lodge, and you can try for white, largemouth, and smallmouth bass as well as channel catfish. Bait and tackle are available at **Lake Country Texaco** at the intersection of US-70 and SH-77S; **Lake Village Grocery** a mile west of the lodge; and at the **Marina store**, 500 feet north of the lodge.

If you don't have your own boat, consider renting a sail boat, paddle boat, canoe, or wind surfer at **Lake Murray Water Sports**, ☎ 580-223-7185. Sightseeing cruises and dinner cruises can be arranged through **Lake Murray Luxury Cruises**, ☎ 580-223-0088. Scuba divers may fill their tanks, take certification lessons, and rent equipment at **Great Escape Dive Center**, inside Lakeside Grocery on 77S and Lodge Road, ☎ 580-226-5357.

❑ Lake Texoma Resort Park

This huge lake sprawls across both North Texas and South Oklahoma, covering 93,000 acres – the second largest lake in Oklahoma (Lake Eufaula is larger) and among the largest manmade lakes in the country. It was created in 1944 when the US Corps of Engineers built 17,200-foot

Denison Dam on the Red River, which separates Texas from Oklahoma. Intended primarily as flood control, the lake was immediately popular with outdoor folk, and today beckons anglers in pursuit of "stripers."

Striped bass are indigenous to oceans and typically swim upstream in rivers to spawn. When a few got trapped in fresh water during the reservoir-building frenzy of the New Deal years, scientists were amazed that they not only survived but multiplied – abundantly. Now this species is stocked in several southern lakes, but they thrive best in Lake Texoma. Maybe it's the high salt content of the lake. Maybe a fish aphrodisiac oozes from the bottom of the tributaries. Whatever, the stripers love it here, and any angler with a smidgen of competitive spirit wants to hook one.

Guide services all along the lake's 530-mile shore do a brisk business and people routinely come home with a nice assortment of bass, catfish, crappie, and sunfish. If you don't want to hire a guide, show up early at any of the cafés along the lake to eavesdrop on conversations among the locals. You'll get a hearty meal and find out who caught what where.

An enclosed fishing dock is located on a peninsula across the road from **Texoma Resort Lodge**, ☎ 580-564-2311 or 800-652-OKLA, at the west end of the Roosevelt Bridge on US-70. The park office, ☎ 580-564-2566 shares a parking lot with the lodge, and rangers provide valuable information, maps, and directions. **Catfish Bay Marina**, just down the road from the park office in the direction of **Catfish Bay Campground**, ☎ 405-564-2307, rents pontoons, ski boats and skis, wave runners, and tubes. For supplies, try **Rick's Lake Country Grocery**, a mile west of the lodge, ☎ 580-564-2906, or the **Phillips 66 Gas Station and Grocery**, a half-mile west of the park on US-70.

Beach bums gather on the white sand beaches along the shore and on the islands, which stretch for six miles through the middle of the lake. Visitors with boats hop from one island to another, soaking up the sun, cooking out near the water, competing in a game of volleyball or frisbee. After dark, when a million stars light the sky, groups set up camp, and couples spread blankets on the soft sand. (Free camping permits are issued at the park office.)

Boats – big boats – cruise the lake every day during every season. On summer weekends the waters are alive with activity, and it's not unusual to see 50-foot craft anchored offshore. They share the huge lake with ski boats, blow-up rafts, waverunners, sailboats – even houseboats. **Willow Springs Resort & Marina**, south of US-70, west of Durant, ☎ 580-924-6240, rents 40- to 56-foot fully equipped and air-conditioned self-drive houseboats to vacationers who want ultimate freedom.

From October through February, ducks, geese, and dozens of species of migratory birds flock to the lake to wait out the bad weather up north. Birdwatchers and nature lovers say this is the best time to visit Texoma. The summer crowds have gone home and visitors have miles and miles of undeveloped, wooded shoreline to explore.

❏ Honey Creek, Turner Falls & the Washita River

Before there was Interstate Highway-35, there was State Highway 77, and many prefer this two-lane scenic road to its successor. The highlight of SH-77 is **Turner Falls**, which plummets 77 feet from **Honey Creek** into a natural swimming hole. Waterfalls pour into streams in several spots in the **Arbuckle Mountains**, and the smaller ones entice visitors to slip and slide over the rocks on their bottoms. But Turner Falls is too high, too slick, too dangerous to maneuver, so even the most adventurous must settle for splashing in the pool at its feet.

Another natural pool, **Blue Hole**, near the entrance to the park that surrounds Turner Falls, has a long, manmade slide that begins high on a rocky cliff and ends abruptly several feet above the water. Good swimmers spend hours here sliding and diving into the deep water, but younger children and lazy sunbathers prefer the park's shallower pools and sandy beaches. Only Blue Hole and the pool at the foot of the main waterfall have lifeguards on duty during peak tourist seasons.

Admission to the park is $2.50 for everyone seven and older during the winter and $6 for adults, $4.50 for children between the ages of seven and 12 in the summer. In addition to the swimming areas, the 720-acre park has an abandoned rock "castle," three natural caves, and hiking trails to explore. Fishermen can angle for trout during daylight hours from November 1 to March 31 at a cost of $1.25 each for up to eight catch-and-keep fish per day. (You must have an Oklahoma fishing license.)

The **Washita River** begins a gentle, 10-mile stretch north of the falls, providing perfect conditions for a lazy float downstream. **Rose Grocery**, two miles north on SH-77, ☎ 580-369-2223, rents canoes for $15 per person and runs a shuttle between the put-in and takeout points.

Reservations aren't necessary and usually there are plenty of canoes available, even on summer weekends. The Washita is muddy because water flow continuously stirs up red dirt that lines the shore and river bottom, but there is no unhealthy pollution. This is a terrific 2½- to three-hour float for families who want a smooth trip and calm swimming waters.

If you have your own canoe or raft, put-in at the SH-77 crossing just east of I-35, southwest of Davis. The best flow level is during spring and fall after adequate rain, but generally the river is floatable year-round. Seven and a half miles downstream from the SH-77 crossing, you can launch or take out at the Dougherty Bridge. The last take out is at the SH-53 bridge; floating the entire distance takes six or seven hours and covers almost 22 miles.

❒ Lake of the Arbuckles

The Plains Indians called this area "The Valley of Rippling Waters" for good reason. A plethora of fresh and mineral springs rise from the marshy ground here, forming natural pools, winding creeks, and lovely waterfalls. Years ago, when people didn't doubt the curative powers of mineral baths and mud wraps, this area was a fashionable resort with grand hotels patronized by health-seeking tourists. Today, visitors are more interested in finding health through recreation.

Chickasaw National Recreation Area, ☎ 580-622-3165, the only National Park in Oklahoma, offers all types of water adventures at **Lake of the Arbuckles** and **Veterans Lake**. Fishermen have good luck catching bass, crappie, sunfish, walleye pike, and catfish. (There is a wheelchair-accessible dock at Veterans Lake.) Sailboats, ski boats, and canoes share water space, and there are launch sites designated at both lakes. Swimmers enjoy the clean, cool water of the park's streams, and the beach on the west side of Veterans Lake on **Rock Creek**.

Chickasaw National Recreation Area encompasses almost 10,000 acres and two districts so visitors need a detailed map to find all the amenities. Call before your trip for information and maps, or stop at a park office once you arrive. Ranger stations are located in three areas: **Buckhorn**, west off US-177 on Buckhorn Road; **The Point**, on Point Road south of SH-7; and the **Bromide Pavilion**, north of Veterans Lake.

Southeast Oklahoma

A full-service **Visitor Information Center** at the **Travertine Nature Center** has interpretive displays, helpful rangers, and a variety of maps and brochures. Take 12th Street south off Broadway in the city of Sulphur to the loop road that circles the Travertine area, then follow the signs to the Visitor's Center.

The most popular swimming spot in the park is **Little Niagara**, near the Nature Center, but all of the streams and creeks are perfect for a dip on a hot day. Just remember, these waters come from artesian springs and they're cold. However, they're also refreshingly pure, so jump in.

❏ Lake Eufaula

This is the largest lake in Oklahoma, with 102,500 acres of water, 600 miles of shoreline, and enough room for two full-facility parks. The lake sprawls in every direction from north of I-40, just east of Henryetta, along US-69 to Brushy Creek, south of McAlester. Maps and information are available from the **Lake Eufaula Association**, ☎ 918-689-7751.

Fountainhead State Park covers 2,800 acres 14 miles south of Checotah on SH-150 off I-40, ☎ 918-689-5311. **Fountainhead Resort**, ☎ 800-345-6343, is a privately-owned deluxe facility overlooking the lake adjacent to the park. There are three boat ramps (one lighted), a heated fishing dock, and a beach inside the park boundaries. **Belle Starr Marina**, ☎ 918-689-2132, south of Fountainhead off Texanna Road in **Belle Starr Park**, rents pontoon boats and waverunners. Two boat ramps and a beach are within the park.

Arrowhead Resort and Gaming Center, ☎ 800-422-2711, is owned by the Choctaw Nation and located adjacent to 2,200-acre **Arrowhead State Park**. The resort has 84 hotel-style rooms with rates in the $50 range, and 70 cabins priced from $52 to $149. Arrowhead Marina, ☎ 918-339-6511, is open 7am to 7pm daily, and features an enclosed fishing dock and boat rentals. Paddleboats rent for $10 per hour, 29-foot pontoons for $140 per day, and all-day fishing from their dock is $2.50.

All kinds of boats are seen on the lake from small fishing dinghies to 95-foot cruisers. If you don't have your own craft, **Getaway Cruises**, ☎ 918-689-2200, rents plush houseboats, and **Evergreen Marina**, ☎ 918-799-5404, rents flashy waverunners.

■ Where to Stay

B&Bs, Lodges & Cabins

Ardmore

 Blackberry Farm Bed and Breakfast, ☎ 580-223-8958, 2715 Hedges Road, is a new French-style country house on 29-acres near Lake Murray. There are two rooms with private baths and guests may use the exercise room. A full breakfast is served and rooms are $75.

Lake Murray Resort Lodge, ☎ 580-223-6600 or 800-654-8240, has suites and standard rooms renting from $40 to $175. There are also cabins, cottages, and villas, which can accommodate up to 14 people and rent from $43 to $250. Everything here books up early, so call a year in advance for peak-season reservations.

Broken Bow/Beavers Bend

Beavers Bend Lakeview Lodge, ☎ 580-494-6179. Take US-259 north from Broken Bow, approximately 10 miles from town, turn east onto Stevens Gap Road and follow it to the lodge. This new state-owned resort is state-of-the-art in design, beauty, and comfort. The view from the two-story greatroom is magnificent, and each room shares it. Rates are $110-$175 and include a continental breakfast. There's usually a waiting list for weekends, holidays, and summers – call early.

Beavers Bend Resort Cabins, ☎ 580-494-6538, in the state park, have fully equipped kitchens, heat, air conditioning, and all linens. They are a nice bridge between camping out and staying in the Lodge. Rates range from a low of $38 for a studio in winter to $94 for a two-bedroom river-view in the summer.

A multitude of cabins are scatted in the forest and along the lakes and rivers from Broken Bow to the Talimena Scenic Byway. You can choose from rustic to deluxe, and find prices ranging from $35 to over $100. All of the following are comfortable, clean, and near the activity. Actual prices are not given because rates fluctuate seasonally and various cabins managed by one proprietor rent for different amounts. However, most of these cabins located off US-259 rent in the $50 to $100 range. Call for directions and reservations.

Southeast Oklahoma

- $/$$$ **Hochatown Resort Cabins/Rustic Retreats**, ☎ 800-550-6521 or 580-494-6521, fax 580-494-6553, offers a wide choice of meticulously maintained cabins. Ask about the honeymoon retreat. Proprietor BJ Zimmerman is a fireball of enthusiasm and information for the Beavers Bend area – stop by to see her at The Cedar Chest on US-259 across from the entrance to the state park.

- $/$$$ **Whip-Poor-Will Log Cabins**, ☎ 580-494-6476, off US-259 at the entrance to Cedar Creek Golf Course, is a tradition in Kiamichi Country. Call early for reservations – the 18 one-room to three-bedroom cabins that sleep up to 10 people fill quickly on weekends and during the summer.

- $$/$$$ **Eagle Creek Guest Cottages**, ☎ 580-244-7597 or 580-244-3851, near Octavia, is hidden in the woods – a great luxury escape with king-size beds and cable TV.

- $$/$$$ **Willow Creek Resort**, ☎ 580-494-6091, has one- and two-bedroom cabins with all the amenities, including cable TV.

- $/$$$ **Lake Pine Retreat**, ☎ 580-494-6464, offers RV hookups, cabins that sleep up to 12 people, and equestrian camping. There's also a swimming pool and laundry room.

- $$/$$$ **Peckerwood Knob Cabins**, ☎ 580-494-7333, half a mile off US-259 near Smithville, has cabins with scenic views, fireplaces, decks, and grills.

- $$ **Cedar Creek Cabins**, ☎ 580-494-6790 or 800-550-6521, is managed by Hochatown Junction Resorts and includes fully equipped cabins and a group lodge near all the activities.

- $$ **Sleepy Hollow Cabins**, ☎ 580-494-6320, has all new cabins half a mile from Lake Access Road off US-259.

- $$ **Three Oaks Cabins**, ☎ 580-494-6144, off US-259, has log cabins with cable TV and a covered pavilion for groups.

- $$/$$$ **Tree Top View Cabins**, ☎ 580-241-5599, are perched above ground on the bank of the Glover River in a remote wooded area near Battiest. A johnboat or canoe is furnished with the rustic but modern fully equipped cabins. They sleep up to six people.

■ **$$/$$$ Kiamichi Country Cabins**, ☎ 580-494-6152, are two-bedroom log and cedar cabins with fireplaces and cable TV.

Scout troops, church groups, or families planning a big reunion will want to check with **Beavers Bend Group Camp**, ☎ 405-326-3351, for information on their two group camping facilities. There are bunk cabins and kitchen/dining facilities to accommodate up to 160 people.

Sojourners' Bed and Breakfast, ☎ 580-584-9324, on Yashau Creek four miles south of Broken Bow, has two rooms with private baths. A full breakfast is served to guests and arrangements can be made for dinner. Room rates are $55.

Clayton

Clayton Country Inn, ☎ 918-569-4165, south of town on US-271, has nine rooms in the main house and two in a duplex cottage with small kitchenettes. The rooms are small and cozy, but many guests come only for dinner. Served Monday through Saturday from 5:30 pm to 9:30 pm in the dining room, dinner includes steak, chicken and fish – you'll need a reservation on weekends. If you stay overnight, rooms rent for about $45.

Big Cedar, ☎ 918-651-3271, http://208.197.10.120/bigcedar/welcome. htm. This has basic but modern cabins and RV hookups with mountain views on the banks of the Kiamichi River. $/$$

Indian Mounds Camp, ☎ 918-569-4761, fax 918-569-4567, www. indianmoundshorsecamp.com, e-mail trailleader@juno.com. This is 2½ miles south of town on US-271 with terrific scenic views. There are 100 RV hookups, a few camper trailers ($20 per night for two people), nine tepees ($10 per person, per night), and tent sites. The best fun and biggest bargain is the three-day guided mountain trail ride led by owner Jess Johnson on the first weekend in May and the third weekend in October. The $75 fee includes everything from meals to entertainment for the three days.

Davis

Cedar Green Bed and Breakfast, ☎ 580-369-2396, 909 South 4th Street, is near Turner Falls in the Arbuckle Wilderness. The house, built in 1938 of cedar and stone, has two guest rooms and a suite with private baths. Breakfast is creative and delicious – hospitality is outstanding. Rooms are priced at $50-$60.

Sandy Creek Cabin, ☎ 580-369-2934, overlooks Sandy Creek in the scenic Arbuckle Mountains near Turner Falls. This rustic cabin is perfect for two, but can sleep four. $

Cedervale Gardens/Mountain Cabins, ☎ 580-369-3224, US-77 south of exit 51 off I-35, is best known for its gorgeous gardens. There are two cabins sleeping four to six people, which rent for $75 to $85 per night. Even if you don't stay overnight, stop at the restaurant for a fresh trout dinner.

Durant

Lake Texoma Resort Lodge, ☎ 580-564-2311 or 800-654-8240, west of town between I-35 and US-75, is across the street from the golf course. Guest rooms in the lodge range from $40 to $92, depending on size, location, and season. There are also cottages and a 40-person group building ranging from $50 to $650. Call at least a year in advance for summer reservations. Most accommodations are full a month in advance throughout the year.

Deer Run Lodge, ☎ 580-367-2687 or 580-924-4402, off SH-22 east of Caddo and north east of Durant, is a 7,200-acre working ranch. Guests stay in one of eight rooms in the two-story ranch house, ride horses with the cowboys, and swim in a nearby pond. Rates are $87 per day per adult and $48 per day per child including meals and activities.

Hugo

The Old Johnson House, ☎ 405-326-8111 or 405-326-3103, 1101 East Kirk, really *is* the old Johnson house, and Johnsons lived here from the time it was built in 1910 until it became a bed and breakfast in 1993. There are six guest rooms and a garden cottage renting in the $60 range. If you visit in the spring, flowers original to the house will be in full bloom.

Two motels in town are worth a mention: $ **Hugo Inn**, ☎ 405-326-HUGO, 1006 East Jackson; and $ **Village Inn**, ☎ 405-326-3333, 610 West Jackson. The Village also has parking for boats and trucks.

Ouachita National Forest Area

National Forest Campgrounds in Oklahoma include Cedar Lake, Winding Stair, and Billy Creek, ☎ 800-280-2267. Cedar Lake also has an Equestrian Camp. All rates are $3 to $12, depending on the camp site's amenities.

Spiro

Aunt Jan's Cozy Cabin, ☎ 918-962-2380 or 800-470-3481, is a single log cabin certified and approved by the Oklahoma Bed and Breakfast Association. It sits on an 80-acre cattle ranch, and breakfast is served in your cabin or in Jan's country kitchen. Rates are $75 to $120.

Stuart

Stuart Hotel, ☎ 918-546-2591, US-270 west of McAlester, is a three-story 1890s hotel that has been renovated with eight rooms and a honeymoon suite. Full breakfast – and a tea room serves lunch. Room rates are from $40 to $65.

Sulphur

Artesian Bed and Breakfast, 1022 West 12th Street, ☎ 405-622-5254, was built in 1904 with a wrap-around porch, complete with a swing. There are two rooms with private baths, and breakfast is served in a cheery breakfast room. Near Chickasaw National Park, rooms rent for $35 to $60.

Four Sisters Inn, ☎ 580-622-4441, 1307 Cooper Memorial Drive, has four rooms and a honeymoon suite with private baths in a ranch-style house with a pool. Breakfast and afternoon tea are served to guests and the rates are $80, with a two-night minimum.

Olde Bathhouse, ☎ 580-622-5930, 1102 West Lindsay, has seven guest rooms, but you can also make a day visit to the two indoor mineral pools. Overnight stays are $65, day visits are $15, and massages are $35.

Wilburton

Windsong Inn and **Windsong Bed and Breakfast**, ☎ 918-465-5174, 100 West Cedar. This 1907 three-story house with a view of the Winding Stair Mountains has original woodwork and stained glass. There are three rooms with private baths and breakfast is served whenever guests are awake and ready. Weekend dinner and Sunday lunch are available and reservations are suggested. Rooms are $60 to $80.

Dome House Bed and Breakfast Inn, 315 East Main, ☎ 918-465-0092, is a 1908 home with a big front porch for relaxing and a turn-of-the-century grand piano for entertainment. Guests stay in five rooms with private baths, and a continental breakfast is served each morning. Rates are from $45 to $75.

Spas

Akia, ☎ 405-405-842-6269, near Chickasaw National Recreation Area in Sulphur, offers health-spa-style retreats for women in a rock cottage compound. Priced from $200 for a two-day hiking weekend to $610 for a seven-day retreat, this simple but comfortable adult camp sends guests home educated and rested.

Lifestyle Center of America, ☎ 405-993-2327, in the Arbuckle Mountains, is a new $12 million center dedicated to healthy living. A one-night, three-meal mini-program costs $95 and includes a massage and use of all the facilities. The 12-day and 19-day programs are geared toward men and women with chronic or serious health problems and are $3,000 to $4,000.

Camping

 There are hundreds of places to camp in southeastern Oklahoma, and you can get several brochures from the State Park Departments by calling ☎ 800-654-8240. The following are worthy of mention because of their facilities or scenic location.

Lake Wister State Park, ☎ 918-655-7756 or 800-654-8240, off US-270 south of Poteau, is less crowded than most other camping areas. There are 15 cabins renting for $48 to $78 per night and 172 campsites renting for $6 to $17.

Robbers Cave State Park, ☎ 918-465-2565, off SH-2 north of Wilburton, has 26 cabins for $48 to $88 and 117 campsites for $6 to $17.

Ouachita National Forest Campgrounds in Oklahoma include Cedar Lake, Winding Stair, and Billy Creek, ☎ 800-280-2267. Cedar Lake also has an Equestrian Camp. All rates are $3 to $12 depending on the camp site's amenities.

The US Army Corps of Engineers operates pleasant campgrounds and recreational facilities at three lakes in the Kiamichi Lake Country: **Sardis Lake**, ☎ 580-569-4131, with 143 campsites (most with electricity), a beach, and three boat ramps; **Pine Creek Lake**, ☎ 918-933-4239, with updated facilities, which consist of 169 campsites with electricity, primitive sites, two beaches, and five boat ramps; **Hugo Lake**, ☎ 405-326-3345, offering 185 campsites with and without electricity, plus three beaches and seven boat launching areas.

■ Where to Eat

Ada

$ **J.D.'s Café**, ☎ 580-332-9750, 911 North Broadway, is still owned by J.D. himself. Stop in for a home-style meal and a piece of his famous pie, Tuesday through Saturday, 5 am to 8:30 pm.

$ **Polo's Authentic Mexican Restaurante**, ☎ 580-332-2710, 219 West Main, serves outstanding fajitas and other typical south-of-the-border meals Monday through Saturday from 11 am to 8 pm.

Ardmore

$ **The Apple Bin**, at Lake Murray Resort, ☎ 580-223-6600, serves a famous catfish dinner. Open daily from 7 am to 8 pm, this is also a popular breakfast spot for resort guests.

Beavers Bend

$ **Riverside Restaurant** in the state park, ☎ 580-494-6551, serves a breakfast buffet on weekends beginning at 8 am. Lunch and dinner include burgers, smoked ribs, fish, and chicken-fried steak. Hours are 8 am-8 pm, Friday, 8 am-9 pm, Saturday, 8 am-2 pm, Sunday, and 11am-8 pm, Monday through Thursday. Closed January and February.

$/$$ **Tootie's By the Lake**, US-259 at Steven's Gap Road, ☎ 405-494-6791. Tootie or his wife, Lillian, will probably greet you at the door and make sure your meal is exactly as you like it. The fried fish is outstanding, and the steaks are a specialty. Lunch and dinner are served from 11 am to 10 pm, Tuesday through Sunday. A Sunday buffet is set up from 11am to 2 pm, and there's a seafood buffet on Friday nights. Prime rib is the special on Saturday.

$ Stevens Gap Restaurant, US-259 at the entrance to Lakeview Lodge, ☎ 580-494-6350, serves breakfast all day. The café is owned by friendly Scott and Chandra Rickey, and the food is down-home good. Get there early for breakfast so you can catch the local fishing gossip.

Broken Bow

$/$$ The Charles Wesley Restaurant, ☎ 580-584-9229, 302 North Park Drive off US-259, has a lunch buffet and also serves steaks and seafood. Open 6 am to 9 pm daily.

Durant

$/$$ Sanford's, ☎ 580-564-3764, US-70 near Lake Texoma, features a salad and soup bar. Dinner is served from 4:30 pm to 9 pm, Tuesday through Thursday, and 4:30 pm to 10 pm, Friday and Saturday. Fish and steaks are the main menu items.

Hugo

$ Cedar Shed, ☎ 405-326-7287, 1300 South F Street, serves barbecue lunch and dinner from 10 am to 9 pm, Monday through Saturday.

$ Mi Casita, ☎ 405-326-5464, on US-271 two miles south of town, serves Mexican meals from 11 am to 9 pm, Monday through Saturday.

Idabel

$ Blue Note Coffee Shop, downtown at 101 Southeast Avenue A, ☎ 405-286-3221, serves gourmet coffee and fresh-baked biscuits and muffins beginning at 7:30 am, Monday through Fridays. Lunch is sandwiches and a hot special served until closing at 2 pm.

Marietta

$ McGehees Catfish Restaurant, ☎ 580-276-2751, off I-35 at exit 15, is famous for its all-you-can-eat catfish feast. Hours are 5 pm to 9:30 pm, weekdays (closed Wednesday), and 1 pm to 9:30 pm, Saturday and Sunday.

$ Denim's Restaurant, ☎ 580-276-3222, east of I-35 and SH-32 intersection, has a salad bar and made-from-scratch meals. Open 6:30 am to 9 pm daily, except Sunday, when they close at 3 pm.

McAlester/Krebs

$/$$ **Gia Como's Italian Cuisine**, ☎ 918-423-2662, off US-69 at 19th Street and Comanche Road in McAlester, is a local tradition. Four generations of family members run this comfortable restaurant that prepares food in either the American or Italian style. Lunch and dinner are served Tuesdays through Saturday from 11:30 am to 9:30 pm.

Pete's Place in Krebs is one of several well-known eateries in the "Little Italy" area near McAlester. (Lynne M. Sullivan)

$/$$ **Pete's Place**, ☎ 918-423-2042, corner of 8th Street and Moore off US-270 in Krebs just south of McAlester, is famous for its Choc beer, but also serves outstanding steaks and Italian food in huge quantities. Open Monday through Thursday from 4 pm to 9 pm, Friday and Saturday from 4 pm to 10 pm, and Sunday from noon to 8 pm.

Ouachita National Forest

$ **Saddle Gap**, ☎ 580-494-6504, sits high in the mountains seven miles south of Big Cedar on US-259. The restaurant is in a recreation area that features camping, entertainment, and hiking trails. New cabins should be complete by now; call for information.

$ **Hillbilly Junkshun**, ☎ 918-653-2128, promises "danged good eatin'" in the café, but you may be more interested in **Dana's Exotic Wings & Things**, which is overseen by pet cougar Bed Johnson. Stop in to see the fascinating creatures while you wait for lunch.

Sulphur

$ **Quail Hollow Depot**, ☎ 580-622-4080, SH-7 one mile west of town, is an antique store and tea room housed in an 1890s Santa Fe depot. Typical tea-room sandwiches and desserts are served Tuesday through Saturday from 11am to 2:30 pm.

$$ The Silver Turtle, ☎ 580-622-3500, SH-7 two miles west of town, serves steak, seafood, and fried green tomatoes. Open for dinner Tuesdays through Saturdays from 5 pm until 10 pm.

Wilburton

$/$$ P & R Cattle Co. Park and Restaurant, ☎ 918-465-5585, SH-2 north of town near Robbers Cave State Park, serves *real* French fries with their steaks, hamburgers, and barbecue. With views of the park, the restaurant is open from 7 am to 8 pm, Tuesday through Saturday, and 7 am to 2 pm on Sunday.

$/$$ Silver Dollar Café, ☎ 918-465-2900, 2900 Carlton Loop, five miles north of town in Robbers Cave State Park, has wonderful views. The owners, Mary and Ert Gailey, promise large portions of excellent food – steaks are a specialty. Hours are 7 am to 8 pm, Monday through Thursday, 7 am to 9 pm, Friday and Saturday, and 7 am to 5 pm, Sunday.

■ Where to Shop

Eufaula

 Wild Woman's, ☎ 918-689-5481, 418 South Main, is not what you think. It's an herb shop, with gifts, books, and medicinal herbs. The tea room serves healthy creations and herbal teas. On the Saturday before Mother's Day, the shop hosts the **Wild Woman's Wild Herb**, **Wild Rose and Wildflower Festival**, with vendors selling all things wild. The shop is closed Tuesday, open Monday and Wednesday through Saturday from 10 am to 6 pm, and Sunday from 11 am to 2 pm.

Hugo

Fallon Road Emporium, ☎ 405-325-3947, on Fallon Road two blocks off US-70, is a restored farm house selling Oklahoma arts and treasures, including antiques and handmade quilts. Hours are Thursday through Friday from noon to 5 pm, Saturday from 10 am to 6 pm, and Sunday from 1 pm to 5 pm. Another shop next door is owned by the same family and sells similar items.

■ Powwows, Festivals, Arts & Crafts Fairs

April

 Idabel Dogwood Days, ☎ 405-286-3305, celebrate spring the first weekend in April. Brochures claim the town is the "Dogwood Capital of Oklahoma," and every year crowds of visitors come to see more than 6,000 trees in bloom. Make overnight reservations early.

May

AdaFest, ☎ 580-436-3032, is held in Ada at the end of May, featuring more than 100 arts-and-crafts booths.

June

Beavers Bend **Kiamichi Owa-Chito Festival** is held for four days in mid-June and includes an art show. The highlight here is forest sports such as chain saw carving and canoe racing, and more than 50,000 attend each year. Every accommodation in the surrounding area books up early, so plan well in advance. For more information, ☎ 800-52-TREES or 580-584-3393.

July

Ada Air Expo draws thousands of spectators each summer. The three-day extravaganza fills the skies with beautiful, colorful hot-air balloons, daring skydivers, and skilled aerobatic airplanes. Call the Chamber of Commerce for exact dates, ☎ 405-332-2506.

Striper Festival is held in Kingston, the "Striper Capital of the World," during three days in early July. You don't have to be a fisherman to celebrate the ocean bass stripers that thrive in the salty lake water at Lake Texoma, ☎ 405-564-4091.

Southeast Oklahoma

September

The **Amish Auction** takes place each year in Clarita to benefit the local school. Amish craftsmen prepare all year for the one-day event that features collector-quality handmade quilts, wooden furniture, and baked goods. Get there early for the opening breakfast that begins at 7:30, ☎ 580-428-3458.

The **Chickasaw Festival** is a week-long celebration and homecoming held at the Chickasaw Tribal Capitol in Tishomingo. Tribe members come from all over the world to dance, eat, parade, and listen to the tribal governor deliver his state-of-the-nation address. Everyone is welcome. ☎ 580 371-2040.

Krebs Ethnic Festival, ☎ 800-854-1417, is on Labor Day weekend at City Park in Krebs and features many types of ethnic food.

Choctaw Labor Day Festival, ☎ 580-924-8280, is held at the Tribal Complex in Durant over the four-day holiday weekend. It includes an arts and crafts fair and camping facilities are available. Call early if you want to camp – reservations are taken after January 1 each year, and most spots are filled by February.

October

Robbers Cave Fall Festival, ☎ 918-465-5154, in the state park near Wilburton, features hundreds of arts and crafts booths and a custom car show.

November

Beavers Bend Folk Festival and Craft Show takes place the second weekend in November, ☎ 580-494-6497. This usually coincides with peak fall foliage color.

Southeastern Oklahoma Arts and Crafts Association Show, ☎ 918-423-7429, features artists and craftspeople from several states the first weekend in November.

Southwest Oklahoma

This is the land most people think of when they imagine Oklahoma. It's "Old West" cowboy country, where cattle were driven along the **Chisholm Trail**. It's Indian territory, where Geronimo became a legend. It's the heart of America, where parts of **Route 66** still stretch back to a simpler time. And, it's ancient earth, where 650-million-year-old mountains jut out of incessant, flat plains.

If you're looking for John Steinbeck's Dust Bowl, you won't find it here. You will find, however, a dramatic landscape, acres of manmade lakes, and infinite opportunity for adventure. Hike the rim of **Red Rock Canyon**, climb the granite rocks of the **Wichita Mountains**, cruise Route 66 with the top down, or explore the historic Western outpost at **Fort Sill**.

Take your time. This section of the state demands it. In fact, time seems to stand still while visitors photograph ageless pink boulders in the **Quartz Mountains**, pause to reflect on history at Geronimo's grave, or browse through an antique store. You will enjoy Southwest Oklahoma most if you come with no expectations, just to see what's here. It's a place of glorious countryside, friendly small towns, authentic Indian traditions, and real cowboys.

■ Touring

If you ever plan to motor west
Try takin' my way,
It's the highway that's the best,
Get your kicks on Route 66.

Bobby Troup, *Get Your Kicks on Route 66*

Route 66 from Clinton to Erick

56 miles

 In 1925, when motor cars had finally taken a solid lead on the horse as America's transportation of choice, the country cried out for a paved national highway system. Oklahoman Cyrus Stevens Avery was a vital part of the planning committee that designed

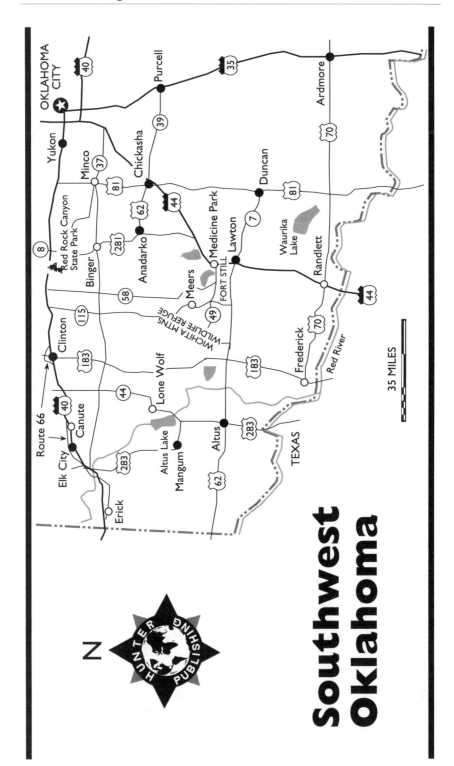

Southwest Oklahoma

a 2,440-mile road to connect Chicago, Illinois to Santa Monica, California – and amazingly enough, it went directly through his hometown of Tulsa. Naturally, the route had to continue conveniently on to the state capital before heading out to California, and that is how Oklahoma (or more specifically, Oklahoma City) became the spot where East meets West.

A decade later, the two-lane road became well-known as the highway that transported destitute farmers from drought-plagued Oklahoma to the "promised land" of California. Ironically, this increased use spurred a frenzy of entrepreneurial venture. Gas stations, motor courts, cafés, and shops sprang up, enabling many residents to survive the hard times. After World War II, Route 66 became the main drag of America's tourist industry, and more businesses opened in little towns all along the way.

About this time, The King Cole Trio recorded Bobby Troup's song, *Get Your Kicks On Route 66*, and travelers sang along as they motored from one town to the next. However, the Federal Highway Act of 1956 put an end to America's beloved *Main Street*. Route 66 was straightened, widened, and routed around towns so motorist could speed to their destinations. By the early 1960s, families were gathering around their TV sets to watch the popular series, *Route 66*, recalling a slower, simpler time. The final blow came in 1985 when crews removed the last Highway 66 road signs.

"The Road of Flight"

"Route 66 was the path of a people in flight, refugees from dust and shrinking land, from the thunder of tractors and shrinking ownership, from the desert's slow northward invasion, from the twisting winds that howl up out of Texas, from the floods that bring no richness to the land and steal what little richness is there. From all of these the people are in flight, and they come into 66 from the tributary side roads, from the wagon track and the rutted country roads. 66 is the mother road, the road of flight." John Steinbeck, *The Grapes of Wrath*

The Oklahoma legislature has since designated old Route 66 as an historic highway, and marked surviving patches with brown replicas of the famous roadside shield. "Shun-pikers" eagerly seek out the original road. It's a game with some – a passion with others. Most just want a break from the sterile, frantic turnpike.

The Mother Road

- "The continent is tilting and Route 66 is a giant chute down which everything loose in the rest of the nation is sliding into Southern California." Frank Lloyd Wright
- Route 66 was the first major automobile highway to cross the United States.
- Route rhymes with "boot," not "out."
- In the 1950s, Route 66 symbolized the American dream. US cars were the biggest and best in the world, and driving became a national pastime.
- In the 1960s, Route 66 was the title of a popular CBS television series that starred George Maharis and Martin Milner. They cruised the Mother Road looking for adventure in a shiny new Chevrolet Corvette.
- Route 66 began at the corner of Jackson Boulevard and Michigan Avenue in downtown Chicago and stretched 2,400 miles west to the corner of Santa Monica Boulevard and Ocean Avenue in Santa Monica, California.
- Route 66 ceased to be an official United States highway in 1985.

Clinton is home to the **Route 66 Museum**, a six-room/six-decade exhibit proclaiming the glory of "The Main Street of America." An audio presentation allows visitors to listen on headphones to Michael Wallis (author of *Route 66: The Mother Road*) describing the route's famous history as they tour the museum. The neon-and-glass building is at 2229 West Gary Boulevard west of US-183 and north of I-40 off Business-40. Hours during the summer are from 10 am to 7 pm, Monday through Saturday, and 1pm to 6 pm on Sunday. The museum is open fewer hours from Labor Day until Memorial Day, so call ☎ 580-323-7866 or 800-759-2397 if you plan to visit during that time. The $3 admission fee includes a headphone tour.

A yellow, vintage Corvette sits in the glass entrance of the museum and sets the mood for things to come. Inside, family station wagons and hippie-era Volkswagen vans depict the character of the traveling public using Route 66 from the 1920s through the 1970s. Nineties-style computers and videos make the museum hands-on visitor-friendly and prevent relics of the gaudy past from becoming tedious.

Across the street at 2128 Gary, you can see where Elvis slept at **Doc Mason's Best Western Trade Winds Courtyard Inn**, ☎ 580-323-2610. If you're hungry, stop next door to enjoy a charbroiled steak at the **Route 66 Restaurant**. Then head west along the route past abandoned gas stations and boarded-up stores to **Foss State Park**, ☎ 580-592-4433.

The town of Foss is almost a ghost town, but the park is a pleasant rest stop. Hiking, biking, and equestrian trails are being constructed, but as of publication date, only blaze-your-own-trail activities are available. Call ahead to check on the status of development. Most visitors come here to enjoy the lake, but even park employees will admit that a strong wind often blows across the prairie, which makes boating difficult. Do notice the unusual three-mile earthen dam that crosses the lake. If you arrive late in the day, watch for a spectacular sunset.

Canute is worth a slow-down, not a full stop. What remains of Mahl Brothers Garage is here if you care to search. The Catholic cemetery is worth a visit because of its bronze statues.

In **Elk City**, stop at the Old Town Museum – a fine turn-of-the-century home containing Indian artifacts and rodeo souvenirs. There is also a one-room school and a chapel. Notice the Parker Drilling Rig #114 as you drive by – it's one of the tallest in the world. **Martin's Antiques** at 2424 West Third is a good place to browse if you're interested in furniture or dishes.

Back on "The Mother Road," stop in **Sayre** for a treat from the antique soda fountain at Owl's Drug, then coast by the Beckham County Courthouse on Main Street, which appeared in the 1940 movie version of Steinbeck's *Grapes of Wrath*. Kids and railroad buffs will enjoy the **RS&K Railroad Museum**, ☎ 580-928-5757, at 411 North Sixth Street. There are 250 model trains on 11 track layouts in this small museum – usually all running at once. Call for the exact hours, but visitors are usually welcome from 9 am until 9 pm on Saturday and Sunday.

A stretch of the early four-lane Route 66 is still driveable from Sayre all the way to Texola on the Texas/Oklahoma border. This patch of history passes through Roger Miller's hometown of **Erick**. On a street named for the award-winning country singer, you'll find the bizarre little **100th Meridian Museum**, ☎ 580-526-3221, located in an old bank building.

The museum's hours are as strange as its exhibits, so call first to see if a docent will be on hand to open the door for you. Once inside, examine the holdings closely since there are some fascinating things to discover. Ask about the surveying error that makes the museum's name significant. A state-operated welcome center is located here, just nine miles inside the state line.

Anadarko Potpourri

50+ miles

This trip actually begins in **Chickasha**, a little prairie town near **Anadarko**. Anadarko is the "must-see" center of this trip because of its Native American history. However, since you're in the neighborhood, you may as well see **Muscle Car Ranch** in Chickasha, just east on US-62. Muscle Car Ranch is a real pasture with grazing cattle – nothing unusual, until you notice a 1969 Camaro half-buried near the stock pond. Every surface of the ranch's buildings and a good part of the landscape is covered by restored signs from old gas stations, diners, and motels. The ranch is famous for its annual September swap meets that feature 1950-1970 muscle cars.

Chickasha Auto Club members staff the small but impressive **Chickasha Antique Auto Museum of Transportation** at the intersection of 18th Street and Chickasha. The irony of Chickasha being a "car town" is that in 1904, when the population numbered 6,370 and considered itself "a city of the first class," an injunction was issued in federal court against driving cars on the main streets because they were dangerous and frightened horses.

When you've seen about all the old cars you care to see, drive to Anadarko to explore **Indian City USA**, ☎ 580-247-5661 or 800-433-5661. There are seven authentic life-size Native American villages here, representing the Apache, Kiowa, Navajo, Caddo, Pueblo, Pawnee and Wichita tribes. This indoor/outdoor exhibit is located 2½ miles southeast of town on SH-8 at the site of a Tonkawa massacre by the Shawnees during the Civil War. Native American guides conduct tours of Indian City from 9:30 am to 5 pm every day. Call ahead to see when the dancers will be performing. During the summer, most tours begin with a dance performance. At other times of the year, dancers usually appear on Sunday.

An Indian affairs agency was established in this area during the 1870s, and continues today as the **Bureau of Indian Affairs Area Office**. It's located on the west side of US-281, north of the city. The **Riverside Indian School**, ☎ 580-247-6673, the oldest US Indian Service boarding school in the country, is also here. It was started in 1871 by a Quaker Indian agent and had only eight non-English speaking students.

Anadarko became one of Oklahoma's instant cities in 1901, when white settlers were allowed to bid on lots of land located on Indian reservations, which were established by the 1867 Treaty of Medicine Lodge. About 20,000 white hopefuls hung around drinking and gambling for three weeks before the August 6, 1901 land auction. Half that number stayed for several months afterwards. Finally, the loiterers moved on and left the newly-founded town to 3,000 permanent settlers. By the end of the year, residents had built saloons, barber shops, meat markets, and law offices. Over a hundred of those buildings are now on the National Register for Historic Places.

While you're in town, stop at the **Southern Plains Indian Museum**, ☎ 580-247-622, to see outstanding examples of arts and crafts. The display of traditional Plains Indians costumes on life-size figures is especially intriguing. Throughout the year, the museum also hosts demonstrations of Native American craft techniques and honors well-known Indian writers and actors. It's on US-62, east of 7th Street, and admission is free.

Directly east of the Southern Plains Indian Museum on US-62, the **National Hall of Fame for Famous American Indians**, ☎ 580-247-5555, exhibits busts of Sequoyah, Captain Black Beaver, and other well-known Native Americans. Hours are 9 am to 5 pm, Monday through Saturday, and from 1 pm to 5 pm on Sunday. Admission is free.

Each August, Anadarko is the site of the largest tribal gathering in the state. The week-long **American Indian Exposition** is held on the Caddo County Fairgrounds and is open to the public. Special highlights include Native American dances, parades, horse races, and an arts fair. There's a printed schedule of events, but it is only an approximation of times since the Indian is not a slave to clocks. Powwows and pageants take place all in good time; the pace of the festival is relaxed and unhurried. Phone the Chamber of Commerce for exact dates, ☎ 580-247-6651.

If you can stay for a few days, check with **Tsain Saw Hay Valley**, ☎ 580-247-3000, about living in a tepee, eating traditional Indian foods, and participating in tribal activities. This cultural adventure is available from April until November.

North of Anadarko, on scenic SH-8, the spectacular landscape of **Red Rock Canyon** spreads across Caddo County. These 200-million-year-old canyon walls were carved when an ancient sea rolled out of the Permian Red Beds leaving deep, long chasms in the sandstone. The Cheyenne, Comanche, and Kickapoo tribes once wintered in these canyons and, later, horse thieves and other outlaws hid out behind the protective rock walls.

In the spring and fall, the stretch of SH-8 between Binger (16 miles north of Anadarko) and Red Rock Canyon is particularly beautiful. The canyon itself has sugar maple trees, which turn brilliant colors each autumn. Camping is permitted in the park, and there are picnic tables, a swimming pool, and hiking trails – the rock walls are particularly popular with rappelers.

When you leave the park, trace your route back along SH-8 to Binger, then turn east on SH-37 and drive to Minco, where US-81 takes a scenic route north through the **Canadian River Valley**. When you reach El Reno, you're just a short drive east on Route 66 to Garth Brooks' hometown of Yukon. There's not much there, but if you're a fan, you must see it. The town was once a large Czech community, and a few celebrations still take place throughout the year, but now you're more likely to find country rather than European food, music, and ambiance.

Lawton, Fort Sill & the Wichita Mountain Range

Approximately 50 miles

Lawton is the fourth largest city in the state and located at the base of the lovely, old **Wichita Mountains**. The town was settled in 1901 by winners of a land lottery. After several land runs on Indian Territory in the state proved to be dangerous – not to mention unfair – Congress decided to allot parcels of land near the mountains to tribal members first, then hold a lottery among white settlers for the 15,000 tracts that remained.

One of the lottery winners was Miss Mattie Beal, who married the owner of a lumber company and built a grand 14-room Greek Revival mansion with gorgeous stained glass windows. Her home has been restored and is listed on the National Register of Historic Places. Visitors may tour

The Mattie Beal Mansion, ☎ 580-353-6884, 1006 Southwest 5th Street. It is open on the second Sunday of each month and a tour costs $2.

The **Red River Trading Post**, on the grounds of the **Museum of the Great Plains**, ☎ 580-581-3461, at 601 Ferris Avenue, holds a Spring and Fall Encampment the first weekends in May and November. Actors in period costumes re-enact everyday activities at the post, and this is the best time to visit. Call for exact dates and times. Throughout the year, the museum and trading post buildings are open to the public from 8 am to 5 pm, Monday through Saturday, and 10 am to 5 pm on Sunday.

Fort Sill, a working military base, is one of the most interesting spots in the Lawton area. Follow the signs on I-44 to the main gate, then take a right to Randolph Road, which leads to the stone visitors center. The exhibits here will bring you up to speed on the history of the fort, which was founded by General Phillip Sheridan during a campaign against the Southern Plains Indians in the winter of 1869. In the beginning, the fort was base camp for operations during the Indian Wars. Then, during World War I, it became an artillery training facility. Still later, it was headquarters for the country's first aero squadron.

While you're at Fort Sill, be sure to visit the Old Post Guardhouse where **Geronimo** was held prisoner. You may be surprised to learn that this famous Apache was not exactly the wild man depicted in most historical stories. He actually was held prisoner at the Guardhouse only on the few occasions when he had too much to drink. Most of the time, he traveled with Pawnee Bill's Wild West Show.

Another interesting display tells the story of **Quanah Parker**, the last Comanche leader to surrender. He was the son of Comanche chief, Peta Nacone, and Cynthia Ann Parker, a white woman who was taken as a child by the Indian tribe after a massacre in Texas. He later became a respected judge on an Indian court and built a big house near Cache, Oklahoma, where he lived with several wives.

Several other historic buildings around the old parade ground are interesting to visit, but save time for **Chief's Knoll** and the Post Cemetery. Geronimo is buried in the Apache cemetery, and Quanah Parker and other well-known Native Americans are buried at Chief's Knoll.

Tales of Geronimo

Geronimo, an Apache chief, was arrested in 1886 for leading his tribe in bloodthirsty warfare. He was held prisoner in Florida and Alabama for eight years.

In 1894, he was transferred to Fort Sill, where he was under military control but allowed to roam about the property.

A notorious alcoholic, Geronimo was often thrown into the guardhouse to sober up.

The public was enthralled by the outlandish Apache and he was in great demand at fairs and exhibitions. Geronimo was granted liberal leave to travel about the country and make public appearances. He entertained at the World Fairs in Omaha in 1898, Buffalo in 1901, and St. Louis in 1904 where he sold his autographed pictures for two dollars each.

President Roosevelt asked Geronimo to be in his inaugural parade, and Pawnee Bill's Wild West Circus featured him in traveling shows.

The Apache chief died of pneumonia in 1909 and is buried in the cemetery at Fort Sill.

When you leave the cemetery, drive north on Fort Sill Boulevard to King Road. Turn west and go to the end of the road and across a bridge. The first left after the bridge leads to **Medicine Bluff**, a sacred Indian spot on Medicine Creek. These sheer granite cliffs overlooking old Apache village sites are considered to have special powers, and Apache descendants come here during the Heritage Fair every Memorial Day weekend to dance the sacred Fire Dance. A small animal park is just north of the creek, and there are picnic tables and fishing docks nearby. Information about Fort Sill and its attractions and events is available by calling ☎ 580-442-5123.

North of the base, off I-44, take SH-49 west to **Medicine Park**, which was a summer resort and health spa in the Wichita Mountains during the 1920s and 1930s. Equally popular among both gangsters and politicians, the town is a unique creation of native granite cobblestones. The Old Plantation Restaurant is on the first floor of what was once a three-story luxury hotel. You can still get a snack or a drink here, but save your appetite for the gigantic Longhorn-beef burger served at **Meers Store** in the goldrush town of **Meers**.

SH-58 is the most scenic route north from Medicine Park, but take a westward jig on SH-49 and a northward jag on SH-115 to get to Meers. Meers Store was once a general store that served prospectors who came to the mountains looking for gold. In the best of times, the town had a population of about 500 people and a dozen businesses. Today, the town is nothing but a building from 1901 that is included on the National Register of Historic Places. This single wooden structure once held a general store, a doctor's office, and a newspaper office. At present, it is home to four people, a federal seismograph station, and a hamburger so big it has to be eaten with a fork. Call ☎ 580-429-8051 for hours and directions – and come hungry.

Wichita Mountains Wildlife Refuge

After you've eaten all you can – or care to – drive back south toward SH-49 and the north entrance to the Wichita Mountains Wildlife Refuge. This is the highlight of southwestern Oklahoma. Not a national park, nor a profit-based animal park, this is a true wilderness – a refuge for all kinds of life in its native and wild state.

At the turn of the century, President William McKinley declared the Wichita Mountains a Forest Reserve. In 1905, Theodore Roosevelt designated the area as a Game Preserve, making this the oldest managed wildlife preserve in the country. Unfortunately, by 1905 there was very little wildlife to preserve. Bison and elk were already extinct because of over-hunting, and other animals had dwindled in number.

Today, thanks to restocking and careful management, the craggy mountain range and vast grass prairie has herds of bison and elk as well as deer, coyotes, Longhorn cattle, raccoons, gray fox, eagles and bobcats. They live a protected existence, which visitors are welcome to witness, but only under the right circumstances. Permits are required in some areas, so call the Refuge Headquarters at ☎ 580-429-3222 for information. You can reserve a camping spot in the restricted areas a month in advance by writing to The Department of the Interior, US Fish and Wildlife Service, R.R. No. 1, Box 448, Indiahoma, OK 73552. Once you arrive in the area, stop at the Refuge Office, located six miles west of the Visitor Center on the south side of the road.

As long as you stay out of restricted land or have the right permits in hand, the refuge is very accessible and visitor friendly. The best orientation comes from driving the scenic route – slowly, and early in the day or just before dusk – to the top of **Mount Scott**. Coming in on SH-115 from Meers to the north or Cache to the south, turn east onto SH-49, stop at Quetone Overlook on the left, then turn north on the curving road up the mountain. At the top, you'll have a panoramic view of lakes, grasslands, weathered boulders, and stony mountains.

If you look for a lush forest, you'll be disappointed. But if you gaze out into the spacious wilderness with an open mind and realistic expectations, you'll be richly rewarded. These granite and quartz mountains were named for the Wichita Indians, relatives of the Pawnees, who farmed the land, built round houses out of grass (they looked much like a haystack), performed the horn dance for agricultural blessings, and believed the spirits of their ancestors inhabited the rugged mountain boulders. Find a quiet place and listen. Some say you can hear the ancient Wichitas still performing their sacred ghost dance.

Holy City, located on the west side of SH-115 near Mount Scott, was built in the 1930s to resemble the city of Jerusalem. An annual passion play is held here in a natural amphitheater the night before Easter Sunday, and visitors can tour the 110-acre area with its 22 native granite buildings all year. The most interesting structure is the World Chapel,

Chapel at Holy City of the Wichitas. (USFWS)

The summit of Mount Scott offers a panoramic view of the wildlife refuge.
(E. Smith)

which has elaborate ceramic brickwork and lovely murals. If you would like a guided tour, ☎ 580-429-3361 or 580-248-4043.

Another great drive is east to west on SH-49. Start early in the day and stop often to explore. Begin at the **Quanah Parker Visitor Center** near the south intersection of SH-115 to pick up maps and information. As you cruise along, watch closely for giant bull buffalo, or maybe a mother deer and her wobbly fawn, or possibly an armadillo waddling clumsily along under the weight of its thick armor-plate. If you want to stay awhile but don't have a reservation in the restricted area, camping is permitted on a first-come basis at **Doris Campgrounds** on the northwest shore of Quanah Parker Lake. The campsites are in wooded areas on sloping ground. Restrooms and drinking water are available.

Rocks, boulders, and granite mountains are scattered throughout the mixed-grass prairie lands in **Charons Garden Wilderness**, a 5,000-acre area at the far west end of the refuge. Oak and Juniper trees grow along the streams, and scaly blue-green lichen clings to the rocks. This is a unique land of contrasts, where endangered birds and animals live a sheltered life. Don't miss **Elk Mountain**, where you can explore the bat caves, or **Twin Rock Mountain**, with its lovely natural bridge. Backpack camping is allowed by permit – only 10 permits are given each day – but day-hiking is unrestricted. From April through October, a different guided tour is offered each month. In April, visitors tour the water-falls; in May, it's wildflowers; June is wildlife month; and in July the tour covers aquatic ecosystems. August is blazing hot, and even the rangers don't like long treks into the refuge, so no activities are scheduled. In September, the tours resume with guided walks to observe bugling elk.

Wichita Mountains to Quartz Mountain

45 miles

From the Wichita Mountains Wildlife Refuge, drop down SH-54 to US-62 and go west to the town of **Altus**. If you have an interest in airplanes, stop at the air force base to see some of the military's largest craft. The C-5 Galaxy, C-141 Starlifter, C-17 Globemaster III, and KC-135 Stratotanker are based here, and visitors are welcome. To get in on a group tour, call ☎ 580-481-7229.

From Altus, travel north on US-283 and prepare for a stunning view. When the road meets SH-44 about 17 miles from town, veer left onto SH-44A to the south shore of **Altus Lake**. This is old Kiowa land, and the nearby town of Lone Wolf (about 10 miles north) is named in honor of the beloved Kiowa chief who died here in 1879 from malaria. The focal point for this area is 1,800-foot **Quartz Mountain**, which pokes up out of the level plains in a splendid wash of burnt rose, cinnabar, copper, and gold. Deep blue Altus Lake and dusty green desert-like vegetation provide an almost surreal contrast. Some compare this landscape to the Mojave Desert, but it looks different in each season and at various times of day.

Because of its unusual beauty and tranquility, artists and photographers come here to work and relax. In the spring, wildflowers cover the ground. During summer and fall, the Oklahoma Arts institute holds programs. Winter brings a plethora of lights and a Christmas Arts and Crafts Bazaar. In addition, bald eagles winter in the park, and the dam off SH-44 is one of the best places to spot them.

Continue the drive up SH-44 along the east shore of the lake to **Lone Wolf**. This stretch of road is designated by the state as a scenic route. Unless you have plans farther north, turn around and drive back through Quartz Mountain State Park. The view will be entirely different from this direction, with the sun at a new angle in the limitless sky.

■ Adventures

On Foot

Hiking

 The truth is, designated hiking spots in southwestern Oklahoma are not so great, with two (possibly three) exceptions. **The Wichita Mountains Wildlife Refuge** is spectacular. **Quartz Mountain** is dramatic. **The Walker Creek Trail** around **Lake Waurika** is long, and parts of it are lovely.

Any adventure you have while hiking in this area involves the weather. Midday treks in the summer can be unhealthy, unpleasant, and seemingly unending. If the infamous wind is blowing anytime of the year, you'll wish you had stayed at home – and think you'll never get the taste of dirt out of your mouth. But take the same hike on a bright, calm day in spring, and you'll be awed by the wildflowers, soothed by the solitude of wide-open spaces, and invigorated by the challenges of the trail. Come back in the fall, and you'll see a whole paint-palette of different colors, smell a hint of winter luring the birds southward, and wonder why you waited so long to try these trails.

❏ Wichita Mountains Wildlife Refuge

The best mix of trails is found in the Wichita Mountains Wildlife Refuge. They require a permit for backpackers in the **Charons Garden Wilderness Area**, but if you're lucky enough to get a permit, you'll be one of only 10 hiker/campers in the 5,000-acre protected space at the west end of the refuge. This is to your advantage if you like solitude bordering on isolation.

Charons is rugged and wild, so the words "garden" and "fragile" seem improper. However, vegetation, geological formations, and wildlife are fragile here, so human access must be controlled to prevent damage. The US Fish and Wildlife Service remembers well the fate of the buffalo the last time man was let loose on the open range. Now that the 15 prolific bison imported from the New York Zoo have increased the refuge's beastly population from zero to 525, the rangers are determined to keep man on a short leash.

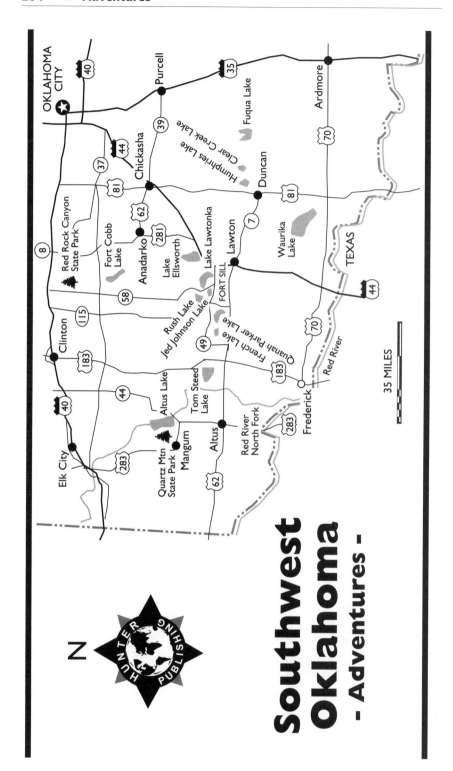

Southwest Oklahoma
- Adventures -

Obtain a permit by writing well in advance to the **US Department of the Interior**, Fish and Wildlife Service, Wichita Mountains Wildlife Refuge, Route 1, Box 448, Indiahoma, OK 73552, or call the **Refuge Headquarters** at ☎ 580-429-3222. They will also send you a map and brochure of the area that indicates the trail from Treasure Lake to Elk Mountain.

Buffalos Were An Easy Kill

Enormous herds of buffalo were slaughtered on the Great Plains between 1870 and 1883 when hunters supplied a seemingly limitless US market using new, cheap railroads.

The nature of buffalo made them easy targets. When one buffalo was killed, the rest of the herd would gather around the fallen beast pawing and bellowing their fury. Hunters took advantage of this instinct to wipe out an entire herd of 100 to 500 animals in one afternoon.

After the hunters finished their job (buffalo hunting was business, not sport), skinners would come in to flay the creatures at the rate of 50 per day per man. Once the skins had been removed, the carcasses were left in the sun to rot.

A buffalo hide, weighing as much as 100 pounds before it dried, sold for only a dollar or two at first. Then, as more and more uses were found for the leather, prices rose to the three- and four-dollar range. This was enough to bring thousands of men out to the plains to join the slaughter, and the days of large herds of free-roaming buffalo were soon over.

It is also possible to visit the "Special Use Area," in the north part of the refuge, to see the big game animals and eagles that live there. But, you must go on a planned tour with a member of the Refuge staff. Again, call Headquarters at ☎ 580-429-3222 for schedules and information.

Other trails in the "Public Use Area" are much more accessible. Stop by the **Quanah Parker Visitors Center** – on SH-49 near the intersection of SH-115 coming north from the town of Cache – for maps and orientation information. The center is open Wednesday through Monday from 10 am to 5:30 pm. Visitors are allowed into the Wildlife Refuge daily from dawn until dark.

Park south of the Refuge Headquarters, six miles west of the visitors center, in the lot near French Lake. **Dog Run Hollow Trail** runs 12

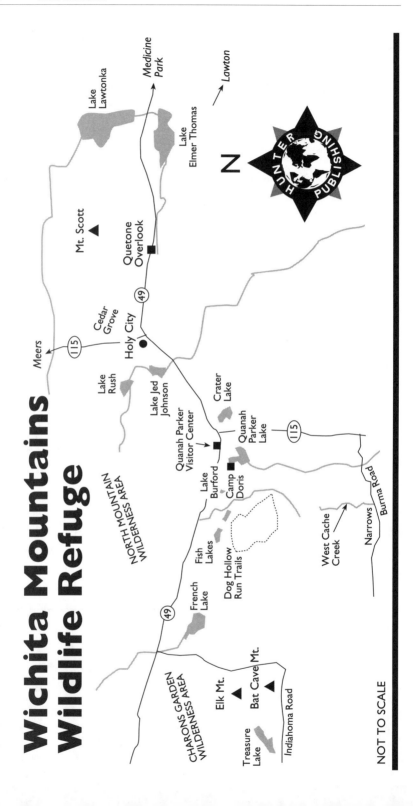

Wichita Mountains Wildlife Refuge

NOT TO SCALE

Cavers find hidden "rooms" at the top of Elk Mountain, named for the creatures that wander over its hillsides. (E. Smith)

miles through the area between French Lake and Lost Lake. The trail makes three complete loops and one semicircle, so hikers can design their own round-trip route. The longest loop is Buffalo Trail at eight miles, with links to **Longhorn Trail** (two miles), **Elk Trail** (.75 miles), and **Kite Trail** (a 1.25-mile half loop).

❏ Quartz Mountain State Park

Quartz Mountain State Park, ☎ 580-563-2424, has two short, but rewarding, hiking paths. The **New Horizon Trail** is a rousing half-mile trudge most of the way up the granite face of Quartz Mountain. Along the way, you can poke around the habitats of various plants and animals, and the views are incredible. You'll see some of the most remarkable scenery in all of Oklahoma. The trail starts on the west side of Altus Lake near the park office (about half a mile from the park entrance off SH-44A).

A nature trail parallels the road between the park office and grocery store – a distance of about a quarter-mile. Many animals come to drink from the stream near the path crossing, and searching for their tracks is entertaining. In addition, the region on the northeast shore of the lake (near Camp Areas 2 and 3) merits a walk – if only along the road. The

*Longhorn Trail is named for the longhorn cattle
that roam freely in the Wichita Range. (E. Smith)*

contrast between pink granite rocks, blue water, and green plains is most conspicuous here.

If you want a more formidable experience, and you're in good physical shape, contact **Quartz Mountain Adventure Tours & Guide Service**, ☎ 800-687-6243, www.intellisys.net/users/advtours/. The staff members know this territory well and lead demanding three-hour backpacking trips and photographic tours several times each weekday. Groups and individuals can arrange tours for weekends. Costs of the guided tours range from $20 for a three-hour backpacking trip to $900 for multi-day, multi-activity packages. As an example, the five-day biking tour rides through the Great Plains, with stops at historic sites, fishing on four lakes, and backpacking in the Wichita Mountains. Package costs include commercial lodging and three meals a day.

☐ Waurika Lake

Walker Creek Trail winds for 13 miles along Waurika Lake about midway between Wichita Falls, Texas and Duncan, Oklahoma. Because of its location, this is a popular trail for hikers from both states. The trail head is 5½ miles north of the dam near a primitive campsite with a parking lot.

Orange posts and wooden mile-markers indicate the route.

This is a multi-use course, so you may encounter horses or bikers but, since the path is so long, you probably won't see many of either. The route takes you along the creek, through wooded areas, over some small hills, and along a level stretch of tall-grass prairie. Wildlife and wildflowers thrive in this area. Watch for tracks and listen for rustling in the underbrush, especially along the trail's two creek crossings.

During hunting seasons, either stay off the trail, or take precautions such as wearing bright clothing. Check with the lake's project office, ☎ 580-963-2111, for the dates and locations most popular with hunters.

Apple & Pear rock formations in the Wichita Mountains. (USFWS)

Rock Climbing, Rappeling & Cave Exploring

Rockers have more challenges in southwestern Oklahoma than in any other part of the state. While this is plains country, it is also mountain country, and the combination creates far-reaching vistas of grassy plains from rocky mountaintops. Just to add interest, accessible caves are found in the mountain areas. Artists and photographers are fond of the beauty in these ancient sculptured boulders, and even seasoned outdoor types are struck by the wonder of the landscape.

Rock climbers and walkers enjoy tough challenges in the Wichita Mountains (USFWS)

☐ Wichita Mountain Wildlife Refuge

The Wichita Mountains run east-west for about 60 miles and offer several climbing and caving opportunities. A permit is required to enter the **Charons Garden Wilderness**. Only 10 are issued per day; you can pick one up at the **Refuge Headquarters**, ☎ 580-429-3222, or **Quanah Parker Visitors Center**. The permits usually are not hard to get, but if you want to be certain you're one of the 10, call well in advance.

Charons Garden Mountain, at the west end of the Wichita Mountains Wildlife Refuge, is an 80-foot rise of granite crag and hard cracks. Fall is the best season to visit, but spring runs a close second. Sections of this partially developed area are perfect for expert climbers who like steep rock. Other sections are less demanding and offer good, but limited, climbs for those with less experience. Park in the lot adjacent to Sunset Picnic Area, a mile west of headquarters on SH-49. Hike west about two miles to the climbing area called Lost Dome.

The Elk Mountain Slab, is the site of the state's first technical rock leads. For more than 50 years, rockers have come here to tackle "Desperate Reality," a classic climb with an expert grade. Other climbs on the west face of this crag-and-slab granite mountain are rated beginner/intermediate, and you may prefer "Great Expectations" or "Buns Up." From headquarters, drive south, then west on Indiahoma Road to Post Oak Lake Road. Turn north and go less than a mile to the parking area. The climbing area is a two-mile intense hike from there.

The most precipitous climb in the wildlife refuge is **The Narrows**. Even if you're not a climber, it's worth the hike just to see these lovely walls.

"Aerial Anticipations," "League of Doom," and "Kirplunk" are fitting names for climbs up this craggy, 300-foot-high granite expanse. This is a developed spot with mixed grades for various proficiency levels, but several climbs require expert skill. Park at the gate a mile down Lost Lake Road south of SH-49 – about three miles west of the SH-115 junction. Hike south down the road for two miles. At the huts, turn east and hike to a creek, which runs through a canyon. Follow the creek another 1½ miles to the climbing area.

Spelunkers have some great choices in the refuge, but this is a wild area and you can easily get lost or confused following one expert's map while using another's directions. To avoid confusion, stop at the Visitors Center or Refuge Headquarters with your map and ask an expert to direct you. The following information will help you know what to ask for.

Bat Cave is a jumble of boulders at the top of Elk Mountain concealing a series of natural rock rooms. Thus, the cave is sometimes called "The Rooms." Whatever you call it, you can get there by parking at Sunset Picnic Area near Headquarters and hiking up the trail to the summit of Elk Mountain – about a mile. Then look northwest for a smooth, rounded boulder. Hike toward this boulder until you see a rock arch about 40 to 50 feet across and five feet above the ground. Follow a canyon west along the north wall and watch for a place to cross to the south side. On the south wall you will find a small opening to the cave.

Now the fun begins. Squeeze and crawl down into the cave through huge boulders. It gets very dark and steep before you reach a pool of water. You can turn around here, but if you wade through the water to the other side, you will have a terrific view as you come out of the cave at its west opening. The climb down this side is tricky, but experienced cavers and climbers can manage without special equipment.

Wind Cave isn't as scary, and the trail leading to it is easy, but you must climb a pole to get into the cave. Find the trailhead on the southeast side of Bat Cave Mountain off Indiahoma Road south of Headquarters. You can see the cave entrance from the road, so park your car and follow the trail that leads in that direction. The cave is about 30 feet deep and half as wide, with plenty of headroom.

The Wichitas are full of old mining tunnels, open-ended caverns, and natural concaves that once sheltered Native America families but now house a variety of wildlife. If this is your particular interest, call the Wildlife Refuge or stop at the Visitors Center for information on how to locate these caves.

❏ Quartz Mountain

West of the wildlife refuge, Quartz Mountain is a favorite of climbers at all skill levels. Respectfully known as **Baldy Peak**, the 160-foot ascent starts with bouldering at the base and progresses to crag. Visitors travel north from Altus for 17 miles on US-283 to SH-44 to reach the Quartz Mountain State Park turnoff. Turn left for two miles, then right on the first paved road past the bridge. After about a mile, watch for a dirt road that crosses a wide gully. Turn east, then take the first right. Parking is the next left. "Bourbon Street" and "Wild Child" are two of the highly rated climbs here.

The following two sites are well-known among climbers, but at press time, both were off limits. Ask around if you're interested in trying either area. Climbing spots open and close rather erratically depending on various conditions, so it is always smart to check before planning a major climb.

The **YCC Quarry**, a mile east of Quartz Mountain, has broken granite wall. If you want to scout for climbing possibilities, go south on the dirt road off SH-44 at the YCC sign. The Quarry gate may or may not be locked.

A better possibility is at the **Rock of Ages Quarry** west of US-183 near Mountain Park. The quarry is on the southeast side of the mountain. You'll need a parking permit from the office, and you may or may not be allowed to climb. The granite is slippery and steep and requires expert skills.

Golfing

❏ Altus

 Quartz Mountain Resort Park Golf Course, ☎ 580-563-2520, is one of the state-run Oklahoma Nine (see page 14). It's 17 miles north of Altus on SH-44A at the southern end of Altus-

Luger Lake. There is an abundance of wildlife on this course, which is laid out on a fairly flat, but often windy, area at the base of colorful Quartz Mountain in a sea of prairie grass and wildflowers. The 18-hole course features bent grass with some water play. Par is 71, and holes number four (nicknamed "Headwinds') and 10 (lovingly called "Forever") are considered the most challenging.

Green fees are $12 for 18 holes and $7 for nine holes on weekends; $9.50 for 18 holes and $7 for nine holes on weekdays. Gas carts are available at a cost of $16 for 18 holes and $9 for nine holes. Pull carts are $2. Golfers may rent clubs, but there are no caddies.

☐ Fort Cobb

Fort Cobb Golf Course, ☎ 580-643-2398, in Fort Cobb State Park, is north of Anadarko and east of Quartz Mountain. The pro shop opens at 8 am and takes tee-time reservations up to a week in advance.

This is a long course with many challenges, especially on the back nine, where tall prairie grass grows thickly along the fairways. Just to make things more demanding, sand bunkers are built around many greens, and the bay below the course is one big water hazard. This is a par-70 course; you should plan on shooting well under on the front nine to compensate for the extra strokes you'll probably take on the back nine.

Green fees are $12 for 18 holes and $7 for nine holes on weekends; $9.50 for 18 holes and $7 for nine holes on weekdays. Gas carts are available at a cost of $16 (18 holes) or $9 (nine holes), and pull carts rent for $2. Rental clubs are available. Caddies are not.

Reach the park by driving west from Anadarko on SH-9 to SH-146. Turn north and go about four miles, then turn west onto a paved local road and drive one mile to a T, where you turn right. Drive past the dam and take a left onto the golf course road.

☐ Other 18-Hole Public Courses in Southwest Oklahoma

Anadarko
Dietrich Golf and Country Club, ☎ 580-247-5075.

Clinton
Riverside Golf Course, ☎ 580-323-5958.

Elk City

Elk City Golf and Country Club, ☎ 580-225-5454.

Weatherford

Weatherford Golf Course, ☎ 580-772-3832.

On Wheels

Biking

 A rather innovative way to see **Route 66** is by bike, and you'll find the longest continuous stretches of the historic road sloping east-west through Oklahoma. The southwestern part of the state has particularly interesting stops along the original route, and biking rather than driving adds a hands-on, good-old-days slant to the trip. I-40 now reigns over stopped-in-time US-66, but many small towns along its course have snubbed modernization, and these nostalgic spots make for a fun ride-and-seek excursion through another era.

If you're game for an ad-lib quest, begin by picking any small town along the old route –perhaps Clinton, home of the Route 66 Museum, or Elk City, where Third Street and a service road at the airport are part of the original old road. The old road is indicated on the official state map, which is available at any Welcome Center or by calling ☎ 800-652-6552. Brown-and-white Historical US-66 road signs mark the route itself. After you've chosen a starting point, pedal west toward the state line at Texola. Your goal is to follow one Historical sign to the next until you're lost, exhausted, or in Texas.

Along the way, detour down country roads and shady lanes in search of whatever is left of yesteryear. Maps are not allowed once you get started if you're playing this game, but you can ask directions at any of the charming shops or cafés. One hint: the service road along I-40 is often the old mother road – and even if it isn't, it provides a good long-distance biking route. Total distance between Clinton and Texola is a little over 60 miles. Spend the night at one of the little mom-'n-pop motels along the way.

☐ Wichita Mountains & Fort Sill

For a more structured tour, start at **Meers**. Chow down on the famous Meersburger at Meers Store, then take the road behind the store, SH-

115, south over the Medicine Creek bridge to the **Wichita Mountain Wildlife Refuge**. SH-49 intersects SH-115 in the refuge and you can take it east to **Mount Scott** or west to **Charons Garden Wilderness Area**.

If you want to go into Charons Garden, write or call for a permit well ahead of your visit. Only 15 bike passes are issued each day through the **US Wildlife Service**, R.R. No. 1, Box 448, Indiahoma 73552, ☎ 580-429-3222. The road up Mount Scott from SH-49 is steep, narrow, and often full of sightseeing motorists. If you must face the challenge, go on a weekday, off-season, and be prepared to call it quits if traffic gets backed up behind you. The road is open daily from 9 am until an hour after sunset.

Get back to your starting point by reversing your route. This ride can be as long as a hundred miles, if you cover the entire area. However, you can just as well take an easy spin through one section of the Wildlife Refuge and call it a day. Either way, consider another burger when you get back to Meers.

Mountain bikers can find unimproved roads throughout the refuge, and the best way to locate them is with a map from the Wildlife Service. A nice 26-mile route starts at Indiahoma on US-62, goes north about 4½ miles on Indiahoma Road toward the refuge and turns west on an unimproved road. You'll be pedaling past Charons Garden, and after you've gone 6½ miles, begin looking for another dirt road and take it north. At the 9.8-mile point, you'll come to a downhill stretch of SH-49. Cruise east down the hill, and continue on until you come to the Refuge Headquarters. Take a right onto the Headquarters road, and go south until the paved road curves west and takes you back along Indiahoma Road to your starting point. Don't try this if it has been raining; the dirt roads turn to muddy sinkholes after a downpour.

You can spend days in the refuge, but when you're ready to move on, head for the old resort town of **Medicine Park**. Go east on SH-49 almost to US-44. At a Y in the road, go north toward Medicine Park and follow it to the creek. If you come this far by car, you can park on the road or at the picnic area in the park.

Pieces of the past combine with eclectic remodeling to make this an arty, fun community to explore. You'll be reminded of 1960s-era hippie hangouts. The narrow roads along Medicine Creek are terrific for biking – except on busy weekends when parked cars line the road near the swimming area and the Old Plantation, the town's centerpiece. If you explore a little, you'll find gravel roads and unsurfaced trails going down to the creek or up to the bluffs. Be prepared to spend a little extra time here. Something about the place is magic

Fort Sill is a short ride east on SH-49 and south on I-44, which is best traveled by car. Once you're on base, park at the Visitor's Center on Randolph Road. Pick up information and a map at the center, then explore by bike the well-known landmarks that date back to the days of Wild Bill Hickok. Fort Sill is an open military base and visitors can roam freely about most of the post as long as they obey signs, respect the privacy of those living in historic (off-limits) housing, and stay out of the soldiers' way. Occasionally, roads or entire areas are closed for one military reason or another, but you can find out by checking with the guard on duty at Key Gate off I-44.

One of the most spectacular sights in this area is **Medicine Bluff**, a gray granite cliff over Medicine Bluff Creek. After you see the historic buildings at the east end of Ft. Sill, bike west on Sheridan to Ft. Sill Boulevard, where you go north, then west again on Punch Bowl Road. Follow the dirt road around to the left and turn left at the next dirt road. This will take you to the Bluffs, where a hiking trail leads up to the rim. The scenery and view are outstanding.

You may be aware that Fort Sill and Lawton's Mud Sweat & Gears Bike Shop host a **"Twelve Miles of Hell"** off-road race each February. And, you may be thinking you'd like to try that route on your own – say, in July. Don't. First of all, it will be hotter than Hell. Second, the route is supposed to be a secret known only to members of a local bike club – and, of course, the bike shop, and the folks at Fort Sill, and anyone who's ever entered the race. Anyway, it's a mean trail. Loose gravel, steep climbs, sudden drop-offs. You've really gotta know what you're doing to tackle this thing – and even then you don't want to be out there without a few buddies to drag your bleeding body home, if it comes to that.

However, and this is top secret information, the great guys at **Mud Sweat & Gears** will tell you how to find the trail if you convince them you know something about technical riding and promise not to do anything stupid to mess up this sweet deal with the military base. Drop by the shop at 5340 Northwest Cache Road in Lawton. You can try calling ☎ 580-355-1808 for the information, but they'll probably make you come in so they can get a look at you – and you're going to need a map to go with those directions. If you want to go legal, call the bike shop and ask about joining the Wichita Mountains Bicycle Club.

❐ Quartz Mountain State Resort Park

Parts of Quartz Mountain State Resort Park are closed at press time because a new, state-of-the-art resort lodge is under construction. This is of little importance to bikers since the park doesn't have a designated biking trail, anyway. However, the area around it begs to be ridden.

Start at Granite, where a local artist is working on the world's largest granite mosaic called "Giant of the Great Plains." This 126-by-116-foot monument honoring Will Rogers, Sequoyah, and Jim Thorpe is on Main Street at the end of town.

In Granite, pick up SH-9 and pedal east past Altus Lake to Lone Wolf. A right turn onto scenic SH-44 takes you south between the lake and Quartz Mountain. Here, the view is dramatic – flat cotton fields and prairie grass extending for miles with gorgeous wild mountains jutting up to surprise and fascinate you with their colors. After Lugert, you can continue on to Quartz Mountain Park, or turn back west to SH-6, which leads north back to Granite. This is a long ride, but the road is mostly flat and small towns provide frequent rest stops.

❐ Waurika Lake

Mountain bikers will like the trails at **Waurika Lake**, south of Duncan near the Texas border, and at **Great Plains State Park,** west of the Wichita Mountains. Thirteen-mile **Walker Creek Trail** loops along the Walker Creek arm on the north side of Waurika Lake. This multi-use path was built by the US Army Corps of Engineers, and you may request information and a map by calling them at ☎ 580-963-2111. Even beginners can manage the varied route that wanders through level tall-grass prairie and over gentle hills. A couple of creek crossings add diversity, and the trail begins and ends at a parking lot on the east side of the road at the north end of the Corum-Hastings Bridge. The paved and dirt roads around the lake are usually uncrowded and perfect for biking.

❐ Red Rock Canyon

One more itinerary is worthy of recommendation. A trip up SH-8 from Anadarko to Hinton will take you through the countryside to an amazing visual treat – Caddo County's red rock canyons. **Red Rock Canyon**

State Park is just south of Hinton, and you will know when you approach it why native Indian tribes used it for a winter camp. Deep canyons cut through the sandstone of the Permian Red Beds providing ideal protection from weather and enemies. So ideal, in fact, that horse thieves and other bad guys hid out there during the cowboy-'n-Indian days.

Of course, this was before a road was sandblasted into the rock. Now, it is possible to get onto the canyon floor rather easily. Getting out is best left to the fittest.

Bike into the canyon by turning east at the sign on SH-8 just as you enter the town of Hinton. This is a speedy down-hill ride into a beautiful two-mile-long valley surrounded by red rock sandstone walls. You'll want to spend some time here, enjoying a picnic beside the little pond or take a dip in the swimming pool located in the canyon depths. In the fall, the sugar maple trees blaze with color. In the spring, migrating cliff swallows swarm about attaching mud nests to the canyon walls. When you begin to suspect that your sudden interest in nature is a shabby cover-up for procrastination, take in plenty of oxygen and set about the arduous task of biking back up the way you came in. The grade will seem twice as steep, but remember, you can always walk it.

Motorcycles & Off-Road Vehicles

 Quartz Mountain Resort Park, 17 miles north of Altus on Lake Altus-Lugert, has an ORV area on the north shore of the lake near Camp #2. From Lone Wolf, take SH-44 south about 4½ miles to a paved access road. Turn west and drive about 2½ miles northwest to the ORV trails. Call the park office at ☎ 580-563-2238 for information.

On Horseback

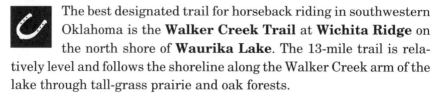 The best designated trail for horseback riding in southwestern Oklahoma is the **Walker Creek Trail** at **Wichita Ridge** on the north shore of **Waurika Lake**. The 13-mile trail is relatively level and follows the shoreline along the Walker Creek arm of the lake through tall-grass prairie and oak forests.

Find the trailhead near the Corum-Hastings bridge off SH-53 south on a lake road leading from Corum to Hastings. The Wichita Ridge public use area is on the east side of the road just south of the bridge, and a parking lot is near the trail entrance. Call the Corps of Engineers project office at ☎ 580-963-2111 for maps, directions, and information.

On Water

 The southern half of western Oklahoma isn't all flat and it isn't all dry. Several spots in this section of the state are stunning specifically because of the dramatic meeting of mountains with water in an otherwise level landscape. The fishing is fine to good on most lakes, and record-sized bass are often taken from these reservoirs. Catfish and bass are the staple fish in this area, but other species have been introduced with great success.

❑ Lake Altus-Lugert

One of the most striking views in this area is 6,260-acre Lake Altus-Lugert at the base of 1,800-foot **Quartz Mountain**. The North Fork of the Red River flows into the reservoir south of Lone Wolf, off SH-44. Trout is good just below the dam in winter, and walleye pikes are plentiful from March until May at dusk in the same area.

The north shore is the quieter side with a campground, boat launch, and off-road vehicle area. State-run facilities on the south shore are more developed and busier. At press time, a new lodge is under construction and

Man-made lakes provide infinite opportunities for adventure in southwest Oklahoma. (E. Smith)

some of the park is off-limits to visitors. However, boat launches, beaches, and campgrounds are open near the golf course at the south end of the lake and, when everything is complete, the area will have outstanding resort accommodations.

A scenic float down the **North Fork** of the **Red River** is one of the most pleasant ways to spend a summer afternoon. Canoes and paddleboats can be rented, or bring your own raft. A good place to put in is at the overpass south of Quartz Mountain State Park on SH-44. This will take you past the mountain and there's a little white-water action to keep you from getting bored. If you want a long trip, travel the river all the way to the Warren Bridge at SH-19, about 10 hours.

The main park also has a miniature golf course, grocery store, and gift shop. Get to the north side of the lake by taking SH-44 south from Lone Wolf for about 4½ miles. Turn right onto a paved country road (signs on the highway point the way) and travel west, cross some railroad tracks, then begin looking for boat ramp signs. Entrance to the south side of the lake is about five miles farther along SH-44, going toward Altus. Bear west onto SH-44A and drive to a Y, where you take the right fork in the road. ☎ 580-683-4249 for information.

☐ Lake Waurika

Lake Waurika, six miles northwest of Waurika, is a typical Great Plains lake. Small trees dot miles and miles of prairie grass surrounding the water, and the wind often stirs up gusts of dust. However, the multicolor wildflowers are beautiful and the crowds are light, so this 10,000-acre lake is a serious fisherman's paradise. A striped bass hybrid (produced at hatcheries by fertilizing striped bass eggs with white bass milt) is stocked here, and is one of the most popular catches. In addition, fishermen can try for largemouth bass, sunfish, crappie, and catfish.

Non-fishermen will like the wide-open space of this large lake for boating and skiing. Big bays and smaller coves cut into 80-miles of shoreline, and sandy beaches lure swimmers and picnickers. All the facilities are available – boat ramps, campgrounds, hiking trails – but it is the quiet spaciousness that sets this lake apart from others. The roads are so lightly traveled most days that bikers and walkers can easily use them without danger.

It's four miles from Waurika to the dam off SH-5. A paved access road leads to the Tulsa District Corps of Engineers Project Office just after the highway curves toward the west. The project office has maps, information, and a small gift shop. An alternate route is a paved country road that runs north from Hastings to Corum on SH-53. The **Walker Creek Equestrian/Hiking Trail** is located in this area nearer Corum. The marina is near Kiowa Park II, half a mile from the project office. For information, phone the project office at ☎ 580-963-2111 or the marina at 580-963-3531.

❏ Fort Cobb Lake

Even if you don't consider yourself a bird watcher, you can't miss the annual "Coming of the Crow" at Fort Cobb Lake. Every October, just when the air begins to have a bit of nip to it and everyone is thinking of all things spooky, up to 10 million crows descend on the lake and proceed to set up the world's largest crow roost. This must be intimidating to the 60,000 ducks who winter here each year. (Don't even think about shooting one of them. Hunting is off-limits in the park.)

This avian infestation only adds to the appeal of the seven-mile long, 63-foot-deep lake, which is popular year-round among fishermen and boaters. Three lighted boat ramps, three unlighted boat ramps, and a marina are located on Fort Cobb Lake along with two swimming beaches. The marina has an enclosed heated fishing dock, bait shop, gas dock, and rental boat slips. The main catch here is largemouth bass and channel catfish, but excellent walleye pike conditions are reported from time to time.

Fort Cobb Lake and State Park is west of Anadarko between SH-9 and SH-152. From a point four miles north of the town of Fort Cobb and six miles south of Albert, turn west onto a paved local road. Drive until you reach a T, turn north (right), go past the dam and golf course, then follow the southward curve of the road to the park office. The marina is across a bay off the golf course road. For information, ☎ 580-643-2249.

❏ Lake Tom Steed

Lake Tom Steed sits in **Great Plains State Park** northeast of Altus between Quartz Mountain and the Wichita Mountain Refuge. The lake has some of the best catfish, largemouth bass, and crappie fishing in the state, and hybrid striped bass are stocked regularly. The name "Great Plains" doesn't take into account the mountains that loom over the prairie grass around the lake. Actually, the park has an unusual landscape, which makes boating and fishing very popular.

Find the lake by driving north from Mountain Park on US-183 toward Roosevelt. Turn west on a blacktop access road about two miles after leaving Mountain Park, then watch for signs for Great Plains State Park. The park office is 1½ miles from the entrance. Call ☎ 580-569-2032 for more information.

☐ Lake Lawtonka

Lake Lawtonka is one of the most beautiful lakes in the Wichitas, near the old resort town of Medicine Park at the foot of Mount Scott. Water covers less than 2,000 acres, but there's room for fishing, sailing, and water skiing. Fishermen can try for black bass, crappie, perch, and catfish. Follow scenic SH-49 west from the junction with US-44 north of Lawton and watch for turnoffs to the lake. For more information, call ☎ 580-529-2663.

☐ Wichita Mountain Lakes & Rivers

The Wichita Mountains Wildlife Refuge has some of the best fishing holes in all of the southwestern United States – but there are a few restrictions. Of the 12 lakes scattered throughout the refuge, only **Jed Johnson**, **Rush**, and **Quanah Parker** allow boats, and even these must be non-motorized or small craft with electric motors. **French Lake** allows only non-motorized boats. There are no trailer ramps at any of the lakes, but there is a handicap-accessible pier near the Visitor's Center.

Sport fishing is allowed at all the lakes in the Public Use Area with, of course, an Oklahoma license. Fishermen can wade into the water, wear a life jacket, or use a one-man innertube for floatation, but fish must be taken only with a rod and reel or a pole and line. Be sure to bring your own bait (collecting it at the refuge is prohibited), and leave the frogs and turtles alone.

Hybrid bass have been stocked at Jed Johnson and Caddo Lakes, but the most likely catches are largemouth bass, crappie, sunfish, and channel catfish. Stop by the Refuge Headquarters off SH-49 to pick up a copy of the regulation booklet and ask the rangers about recent fishing reports. The phone number there is ☎ 580-429-3222. General information about the refuge is available at the Quanah Parker Visitor's Center six miles east of headquarters near the junction of SH-115 and SH-49 adjacent to the Doris Campground.

Cache Creek flows through Fort Sill and Lawton. Bring your own canoe and get permission from the military base to put in at the low-water bridge on Fort Sill property. Then float to one of the bridges in Lawton at Rogers Lane, Gore Boulevard, or Lee Boulevard. The current usually moves quickly through this area.

❒ Lake Ellsworth

Lake Ellsworth, on the eastern fringe of the Wichita range between Lawton and Anadarko, is especially pretty because of its view of the mountains. The 5,600-acre lake is well stocked with largemouth bass and catfish, and walleyes bite during the spring. Fishermen and boaters need a state license and city permit, which is available at Lake Patrol Headquarters. For directions and information, ☎ 580-529-2663.

❒ Fuqua, Humphries & Clear Creek Lakes

Triplet lakes, Fuqua, Humphries, and Clear Creek stretch along SH-29 north of Duncan. Clear Creek is the most developed, Fuqua is the largest, and all three have basic facilities such as boat ramps, campsites, and nearby restaurants. Largemouth bass is the main catch here, and jumbo-sized fish have been pulled from the water at each lake. Get information on all the lakes in the Duncan area by calling ☎ 580-255-9538 or 580-252-0250.

■ Where to Stay

Hotels & Inns

Altus

Quartz Mountain Resort, ☎ 580-563-2424, 17 miles north of town on SH-44A, is under construction at press time. The original lodge suffered severe fire damage in 1995, and a new $12 million facility will be open by the time you read this. When completed, the lodge will include 100 new rooms in addition to the original 45-room wing, which is being remodeled. Prices will not be available until the lodge reopens, but previous summer rates were in the $60 range. Room

Native wildflowers grow abundantly along roadsides and on untamed land throughout the state. (E. Smith)

rates at the new, comparably deluxe, state-run Lakeview Lodge at Beavers Bend are $80 off-season and $110 during the summer. Expect the rates at Quartz Mountain to be about the same.

Ramada Inn, ☎ 580-477-3000, fax 580-477-0078, 2515 East Broadway, features an indoor pool and recreation center. Guests receive complimentary newspapers, full breakfast, afternoon cocktails and cable TV. Rates are $60 to $100.

Clinton

Doc Mason's Best Western Tradewinds Motel, 2128 Gary Boulevard, ☎ 580-323-2610, fax 580-323-4655, is the motel where Elvis stayed during road trips to Las Vegas. Rates are $40-$70. If you want to stay in an *Elvis Room*, ask for 215 or 238.

Cordell

Chateau Du Rhe, on a private drive off Grant Street, ☎ 580-832-5564, is a bed and breakfast with horseback riding, trap shooting, hot tub, and full breakfast. Prices range from $75 to $100.

Grape Arbor Inn, 114 East Main, ☎ 580-832-2200, is above the Grapevine Galleria and Tea Room on the town square. Room rates are $75 per night.

*The restored Lindley House offers luxury lodging
in an historic home near downtown Duncan.*

Duncan

Lindley House, ☎ 580-255-1719, 1211 North 10th Street, is a 5,000-square-foot house on two acres of land. The house was built in 1939 for the town's doctor, and restored as a first-class bed and breakfast in 1997. Two deluxe bedrooms with private baths are upstairs, and three garden cottages are out back. Most have fireplaces, whirlpools, and private patios. A continental-plus breakfast is served each morning. Rates are $110 to $150. Ask about the honeymoon cottage.

Elk City

Holiday Inn Holidome, ☎ 580-225-6637, I-40 and SH-6 south at exit 38, has a covered dome with an indoor pool, miniature golf, game room, and an outdoor sundeck. King rooms have sofas. Rooms and suites are $60 to $100.

El Reno

Nelson's Homestay Bed and Breakfast, 315 East Wade, ☎ 580-262-9142, is a turn-of-the-century home with three rooms, an outdoor hot tub, garden, and full breakfast. Rooms are priced from $45 to $95.

Campgrounds

 Doris Campground, ☎ 580-429-3222, near the intersection of SH-115 and SH-49 in the Wichita Mountains, has 70 sites renting from $6 to $10. Campsites are in a wooded area above the northwest shore of Quanah Parker Lake, one of the most shaded camps in this section of the state.

The following three campgrounds are state-operated and conveniently located with better-than-average facilities or scenery. RV rates range from $11 to $17 and tent site fees are $6. Senior citizens and disabled persons may apply for lower rates, and assigned areas rent for $1 more than regular daily fees. The central reservation number for all state parks is ☎ 800-654-8240.

Red Rock Canyon State Park, ☎ 580-542-6344, a half-mile south of Hinton on US-281 off SH-8, has 76 campsites, some with full hookups. There's a swimming pool, hiking trail, and snack bar. Rates are $6 to $17.

Fort Cobb State Park, ☎ 580-643-2249, six miles north of town on SH-146, has 700 primitive campsites, and 264 sites with electricity and water. The park offers a variety of facilities including an 18-hole golf course. Rates are $6 to $17.

Quartz Mountain State Park, ☎ 580-563-2238, 17 miles north of Altus on SH-44 on Lake Altus-Lugert. Five camping areas have 214 campsites. Facilities include a swimming pool, 18-hole golf course, and outdoor adventure programs.

■ Where to Eat

Amber

Eight miles north of Chickasha

 $/$$ **Ken's Steak and Ribs**, 215 East Main Street, ☎ 580-222-0786, is open Thursday through Saturday from 5 pm to 9 pm and Sunday from 11 am to 2 pm. This plain little restaurant doesn't even have a menu, but the crowds come anyway. Arrive early to avoid waiting in line.

Clinton

$ **Pop Hicks Restaurant**, 223 Gary Boulevard, ☎ 580-323-1897, open all day every day except Christmas. This famous café opened in 1936 and became a Route 66 tradition. Save room for dessert.

Cordell

$ **Grapevine Galleria and Tea Room**, 114 East Main, ☎ 580-832-2200, open Tuesday through Friday from 10 am to 2 pm, serves delicious homemade desserts in a 1902 building with its original tin ceiling.

Elk City

$ **Country Dove Tea Room**, 610 West Third on Historic Route 66, ☎ 580-225-7028, serves lunch from 11 am to 2 pm Monday through Saturday (desserts are available until 5 pm). This little spot is famous for French silk pie but also serves the traditional soup-and-sandwich lunch.

El Reno

$ **The Wilds**, Britton Road east of US-81, ☎ 580-262-7275, open Wednesday through Saturday from 5 pm to 10 pm and Sunday from noon to 8 pm, serves fresh catfish, barbecue, and buffalo soup.

Erick

$ **Cal's Country Cooking**, I-40 at Exit 7, ☎ 580-526-3239, is open every day from 6 am to 10 pm, except Thanksgiving and Christmas. Cal and his daughter Cheryl prepare country favorites from scratch and serve them in this log building on the northeast corner of the intersection of I-40 and SH-30. Take some cinnamon rolls home with you.

Lawton

$/$$ **Pisano's Italian**, 1320 Northwest Homestead Land, ☎ 580-357-4033, is open Monday through Saturday from 11 am to 2 pm and from 5 pm to 10 pm; Sunday from 11 am to 9 pm. This upscale restaurant serves steaks in addition to traditional Italian cuisine and a large variety of cheesecakes.

Marlow

$/$$ **Giuseppe's**, 201 West Main, 10 miles north of Duncan, ☎ 580-658-2148, is an Italian restaurant open Tuesday through Saturday from 11 am to 9 pm in a renovated 1911 bank building. Tablecloths and classical music make this a special-occasion place; it has excellent food and reasonable prices.

Meers

$ **Meers Store and Restaurant**, SH-115 north of Lawton at the edge of the Wichita Mountains Wildlife Refuge, ☎ 580-429-8051, is open Monday through Friday from 8 am to 9 pm and Saturday and Sunday from 7 am to 9:30 pm. This old general store now serves the famous seven-inch "Meersburger." If a tour bus has unloaded there, and you can't get inside the door, walk across the street to the **Longhorn Café**.

Medicine Park

$$ **Old Plantation Restaurant**, Eastlake Drive, ☎ 580-529-9641, is open Tuesday through Saturday from noon to 9 pm and Sunday from 1 pm to 7 pm. The restaurant is well-known for serving sirloin steaks so big they hang over the plate.

$$ **Riverside Restaurant**, Eastlake Drive, ☎ 580-529-2626, serves lunch from 11:30 am to 2:30 pm and dinner from 5 pm to 9 pm, Thursday through Monday. Choose from healthy veggie plates or meat-and-potato meals. Reserve a table outside on the deck overlooking Medicine Creek during good weather.

Waurika

$ **Moneka Tea Room**, US-70 south, ☎ 580-228-2575, serves lunch from 11:30 am to 2:30 pm, Tuesday through Saturday, in the Moneka Antique Mall, a former boarding house. The menu includes sandwiches, soups, and salads.

■ Where to Shop

Altus

 Scott Farms, US-283, 6½ miles north of Altus, ☎ 800-482-1950, open Monday through Friday from 9 am to 5 pm. Stock up on seasonings, spices, party mixes, and flavored snacks at this outlet shop. Call for a catalog if you can't stop by the store.

Anadarko

McKee's Indian Store and **The Susan Peters Gallery**, 116 West Main, ☎ 580-247-7151 or 800-972-7653, sells rugs, baskets, pottery and beadwork plus original art, sculpture, and jewelry.

Apache

US-281 south of Anadarko

Mo' Betta Store, 104 East Evans Ave, ☎ 580-588-9222, open Monday through Saturday, 9 am to 5 pm. This is the store made nationally famous by country music singer Garth Brooks, who wears their Technicolor shirts on stage.

Carnegie

SH-9 west of Anadarko

Horn Canna Farm, west of the junction of SH-9 and SH-58, ☎ 580-637-2327, produces the largest number of canna bulbs in the country. Pick out the color you want for your yard and the bulbs will be mailed to you in time for planting. If you're in the area the last Saturday of September, stop at their festival, where you'll be allowed to cut "all you can carry."

Clinton

Mohawk Trading Post, east of town on Historic Route 66, ☎ 580-323-2360, open Monday through Saturday from 9 am to 5 pm. This is the oldest Indian trading post in the state – part museum, part store. You can see turn-of-the-century pictures of Cheyenne chiefs and antique beadwork, or purchase pottery, moccasins, and other Native American crafts.

Antique Mall of Clinton, 815 Frisco, ☎ 580-323-2486, is a huge building with more than 50 booths selling top-quality antiques and gifts.

Bessie

Eight miles south of Clinton

The Kachina Gallery, 705 Main Street, ☎ 800-367-4094, is open Monday through Saturday from 10 am to 5 pm – closed for lunch from noon to 1 pm. This is a big-bucks shop for serious collectors of Native American artifacts and antiques. The Kachina doll collection is said to be the largest in the world. Browsers are welcome.

Duncan

Antique Marketplace and Tea Room, 726 West Main, ☎ 580-255-2499, is open Monday through Saturday from 10 am to 6 pm. More than 40 booths sell furniture, jewelry, and clothing.

Serenity Day Spa, 1205 West Main Street, ☎ 800-708-4372, offers custom-blended makeup, essential oils, and specialty teas, as well as personal spa services such as facials and massages. Call for a brochure or appointment.

Cow Creek and Company, 17 miles south of Duncan on US-81 in the tiny town of Addington, ☎ 580-439-6489, is open Thursday through Saturday from 10 am to 5:30 pm. This former bank sells antiques and "cow patties" – a tasty homemade chocolate treat.

Peachtree Plantation, SH-5 south of Duncan near Lake Waurika, ☎ 580-963-3311, www.peachtreeplantation.com, is open Tuesday through Saturday from 10 am to 5 pm (until 8 pm on Friday and Saturday). Fine art, pottery, Native American crafts and unique gifts are sold in this refurbished 1906 building. The true standout here is custom-designed clothing made from hand-spun yarn.

Erick

OK Honey Farm and Candle Company, I-40 and Honey Farm Road, ☎ 580-526-3759, is a working honey farm and candle business, with a gift shop. It's open Monday through Saturday from 8 am to 6 pm and Sunday from 1:30 pm to 5:30 pm. The farm and store are closed in January and February. All types and flavors of honey are sold, along with various wax products such as candles, lip balm, and furniture wax.

Lawton

Prairie Crafters Gift Shop, ☎ 580-353-7055, near the historic chapel at Fort Sill in Building 372, is run and stocked by soldiers and their families. You'll find baskets, candles, and all types of crafts in this multi-room building, which is open from 10 am to 5 pm, Monday through Saturday.

Medicine Park

Happy Hollow Gifts, US-49 near the entrance to Wichita Mountain Wildlife Refuge, ☎ 580-529-2677, carries imported gifts, Indian beadwork, pottery, snacks, and cold drinks.

Waurika

Moneka Antique Mall, ☎ 580-228-2575, west of the intersection of US-81 and US-70, is a 100-year-old former boarding house turned tea room/antique shop. The locals say ghosts from a lawless past still move around in the old building, but no one seems concerned. Antique and art fans will want to spend hours here. The shop is open Tuesday through Saturday from 9:30 am to 5:30 pm. Plan your visit to coincide with lunch, which is served in the tea room from 11:30 am to 2:30 pm.

■ Powwows, Festivals, Arts & Crafts Fairs

March

Weatherford World Championship Hog Calling Contest, ☎ 580-772-0310, is a crazy, family-style event attended by hog callers from around the world. Festivities include a Hog Call Ball, a barbecue, and craft demonstrations. Usually held in Weatherford the first weekend in March. Call for exact dates.

Easter Weekend

Wichita Wildlife Refuge, **Holy City of the Wichitas**, ☎ 580-248-4043. The longest running Easter passion play is held in a natural amphitheater at the Holy City on the Saturday evening before Easter.

April

Beaver, Cimarron Territory Celebration, ☎ 580-625-4726. This mid-April event includes the annual World Championship Cow Chip Throw, a competition you must attend at least once in a lifetime.

August

Anadarko American Indian Exposition, ☎ 580-247-6651. This is the oldest fair in the United States owned and operated by Native Americans. Usually held in early August, it features ceremonial dancing, an all-Indian rodeo, and an arts and crafts sale. Admission is free, but there is a charge for some events.

September

Chickasha Muscle Car Ranch Swap Meet, ☎ 580-222-4910, off Country Club Road south of town on Sixteenth Street. Car and antique fans will want to attend this three-day meet held near mid-September each year. There's always plenty of buying and selling in a fair-like atmosphere that includes an outdoor concert.

November

Chickasha Festival of Light, ☎ 580-224-0787. About three million lights decorate the city the weekend after Thanksgiving through the first of the year. Opening ceremonies are held at Shannon Springs Park.

Northwest Oklahoma

Surprise! Northwest Oklahoma is not "No Man's Land," "Wasteland," or "Endless Miles of Hell." It's a wonderland of nature, created over millions of years and compacted into an area that can be seen over a long weekend.

Alabaster Caverns is the world's largest publicly accessible gypsum cave. Over 1,500 acres of sand shift and mound at **Little Sahara State Park**. Selenite crystals form in the wet sand of **The Great Salt Plains**, and an underground river pumps water into the cedar-filled canyon at **Roman Nose**. Cimarron County stretches long and lazy into the panhandle and ends with a lava-coated plateau hiding dinosaur bones and prehistoric footprints at **Black Mesa**.

All of this unusual geography is made more interesting by tales of rowdy cowboys, determined pioneers, exploited Indians, the US Cavalry – and artistic German war prisoners. There's probably not another section of the country with more adventure to offer.

■ Touring

 In this section of the state, towns are small, conveniences are basic, and there's often a great deal of uninteresting distance in between. Driving just to enjoy the scenery is usually not a good use of time. However, in the spring when the wildflowers bloom, and again in the fall when the trees turn breathtaking colors, the following short routes are worthy of a leisurely, purposeless road trip.

Woodward to Alabaster Caverns

24 miles one-way

From the town of **Woodward** drive north on SH-34 for a mile and a half to SH-34C. Turn east and drive five miles to **Boiling Springs State Park**. This is a shady little park full of oak, elm, walnut and hackberry trees that have grown tall and wide since they were planted by the Civilian Conservation Corps in the 1930's. Turn right (east) into the park and follow the road to the park office, where you will see the reason for the park's name. A natural spring behind the office gushes 30 gallons of water per minute resulting in a bubbly, rolling action. At the time that the

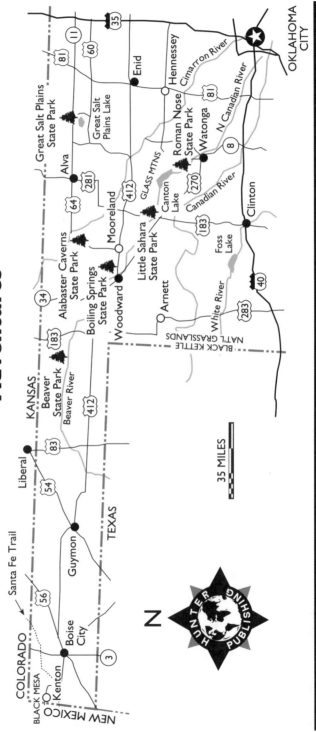

Northwest Oklahoma
- Adventures -

park was named, the spring produced about 90 gallons of water per minute, causing the sandy bottom to churn and appear to be boiling. The water, however, is subterranean cold, not boiling hot.

After Boiling Springs, drive east on SH-50B to Mooreland, then turn north onto SH-50 and go 18 miles to **Alabaster Caverns State Park**. A right turn (east) onto SH-50A will take you to the park office, where you can pick up a map and information about the caves. Take a jacket for exploring the caves. Or just walk through scenic Cedar Canyon.

Boise City to Black Mesa

27 miles one-way

Only one town in the continental United States was bombed during the war. That town was Boise (rhymes with voice) City. The bombers were American pilots from Dalhart Air Force Base in Texas. Seems the crew's navigator called in sick that night, and the guy who took his place got a little off course, thought the lights around the courthouse in Boise City were target lights on a bombing range in the Texas Panhandle, and directed the crew to drop six 100-pound bombs on the small Oklahoma town. Fortunately, the damage was relatively light and no one was hurt.

After you view the bomb memorial at 6 Northeast Square in town, fill the gas tank and ice chest (you won't see a mini-mart with gas pumps out front for a long time), and begin driving west on SH-325. Fifteen miles from town, after the highway turns north, you'll cross the Cimarron Cutoff of the **Santa Fe Trail**, which ran from Franklin, Missouri to Santa Fe, New Mexico more than a century ago. Most of the identifiable historic sites are on private land, and your best chance to see them is during Santa Fe Trail Daze, held the first weekend each June (☎ 580-544-3344 for information and specific dates.) You can, however, find deep ruts left by the wagon trains near historical markers on SH-325 and US-287.

The scenery turns dramatic as you near **Black Mesa**. Just before the town of Kenton (where the time zone changes from Central to Mountain), turn west onto a paved access road off SH-325 that leads to **Lake Carl Etling**. The state park is located near the lake (follow the signs turning north at the T). **Black Mesa Nature Preserve** – and the actual mesa – is about 15 miles northwest at a point where Oklahoma meets New Mexico and Colorado. Find the mesa by driving west on SH-325 to a blacktop road marked "Colorado." Towering, weather-carved sandstone formations in this area have names such as "The Wedding Party" and "Old Maid." Turn north onto the blacktop road and travel about five miles to the preserve, which is open daily from sunrise to sunset.

Black Mesa is near the foothills of the Rocky Mountains, covered with a thick layer of lava that flowed out of the mountains in Colorado about 30 million years ago. Fossilized remains of dinosaurs from the Jurassic and Triassic Periods have been excavated from this region, and you can still find tracks left by the huge beasts. The best place to see them is along Carrizo Creek near the dinosaur road sign on the *Colorado* road leading to Black Mesa. The sign is four miles north of SH-325, and parking is on the left.

Robber's Roost

You can see a hill from this same road, off to the east with a house at the base and rock around the rim. This is Robber's Roost, the legendary hideout for all manner of bad dudes. Outlaw gangs used to hang out here in a fortified rock building waiting for wagon trains to come down the Santa Fe Trail. Then they would rob the wagons, maybe stop along the way to steal some grub from one of the nearby ranch houses, and return to "the roost" to count their loot. At other times, they would steal cattle and horses, change the branding marks, then sell the animals to ranchers in Kansas.

Make a pit stop in Kenton when you leave Black Mesa. The **Kenton Mercantile**, ☎ 580-261-7447, on SH-325, has been a well-known provision spot in this area since 1898. You can refuel, mail a postcard, refill the ice chest, grab a meal, and look at dinosaur fossils while you're there.

Jet to Great Salt Plains State Park

30 miles round-trip

State Highway 38 north of Jet leads to the moonscape of **The Great Salt Plains Lake** eight miles away in a National Wildlife Refuge. The state park office is a left turn (west) off the highway in the South Spillway Area, ☎ 580-626-4731. Stop here or at the Refuge Headquarters,

☎ 580-626-4794, for information and a map of the area. Also ask for a brochure on the **Harold F. Miller Auto Tour Route**, which begins near Refuge Headquarters on a gravel road north of the lake off SH-38 south of SH-11.

Salt covers a section measuring seven by three miles that was an inland sea millions of years ago. When the water dried up, it left salt – tons and tons of salt. The Osage Indians brushed up the salt from the plains with feathers and used it to preserve buffalo meat, which was plentiful because the buffalos were drawn to the area by the salt. Today, a wide variety of animals and birds come to the lake, which was formed when the Salt Fork of the Arkansas River was dammed in 1941. Visitors come to view the wildlife and dig crystals from the sand.

Begin the Wildlife Refuge auto tour route near the Eagle Roost Nature Trail west of Refuge Headquarters. A printed map and brochure will guide you along the 2½-mile route, which takes you past ponds, marshes, wheat fields, and an observation tower. The tour route ends at SH-11. Turn left (west), cross over several streams where fishing is allowed from April until October, then head south on SH-8 to a paved road that leads to the west side of the lake, where crystal digging is allowed during the summer. If you plan to dig, bring a shovel, hand trowel, bucket, towel to sit on, and plenty of water to drink and wash crystals. You'll also want a camera and binoculars.

When you're ready to leave, take SH-8 south to US-64, where you can go east to Jet, or continue south about 12 miles to the only remaining original sod house in Oklahoma. The *soddie* is furnished with pieces from the pioneer era, and you'll get an authentic idea of what it was like to be an early settler. Admission is free and visitors are welcome Tuesday through Friday from 9 am to 5 pm, Saturday and Sunday from 2 pm to 5 pm, ☎ 580-463-2441.

Watonga to Roman Nose State Park

7 miles one-way

Try to be in **Watonga** the first weekend in October for the **Cheese Festival**. There's cheese tasting and rat racing as well as an art show and flea market. If you miss the festivities, stop by the **Cheese Factory** at 314 East 2nd Street, ☎ 580-623-5915. The factory in back turns out over 2,000 pounds of cheddar each day, and the shop in front sells it along with other goodies made in the state. The Oklahoma-shaped cheddar is a nice gift to take home to friends.

If you liked the book and movie, *Cimarron*, by Edna Ferber, drive by the **T.B. Ferguson Home**, 580-623-5069, 519 North Weigel. Ferber was staying here with the Fergusons in 1927 when she began her book about Oklahoma settlers, which includes a character much like newspaperman Thomas Benton Ferguson. The house, porch, and back yard pretty much tell the whole story, but you can also look around inside, Wednesday through Saturday from 10 am to 5 pm and Sunday from 1 pm to 5 pm.

Watonga was named for an Arapaho chief. The multi-colored canyon seven miles to the north on SH-8 was named for the last Cheyenne warrior-chief, Henry Carruthers Roman Nose. Driving into **Roman Nose State Park**, ☎ 580-623-7281, visitors are struck by the contrast of silver-streaked canyons and deep green trees. In the fall, the leaves become a flash of color. The park sits on the canyon floor, with two small lakes and a large collection of freshwater springs. This is truly a geologic masterpiece in the middle of the prairie.

■ Adventures

On Foot

Hiking

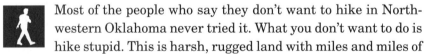

Most of the people who say they don't want to hike in Northwestern Oklahoma never tried it. What you don't want to do is hike stupid. This is harsh, rugged land with miles and miles of Nothing before you come to Something. If you get lost or underestimate your need for water or overestimate the amount of gas in your tank, you'll be in serious trouble. On the other hand, if you do a little research, get the right maps, and double-check your supplies, you'll have a great adventure.

If you just want a little nature hike complete with interpretive signs and restrooms, perhaps you'll be happier east of I-35. But, if you consider yourself an independent, broad-minded, reasonably fit adventurer open to all types of experiences, read on.

Some of the following areas have newly constructed, well-marked trails suitable for most hikers. A few, such as **Black Kettle** and the hunting grounds around the Panhandle town of **Beaver**, are more suitable for the aforementioned *IBMF* (independent, broad-minded and fit) hiker.

❒ Roman Nose Canyon

Old Shotnose, Cheyenne warrior-chief and father of Roman Nose, used to hike this canyon. He brought his family here for shelter during winter, made medicine from the cedar trees and took comfort from the sound of running water in the eternal springs. Today, the canyon still is protected from most of civilization's maladies, even though Oklahoma City is only an hour's drive. A state park and resort lodge have taken over some of this area, but there is still plenty of wilderness to explore. Three short nature trails and three longer multi-use trails are located in the park, and you can get a map and directions to the trail heads at the park office on SH-8A or by calling ☎ 580-623-4215. The best route is along 10½-mile **Wineglass Trail,** rated Intermediate to Difficult because of steep climbs up gypsum buttes and demanding treks through thick undergrowth along wooded ravines.

Consider taking an interpretive trail ride on horseback if you want a quick orientation of the area or just don't want to contend with the terrain on foot. The night rides are especially fun. Call the stables at ☎ 580-623-4354 or 580-623-7281 for times and information. Another option is simply to set out into the canyon on your own. There are animal paths on the grassy slopes and along the stream beds, and the entire canyon is relatively small. Check with park rangers if you plan on primitive camping since some areas are off-limits – and, as always, tell someone where you're going and when you'll be back.

❒ Boiling Springs

The last stand of Big Timber in the western part of the state provides shaded hiking at **Boiling Springs**, ☎ 580-256-7664. There are three designated trails ranging in length from .75 miles to 1.75 miles. **Chisholm Trail** is marked with interpretive signs and makes a loop just north of Group Camp #2. The 1½-mile **Burma Trail** connects at both ends to the main park road near Group Camp #1 and is popular with hikers and bikers. **River Trail** runs from Boiling Springs Well behind the ranger office to the bank of the North Canadian River, then back to the main park road, a distance of one mile. Other parts of this area beg to be explored, and you'll find tempting spots along the river and also north of the campgrounds along the park's border.

☐ Alabaster Caverns

The best hike here is into the gypsum caves. A .75-mile guided walk deep into the main cave is a nice beginning, but the real fun comes when you obtain a permit to explore one of the five other caves on your own. If you'd rather stay above ground, four designated trails wind through the park. Check at the park office for guidance on the best trail for your skill/endurance level. The best trails wind through Cedar Canyon, where outlaws once hid out among the dense trees. Ask a park ranger to point out the "Difficult" trail leading to an area once spanned by a natural bridge. Call ☎ 580-621-3381 for information.

Legend of a Golden Treasure

Old-timers who live near the moonscape of the Great Salt Plains tell a story of hidden treasure and friendship gone bad. Back in 1854, a group of miners was returning from California with more than a thousand pounds of gold when they were threatened by a band of Indians. To safeguard their treasure, the miners wrapped their cache in buffalo skins and buried it near red bluffs just after they crossed the Salt Fork River.

Indians soon attacked and killed all but one of the miners. The single white survivor drew a careful map marking the location of the treasure, then, happy to be alive, left Indian Territory and went on with his life. Years later, a homesteader named Carl Joseph Sheldon showed up in Cherokee country near the Salt Fork River with a map, a friend, and digging equipment.

The two men located a pole in the ground where the map indicated the treasure was buried and set about drilling into the crusty salt flats. They quickly hit quicksand and water, and Sheldon rode off to town to have a core sample analyzed. By the time he got back with the report showing traces of gold and buffalo hide, his friend had removed the marker and drill (and possibly more) and disappeared.

Sheldon, in a fit of greedy fury, bought 20 acres of land on the river near the red bluffs for $400 and spent the next three decades searching for the gold. When the state of Oklahoma built a dam on the river in 1936, Sheldon was forced to give up and sell his land to developers for $50 less than he paid for it.

No sign of gold was found during construction of the dam. Some say it never existed. Some say, if it did exist, it would have been impossible for Sheldon's friend to move all thousand pounds in such a short period of time; therefore, some or all of it is still buried somewhere near the dam.

When you're out there hiking, watch for decaying markers, forgotten buffalo hides, specks of dropped gold, and suspicious pockmarks in the salty terrain. And remember, if you find anything, send a nice token of thanks to the author who told you where to look.

❒ Great Salt Plains State Park

This area is full of hiking possibilities. In Great Salt Plains State Park, ☎ 580-626-4731, you'll find **The Salt River Trail** near the lake's North Spillway. Other hiking areas are near Sandy Beach, west of the dam. In the National Wildlife Refuge, ☎ 580-626-4794, **The Eagle Roost Nature Trail** is a nice 1.25-mile path with numbered interpretive stops and interesting animal tracks. The new **Sandpiper Trail** gets you up-close-and-personal with a variety of refuge habitats, including the endangered whooping crane. Walk to the Casey Marsh Observation Tower from a parking area near the Miller Auto Tour for a good view of the entire area.

If you're more interested in raising your heart rate into the aerobic zone, strike out across the salt flats on the west side of the lake. This is a strange geological site, and you'll feel a weird freedom – and, of course, the thrill of trying to guess which spots may be quicksand. A number of gravel roads branch off from the paved roads all around the lake, and they make fine hiking and jogging paths, especially during bird-migration season. However, the real adventure here is digging for selenite crystals, so pack a shovel along with your running shoes.

❒ Glass Mountains

By the time you read this, there may be some type of development taking shape on US-412 about six miles west of Orienta in 24 miles of painted hills called **Glass Mountains**, ☎ 580-521-3411. Locals have been trying to interest the state in "doing something" here for several years, and finally a few information signs have been put up at a rest stop on the north side of the highway. Don't expect designated trails anytime soon, but you can get out and climb up the buttes or hike around the red-colored mesas.

 Maintain a healthy respect for the snakes and their hangouts. Chances are you won't see a single one, but they are here; this isn't a botanical garden.

◻ Black Kettle National Grasslands

After years of struggle and debate, the Oklahoma Historical Society and National Park Service finally acquired the 326-acre **1868 Washita Battlefield** near Black Kettle National Grasslands, ☎ 580-497-2143, for development of the **Battle of Washita National Historic Site** and cultural national park. This far-west tract of land is slowly being "improved," but if you hurry, you can get there before too much harm is done.

The sacred Cheyenne soil near the Washita River has a fascinating and confusing history. Visitors can pick up brochures about the battle/massacre site at the **Black Kettle Museum**, ☎ 580-497-3929, on US-283 just south of SH-47. Eventually, historians plan a high-quality museum at the site itself, which promises to present all the facts of the 1868 attack from both sides – the Cheyennes' and Custer's.

Black Kettle National Grasslands. (Fred W. Marvel)

The Washita River flows through the 30,710-acre national grasslands near the town of Cheyenne. A monument to the 1868 battle is located west of town on SH-47A, but the specific location of the Cheyenne camp where the battle/massacre took place is still being researched. When the national cultural park is complete, there will surely be markers for Chief Black Kettle's lodge, sacred burial grounds, and the Cheyenne camp of tepees, which faced east towards the rising sun.

At present, you can tromp around the undeveloped 326-acre site and imagine the life of the Cheyennes. Remember that the grass was taller. And there were cottonwood trees in the valley then. And the wind blew gently over the river through the trees cooling the Indians camped in a clearing circled by tall grass. When the tourists arrive, as they doubtless will, it may be harder to image the peace of earlier days.

The grasslands provide miles and miles of dirt trails and unimproved roads for hiking. Try the bank along the Washita River beginning near the ranger office at SH-47 and US-283, or head north up the highway to Dead Indian Lake for a sunset hike. The area is so vast, you'll need a detailed map, which you can request from the **Cibola National Forest** office in Albuquerque, New Mexico, ☎ 505-761-4650.

From Black Kettle National Grasslands, you can see red hills to the north. Reach them by driving north on US-283 then west on SH-33 to **Antelope Hills**, once the boundary between Mexico and the United States. These six flat-top hills are on private land, so you should get permission from the owners to hike here. You didn't read it here, but you probably won't encounter any trespassing problems if you "act right, don't hurt nuttin' and clean up yur mess." Don't plan to set up camp out here, though.

❑ Beaver River & Black Mesa

Hiking in the high plains of "No Man's Land" is a terrific experience. There are miles of open land around the town of Beaver, site of the annual World Championship Cow Chip Throw. You can camp and hike in the **Beaver River Wildlife Management Area,** except during hunting season from October through January. The town is on SH-23 north of US-412. A 360-acre state park is north, across Beaver River, and the wildlife management area is west on an unnumbered country road. Hikers probably won't hang around here long, unless they also like hotdoggin' off-road vehicles that race over 120 acres of sand dunes in the park.

Black Mesa, so many miles west through nothingness you'll be tempted to turn back, is worth the drive – and you gain an hour of hiking time when you get there. (This is the only section of Oklahoma on Mountain Time.) You'll need that hour because it takes about two to hike to the top of Black Mesa, which is 4,973 feet high, and another two to hike down. At the top, the view is other-world fantastic. The trail up is an old eight-mile ranch road, but it's steep and rugged, so wear hiking boots and carry a couple of water bottles in some sort of wearable pack. Best times to hike are spring and fall because temperatures can reach 112° in summer and dip to minus 30° in winter. Sudden, heavy thunderstorms also occur in summer. And, by the way, there are rattlesnakes.

Caving

❒ Alabaster Caverns

The 2,256-foot-long **Alabaster Cavern**, ☎ 580-621-3381, is the world's largest gypsum cave open to the public. Guided tours take visitors along a 3½-mile trail that winds down into the multi-colored rock hollow created 200 million years ago by an inland sea. The cave is strung with electric lights and steps are carved into the rock to provide a fairly easy descent, but the tour is not recommended for anyone with health problems or claustrophobia.

Tours are $5 for adults and $2.50 for kids, last about an hour, and begin on the hour from 8 am to 5 pm daily from May 1 to September 30. The last tour is at 4 pm during the rest of the year, and special tours take place at various times during October. You'll see rare black alabaster, which is found in only two other caves worldwide, plus many other minerals and crystals. Wear a sweater – the temperature is about 50° year-round – and shoes with good traction.

 Check out the little cracks in the cave's ceiling as you walk along. Five different types of bats live in these crevices, but you may not see one as they sleep all day and eat all night. Each one devours about 40% of its body weight in mosquitoes and other bugs every night.

Several lesser caves within Alabaster Caverns State Park can be explored independently, but you must prove you have the proper equipment before you can get a permit and map from the park office. If you want to try the "wild caves," you'll need a hard hat, three sources of light, a long-sleeved shirt, long pants, heavy-duty shoes or boots, a first-aid kit, and plenty of water. Once you have the permit and maps, keep the park office informed of your plans. You'll be allowed to explore from 8 am to 4:30 pm, and if you don't report back to the office by 5 pm, the rangers or Explorer Scouts will set out on a search-and-rescue mission.

Bat Stats

The bats living in **Alabaster Caverns** belong to several *non-migratory* species, so the best time to get close is during the winter months. From November through March, the bats can't distinguish night from day, and humans can walk right up to the critters hanging out on the gypsum walls.

Don't scream when your night vision kicks in and you find yourself face to face with an open-eyed bat. The little beasts appear asleep, but they're just in the groggy grip of semi-hibernation. About the time your heart regains a normal beat, the guide turns out all the lights and plunges the cave into total, absolute, pitch-black darkness. This is a heady experience. Suddenly you are disoriented, blind, and helpless. So how do bats cope with these conditions on a daily basis?

Exceedingly well, thank you.

In total darkness, bats can locate and eat about 600 insects an hour using an instinct called echolocation. This method of sensory perception allows the mini mammals to recognize objects, communicate among themselves, and orient themselves to their surroundings by emitting a series of short, high-pitched sounds that bounce off surfaces and create an echo. They never bump into anything and can hunt down a meal one gnat at a time.

The bats at **Selman Cave** are *migratory* Mexican free-tailed bats that fly in from Central America each spring. They won't be caught languishing about for face-to-face human encounters, but their nightly emergence from the cave on summer evenings is a splendid sight.

You can make your own bat house with a kit available at nature stores or from the Oklahoma Department of Wildlife Conservation, ☎ 405-521-4616, e-mail natural@oklaosf.state. ok.us. These habitats are designed to attract and house bats, which eat thousands of mosquitoes and other insects each night.

There is no cleared path through the smaller caves, so you should expect to do some crawling-over and squeezing-through. Again, this will be too much adventure for anyone with health problems or claustrophobia. The charge to explore the wild caves is the same as the guided tour through the main cave – $5 for adults and $2.50 for children – and spelunking is allowed from March 1 through September 30. Consider taking the guided tour through the main cave before you try the wild caves. This will give you some basic history and information about features inside the caves so you'll enjoy your independent explorations more.

❏ Selman Bat Cave

The cave is on private property, so the only time you can visit is during a scheduled Wildlife Diversity Program sponsored by the Oklahoma Department of Wildlife Conservation. These bat-viewing tours are held during July and August after mother bats wean their babies and the pups are able to fly.

Call ahead for tour dates and information, ☎ 580-521-4616, e-mail natural@oklaosf.state.ok.us. Only a limited number of permits are issued for each viewing, so apply as early as possible. Tickets are $4 each and include bus transportation to Selman Cave.

During the bat emergence tours, which run from approximately 6 pm to 9 pm, you'll see a million (literally) hungry Mexican free-tailed bats rush from the cave in search of dinner. Selman cave is the bat equivalent of a maternity ward and newborn nursery. Each spring, approximately 500,000 pregnant bats arrive from Central America, bed down in the cave, and give birth to, usually, one pup. For the next few weeks, while the newborns feed on mother's milk, visitors are not welcome. Beginning in July, when the babies can fly and feed themselves, the Wildlife Conservation Department leads groups across private property to Selman Cave to view the nightly food-flight.

Try to get a ticket for one of the first tours, when baby bats are fresh out of flight school and still a little clumsy. You won't be allowed to bring anything that makes noise or light – including crying kids, the family dog, flashlights, flash cameras, or radios. However, you can use binoculars and non-flash cameras and camcorders. It takes several hours for a million ravenous bats to emerge from the cave in search of 10 tons of insects, and the sight is spectacular. Don't miss it.

Bat Trivia

- They can see, but use their sonar instinct in the dark.
- Their wings are actually "hands," with skin stretched between long "fingers."
- They can live for up to 30 years.
- There are 1,000 different species of bats, and all of them are mammals.
- Mexican free-tailed bats will fly two miles high to catch a tasty bug.
- At high altitudes, tailwinds help bats reach flight speeds of more than 60 mph.
- Mexican free-tailed mama bats recognize their own young in colonies of up to 500 babies-per-square-foot at nursing time.
- Bat droppings in caves provide breeding grounds for unique organisms that can be used to detoxify wastes and produce fuel.

Digging for Crystals

The Great Salt Plains is the only place in the world where hourglass-shaped figures form inside selenite crystals. You can hunt for these unique rocks from sunrise to sunset, April 1 through October 15, in the Selenite Digging Area six miles west of Jet off US-64. Signs on the highway direct visitors to the observation tower at the entrance to the digging area.

Salt Flat Treasures

- Iron oxide causes the crystals in the Great Salt Plains to be amber or tea-brown in color.
- Crystals are usually found less than two feet below the surface.
- No two crystals are ever the same.
- Selenite crystals are made of gypsum, a white mineral.
- Great Salt Plains State Park is the only place in the world where hourglass-shaped crystals form.
- Crystals clump together in large freeform designs.

Pick up a brochure explaining crystal-digging techniques at the **Wildlife Refuge Headquarters**, ☎ 580-626-4794, off SH-38 north of Jet, or near the dig site. Bring a shovel and hand trowel for digging, jugs of water for washing sand from the crystals, and some type of container for transporting your treasures. (An empty egg carton will work for small crystals.)

The best time to find crystals is during a dry period, when salt appears snow-white on top of the sand. The crystals are found as singles, twins, and clusters, ranging in size from a few inches to several pounds, and are usually less than two feet below the surface. Selenite is a crystallized form of gypsum, and, on the Salt Plains, sand and clay particles form an unique hourglass shape inside the crystal.

How to Find Crystals

Start your treasure hunt by digging a hole two feet deep and two feet across. You'll probably hear or feel crystals breaking as you dig, but there is no way to avoid this since it is impossible to predict where a crystal bed is located. After two or three inches of water seep into the hole from the bottom, splash the sides of the hole to expose crystals hiding within the soil. When you locate a crystal, continue splashing it until it is freed from the sand and clay, then carefully place it in a safe place to dry. The crystals are extremely fragile until they dry and harden.

Golfing

❑ Watonga

Roman Nose Golf Course, north of Watonga, has only nine holes, but they are challenging. The fairways are surrounded by native trees, the rough is buffalo grass, the greens are narrow and sloping, and 30-foot canyons drop off to the left of some holes. Par is 35, and the signature hole is a 415-yard, par-4 known for its natural canyon hazard.

Green fees are $6.50 on weekends and weekdays, and gas carts are available at a cost of $9. Pull carts can be rented for $2. There are no caddies, but players can rent clubs.

Take US-281 north from Watonga to SH-8A – about eight miles from town. The golf course is in Roman Nose State Resort Park, which is located in a large canyon on the west side of Lake Watonga. The pro shop takes calls beginning at 7 am for tee times up to three days in advance. The pro shop phone is ☎ 580-623-7989; and the resort number is ☎ 580-623-7281.

❏ Guymon

Sunset Hills Golf Course, ☎ 580-338-7404, two blocks west of US-54 on Sunset Lane, is an 18-hole course with 6,236 total yards. The greens are bent grass; par is 71, with a slope of 115 and a USGA rating of 70.1. Green fees are $12 on weekends and holidays, $9 on weekdays. Carts rent for $8 for nine holes and $16 for 18 holes.

❏ Woodward

Boiling Springs Golf Course, ☎ 580-256-1206, east on SH-34C north of town in the state park, is an 18-hole course with 6,511 total yards and a par of 71. Don Sechrest designed the course, which is surrounded by trees. The USGA rating is 69.6 and the slope rating is 117. Green fees are $16 for all-day play Friday through Sunday, and $11 for play from Monday at noon through Thursday. Cars rent for $16 for 18 holes and $8 for nine holes.

On Wheels

Biking

 It takes a certain type of cyclist to enjoy the far corners of the northwest panhandle, but if you're that type, you'll have some marvelous bike trips. Facilities are scarce and far between, but the wide open wildness of the place makes many bikers' hearts beat faster. A tamer ride is possible farther east, where several state parks and a diversity of natural wonders cluster along routes seemingly built for two-wheel travel.

There are some designated bike trails, but most of the rides suggested here follow paved or graveled roads with little motor traffic. Along the way, you'll find plenty of ranch roads and narrow paths leading to something spectacular, or maybe nothing at all. When bikers get together, the stories they tell most passionately are about solo rides with unplanned itineraries, and this section of the state provides abundant opportunity for just that sort of trip.

❏ Panhandle

Start in Boise on a fall morning, and head west on SH-325 toward **Lake Etling** and **Black Mesa**. There isn't much to see – and that's the point. Notice the wildflowers and yucca, but pay special attention to the way the road goes forever and then meets the cloudless sky. And listen to the silence. Awesome.

Stop at Lake Etling and Black Mesa State Park for a picnic and rest – the elevation is 4,400 feet here, so expect to feel more winded than usual. You may even decide to camp overnight and ride to Black Mesa the next day.

When you're ready, push on another 15 miles to the mesa and nature preserve. You'll gain another 573 feet of elevation as you travel closer to the state's highest point. Turn right onto black-topped Colorado Road and follow it to a parking lot, where a trail leads up the butte. The hike up and back takes four to six hours, and camping is not allowed in the nature preserve, so watch the time and be out by dusk. If you don't have time – or energy – to tackle the hike, ride on to the Dinosaur Quarries where tons of fossilized dinosaur bones have been excavated since the 1930s. You can also explore the rock formations in the area, and hunt for prehistoric markings on the canyon walls.

❏ Four Bizarre Sites

This multi-day route covers about 90 miles and includes four of the strangest sites in the state. Start at **Alabaster State Park,** where you can warm up with a walking tour of the world's largest publicly accessible gypsum cave. Cycle south on SH-50 about 18 miles to Mooreland, where you go west for five miles to **Boiling Springs State Park**. The park contains cold springs that bubble up to the surface in a boiling action. There are tall trees here on the north side of a valley along the North Canadian River, which makes this a pleasant place to break for lunch or camp overnight.

Continue the trip by returning to Mooreland and picking up US-412 going east. At the junction of US-281/SH-14, turn north and pedal eight miles to **Little Sahara State Recreation Area**. The attraction here is

1,800 acres of sand dunes, and you'll have to catch a ride on something with a motor to make it through off-road areas.

At this point, you can continue north on SH-14 to US-64 and turn west to get back to your starting point on SH-50, or go back south to the junction of US-412 and turn east. Soon after the junction, you will begin to see the **Glass Mountains** in the distance. The road is a little steeper here, but the shiny red mesas and the "painted" landscape around them are worth the effort. The quickest way back to Alabaster State Park is US-412 west to SH-50, where you turn north.

If you're pumped up and want to take the long route, go back to US-281/SH-14 and take it north to US-64. You'll go past the dunes again, but maybe they'll look different to you this time through. (They're called the "walking hills" because of their penchant for wandering about when no one's looking). Take a break in **Waynoka**, just north of the sand pile, to see the paintings created by German World War II POWs, who were held in the basement of Congregational Church. The art was discovered hidden in the walls in the 1980s, and some of the artists have traveled from Germany to see where their art hangs in the church museum.

When you get to **Freedom**, at the junction of US-64 and SH-50, slow down to see the cedar-fronted buildings on Main Street. This is the site of the annual Old Cowhand Reunion every August, and the town has gone to the trouble of creating the appearance of an early frontier community. When you turn south on SH-50, you'll be in the final stretch – only six miles to Alabaster State Park.

☐ Roman Nose State Park

Leave your car at Roman Nose State Park, seven miles north of Watonga. From here you can map out several short or long road trips or just ride the narrow six-mile **Wineglass Trail** through the park. This multi-use loop is taken over by "Slime Fest" every October, and knowledgeable mountain bikers say the route is a wild-west thriller. Gypsum bluffs. Beautiful canyons. Western-movie scenery.

Wineglass links up with other multi-use trails to create a total of 10 miles of riding inside the park. However, if you crave the open road, head south on SH-8 to **Watonga**. This is a fine town with several options for refreshment, including a cheese factory at 314 East Second Street. From here you can take on the hills near the North Canadian River on

SH-51A, or try the longer route west on US-270, then north on SH-58. The prettiest ride is simply back the way you came on SH-8.

❏ Foss Lake State Park

Mountain bikers have a wide choice in the ranching area around Foss Lake State Park and **Washita Wildlife Refuge** between the towns of Hammon and Butler. **Warrior Trail** crosses rolling prairie and wooded ravines for about 14 miles in the southern part of the park, and a network of dirt paths and old oil-field roads are open in the refuge. Most of the park trail is beginner-level, but one three-mile stretch along the south shore of Foss Lake is rough-intermediate. To get to the refuge from the park, go north on SH-44 to SH-33, turn west and watch for the entrance on the south side of the road. Traffic will probably be light unless it's a holiday, but there are no shoulders on either state road, so plan accordingly. If you want to extend the road ride, do the entire 36-mile route from Foss State Park north on SH-44, west past the refuge on SH-33, south on SH-34, then east on SH-73 to the junction of SH-44.

Motorcycles & Off-Road Vehicles

❏ Little Sahara State Park

Four miles south of Waynoka off US-281, the hills are alive with the sound of motors. Dune buggies, motorcycles, and 4x4s roar over 1,200 acres of quartz-sand hills that mound as high as 75 feet. If you own your own off-road vehicle, entrance fees are $5 per vehicle per day or $10 per vehicle for a three-day pass. The park is never closed, but quiet hours are observed from 11 pm to 7 am, so don't plan to ride the dunes during those hours.

You don't have to miss the fun if you don't own an ORV. Six-passenger dune buggies are available for 45-minute guided rides through parts of the park that can only be reached by ORV. This multi-passenger ride may be rather calm for experienced off-roaders since the driver/guide controls the speed and route, but the trip up and down the dunes is thrilling enough for most.

Rides are available Monday through Friday from 9 am to 5 pm, Saturday and Sunday from 8 am to 10 pm, at a cost of $6 per adult and $4 per child.

The park entrance is on the west side of SH-281, 10 miles north of the junction with SH-412. Arrange for dune buggy rides and pick up ORV regulations at the office near the entrance, ☎ 580-824-1471.

❒ Beaver State Park

Off-road vehicles are allowed on almost 300 acres of sand dunes at **Beaver State Park**, north of the Panhandle town of Beaver. Fewer people come to this part of the state, so the ORV trails here are less busy than at Little Sahara. You can ride from 7 am to 10 pm daily, but you must bring your own vehicle since there are no rentals in the park. From US-270, turn west onto an access road leading to the park – an access road a quarter-mile farther north leads to the campgrounds – ☎ 580-625-3373.

On Horseback

❒ Roman Nose State Park

Experienced horse owners and novice riders will find great horseback adventures at **Roman Nose Resort Park Stables**. This new equestrian facility offers more than 10 miles of trails over rugged terrain in beautiful canyon country.

If you have your own horse, **Pack Saddle Camp** has pens and stock tanks near tent sites. Horse pens are also within walking distance of resort cabins number 13 and 14, and downhill from the resort lodge. Trail maps are available at the stable, and fees are $3 per day per rider. Knowledgeable guides are also available for tours through the countryside at a rate of $10 per hour.

Horses may be rented for a fee of $10 per hour for one to three hours. Guided trail rides are led by a Western character right out of the 19th century, who tells tales of outlaws and lost treasure as you travel the trails through red-shale canyons. One of the most popular rides is a horseback trip to a remote area where dinner is prepared over an open campfire. The meal includes a ribeye steak with all the "fixin's" and costs $40 per person.

For equestrian camping or horseback riding reservations, call ☎ 580-623-4354. Maps and information about the equestrian program are available at the stable north of park headquarters, seven miles north of Watonga on SH-8A.

❏ Foss State Park

Warrior Trail is a multi-use path open to horseback riders along the southwestern shore of **Foss Lake**. Future plans are to expand and improve the trail; the present path is badly overgrown in most spots, but rideable. Eventually, an equestrian campground will be built at **Mouse Creek**, off SH-73, west of SH-44. Check with the park office, ☎ 580-592-4433, for updated information on construction.

The 14-mile **Warrior Trail** crosses open prairie and forested ravines with views of the lake. Stop at the park office on SH-44 near the junction with SH-73 for a map and directions to the trailhead. South Campground, Sandy Beach, Mouse Creek, and Panther Creek recreation areas are linked by the trail, and the best access is from the parking lot at Mouse Creek. There are no rentals at Foss State Park, so riders must bring their own horse.

On Water

 Fishermen and boaters don't give northwestern lakes much respect – and that's regrettable, but probably justified. With few exceptions, the lakes in this region are small, shallow, underdeveloped, and understocked. However, the US Army Corps of Engineers operates a system of three lakes within the North Canadian River Basin, and the state maintains facilities at three additional lakes.

If you have a choice, haul your boat and fishing gear to another part of the state. But, if you're in this region for one of its many other attributes, you might try **Canton Lake**, north of Roman Nose State Park off SH-58, or **Foss Lake**, a decent-sized reservoir, which sneaks into the northwest category by being two miles north of I-40. **Great Salt Plains Lake** within the National Wildlife Refuge is another choice. It's stocked, but boating is restricted in some areas at various times.

Rivers in this area offer solitary floats through scenic areas – if there's been enough rain. Fishing in these streams is fair to good, depending on the season. The best opportunity for river fun in the northwest is during the spring.

❏ Canton Lake

This 7,950-acre high plains lake is the best place in the state for walleye fishing. In fact, walleye eggs from Canton Lake are sent to fish hatcheries for stocking other lakes. Anglers also have a fair chance of hooking largemouth bass, hybrid striped bass, crappie, and channel catfish. Boat ramps and other facilities are available at **Big Bend** (west side), ☎ 580-886-3576; **Cheyenne-Arapaho Park** (west side), ☎ 580-262-0345; **Canadian Campground** (south end), ☎ 580-886-3454; **Sandy Cove** (east side), ☎ 580-274-3576; **Longdale** (east side), ☎ 580-886-2989. Pick up maps and information at the project office, north on SH-58A a mile off SH-51 west of Canton, ☎ 580-886-2989. The best source of supplies is in Watonga, about 16 miles south on SH-51A.

Float trips are possible from the Canton Wildlife Management Area down the **North Canadian River** to the lake. Fishermen like this trip in late spring when the sand bass are plentiful. The entire trip from the wildlife area to the lake takes about two hours.

☐ Foss Lake

Washita National Wildlife Refuge surrounds Foss Lake, the largest body of water in western Oklahoma. Walleye, bass, hybrid bass, and crappie are abundant in the 8,800-acre lake, along with catfish and bluegill. Recent improvements at the state park include additional campsites, new access roads, and an enlarged marina. Stop at the park office on SH-44 at the south end of the lake for a map and information, ☎ 580-592-4433. The state plans to expand its facilities here, so be sure to ask about new developments.

Marina Del Rey, in the main park at the south end of the lake, is open year-round, ☎ 580-592-4577. Besides the usual supplies and boat stalls, the marina also offers boat rentals, an indoor heated fishing dock, and a floating restaurant – the **Portside Café**, ☎ 580-592-4490. More boat ramps are located at **Mouse Creek, Sandy Beach** and **Panther Creek** on the west side of the lake off SH-73. East side ramps are at **Cutberth** and **Northside** campgrounds off SH-44, and supplies are available at **Toot's Bait House** near the east-side overlook, ☎ 580-664-5781.

The Washita National Wildlife Refuge, ☎ 580-664-2205, oversees the north end of the lake, and there are various public use areas along the shore.

Northwest Oklahoma

❐ Great Salt Plains Lake & The Salt Fork River

This 8,690-acre lake is shallow – about four feet in many spots most of the time – so boaters often have a tough time here. However, there are ramps in the **South Spillway Area** and the **Sandy Beach I & II Areas** in the state park off SH-38. Channel catfish and saugeye fishing are fair to good; striped bass, and blue catfish have been stocked in the lake by the Wildlife Department. A handicapped-accessible fishing dock is at the South Spillway near the park office, ☎ 580-626-4731. Swimming is allowed at Sandy Beach I on the north side of the park, but there is no lifeguard. For more information and maps, contact the Wildlife Refuge, ☎ 580-626-4794, or the Recreational Development Association, ☎ 580-596-3053.

If you have your own equipment, you can float the **Salt Fork River** from below the dam on SH-38 to Pond Creek. Depending on the river flow and how hard you paddle, this trip will take about five leisurely hours.

❐ Notes on Lesser Lakes & Rivers

Roman Nose Resort is a terrific park with two pretty lakes, 83-acre **Lake Watonga** and eight-acre **Lake Boecher**. Fish for white bass, black bass, and crappie year-round and for trout during the winter. The resort rents paddleboats and canoes. Contact the park office at ☎ 580-623-4215 and the resort at ☎ 580-623-7281.

Fort Supply Lake stretches for eight miles over 1,820 acres from a dam on Wolf Creek about 12 miles northwest of the town of Woodward. The outstanding feature here is natural white sand beaches. Fish species include largemouth bass, crappie, white bass, walleye, and catfish. Boat ramps are located at **Supply Park** and **Cottonwood Point**, south of the Corps of Engineer project office, ☎ 580-766-2701, and at **Beaver Point**, east on the dam road.

Float trips are possible on **Wolf Creek,** just below Fort Supply Lake all the way to the **North Canadian River**. Put in for this six-hour trip at the bridge on US-270 and take out at the bridge north of Woodward on SH-34.

Near the town of Aline, you can begin a day-long river trip on **Eagle Chief Creek**. Put in at the bridge on SH-8B and float to the bridge on US-412 at the **Cimarron River,** just past the town of Cleo Springs.

Visitors to Black Mesa State Park can boat and fish at 159-acre **Lake Carl Etling**, ☎ 580-426-2222. The lake is stocked with trout and ice fishing is popular during the winter. The Corps of Engineers operates facilities at Hardesty Point on the south side of **Optima Lake**, ☎ 580-888-4226, off SH-3 east of the panhandle town of Guymon. The **Black Kettle National Grasslands** near Cheyenne include **Dead Indian**, **Skip-Out**, and **Spring Creek Lakes**. For maps and information, contact the National Grassland office in Cheyenne, ☎ 580-497-2143.

■ Where to Stay

Hotels, Inns & Ranches

Aline

Heritage Manor, ☎ 580-463-2563 or 800-295-2563, is one mile east of Sod House on SH-8 between Aline and Cleo Springs. This rambling turn-of-the-century house has four guest rooms with private baths, eight staircases, three decks, and a rooftop hot tub. Breakfast is served in one of the two parlors each morning, and arrangements may be made for lunch, dinner, high tea, and special occasions. Rates are $55 for one person, $75 for two people, and $150 for a suite.

Cheyenne

Coyote Hills Ranch, ☎ 580-497-3931. Follow the signs on SH-47 west of town to this guest ranch with an air-conditioned bunkhouse. Built with guests in mind, this Old West spread sits at the edge of Black Kettle National Grasslands in rugged red hills filled with wildlife. The ranch has a bunkhouse with 20 rooms (all with private baths), five tepees, and a social barn with a theater and library. Guests may use the mountain bikes, ride the horses, and relax in the hot-tub. Five times each year, the ranch leads wagon-train trips. Rates are $150 per person per day in the bunkhouse and $100 per person per day in the tepees. The prices include meals and activities.

Enid

Island Guest Ranch, ☎ 580-753-4574, 35 miles southwest of Enid on an island in the Cimarron River, accepts guests from April 1 through September 30. This 3,000-acre working ranch is run by *real* cowboy Carl White and his family. It features rooms with two queen-sized beds and private baths. Guests participate in horseback riding, square dancing, powwows, and – if they want to – actual chores such as feeding and penning the livestock. Rates are $70 per person per day and include everything from buffet meals to a choice of activities.

Worthington House, ☎ 580-237-9202, 1224 West Maine, is a three-story house built in 1906 and decorated with antiques. Guest rooms have private baths and a gourmet breakfast is served each morning. Rates are in the $75 range.

Keyes, Near Boise City

Cattle County Inn, ☎ 580-543-6458, off US-64 between Guymon and Boise City, is really, really out in the country, and you'll want to get good directions when you call for reservations. There are six guest rooms with semi-private baths (two rooms share one bathroom), and a big family-style breakfast is served each morning. Room rates are $40 to $70.

Mooreland

Three Sisters Inn, ☎ 580-994-6003, 609 South Laird, is on the National Register of Historic Places. There are four guest rooms with private baths, and a full breakfast is served each morning. Rates range from $45 to $60.

Watonga

Kennedy Kottage, ☎ 580-623-4384 or 800-511-0141, 1017 North Prouty, is a two-story house with two guest rooms. Each room has a private bath, a queen-sized bed, and a TV. Guests are served a full breakfast each morning in the dining room or on the patio. Room rates begin at $65.

Redbud Manor, ☎ 580-623-8587, fax 580-623-4549, 900 North Burford, is a unique house enclosed by a rock wall and surrounded by big trees. There are flowering gardens, a swimming pool, and a full breakfast is served each morning. Ask about the Garden Suite, which opens onto a patio. Rates are in the $75 range.

Woodward

The Anna Augusta Inn, ☎ 580-254-5400 or 800-864-8320, fax 580-254-3388, 2612 Lakeview Drive on the east side of town, is a restored 1904 house with four guest rooms. They claim "the most comfortable beds in town," and the bathrooms have claw-foot tubs. Breakfast is served each morning. Guests can make reservations for other meals at the Inn. Lunch is served Monday through Thursday, and dinner is served on Friday and Saturday. Room rates include breakfast and range from $65 to $85.

Adams Farms, ☎ 580-866-3344, is south of town off SH-34. This log cabin sleeps up to six, and breakfast is brought to the door each morning. Rates are $65.

Guest Ranches & Cattle Drives

Boise

 West End Roping, **Inc.**, ☎ 580-426-2723, begins their cattle drives and chuckwagon dinner rides in Boise. The three-day cattle drives are a city slicker's dream. Everyone pitches in to round 'em up and move 'em out, then real cowboys take the fake cowboys on sightseeing tours of unusual places in No Man's Land. Guests hunt for dinosaur bones and relics from ancient civilizations, then chow down on meals cooked over an open fire and sleep under the stars (tents are also available). The cattle drives take place from May until September. Everything is provided. The three-day package price is about $500 per person.

Rosston

Lotspeich Cattle Company, ☎ 580-533-4718, is northwest of Woodward, near the town of Laverne at the eastern edge of the Panhandle. Ask for detailed directions when you call for reservations. This ranch is different from most guest ranches because visitors just dive right into daily life on the open range. If it's time to brand the new calves, guests can help. If it's harvest season, they can bale hay. Of course, all this labor is optional, and if you'd rather float in the swimming pool, that's fine, too. Guests eat with the family in the dining room and may ride one of the ranch horses.

Woodward

Dewey County Great Western Cattle Drive, ☎ 580-995-3120, is organized by the South Canadian River Cattle Company to benefit historic renovation in Dewey County and college scholarships for area students. The three-day cattle drive takes place the first weekend in June, and everyone helps move about 200 cows eight to 10 miles each day. Bring your own horse, or ride in one of the wagons. Participants supply their own camping equipment, but meals are provided. The cost is $145 for adults and $85 for kids under 17.

Camping

Woodward

 Boiling Springs State Park, ☎ 580-256-7664, on SH-34C north of town, has four one-bedroom cabins that sleep up to four people each. Each cabin has a living area, kitchen, fireplace, and a TV. Rates are $43. There are also RV hookups and tent sites in two camping areas. Rates are $6 to $17.

Jet

Great Salt Plains, ☎ 580-626-4731, on SH-38 north of town, has five one-bedroom cabins that sleep up to four people each, and a larger cabin will accommodate up to six people. Each cabin has a kitchen and living area. The rate for the one-bedroom studios is $43. The larger cabin rents for $53. There are also 171 campsites in three areas. Rates begin at $6 for a tent site, and go up to $17 for a modern RV site.

■ Where to Eat

Enid

 $$/$$$ **The Sage Room**, ☎ 580-233-1212, 1927 South Van Buren, is a special place for a special occasion – and you should arrive early if you don't want to wait for a table on weekends. Steak and seafood are the most popular entrées, but some customers

drive long distances for the stir-fry meals. Live piano music plays in the background, and candlelight shines on white tablecloths. Dress up a bit for this place. Dinner is served Monday through Thursday from 5:30 pm to 9:30 pm and weekends from 5:30 pm to 10 pm.

$ **Best of the Orient**, ☎ 580-234-2737, 518 South Van Buren, has a huge selection of oriental dishes. The atmosphere is casual and the price of a complete meal is in the $5 to $10 range.

$$/$$$ **High Voltage**, ☎ 580-237-3224, 3205 South Van Buren, is only open Friday and Saturday from 5:30 pm to 10 pm. This bistro-style restaurant specializes in custom-cut steaks, but also has seafood and pasta on the menu.

Guymon

$ **LeAnn's**, ☎ 580-338-8025, 205 East 2nd Street, has sandwiches and hot daily specials. Lunch and dinner are served every day from 11 am to 9 pm. Save room for the homemade pie.

$/$$ **Eddie's Steak and Seafood**, ☎ 580-338-5330, 421 Village Shopping Center on SH-54 and East Street, is known for serving the best steak and seafood in town. Dinner is served from 4 pm until midnight, Tuesday through Saturday, and Monday from 4 pm to 10 pm.

Watonga

$ **Noble House Restaurant**, ☎ 580-623-2559, 112 North Noble Avenue, is a renovated boarding house. Built in 1912, the two-story, red brick house has three dining rooms, and is often crowded. The menu features a variety of soups, salads, sandwiches, and hot entrées, but the local favorite is cheese soup made from hometown Watonga cheddar. Open from 11 am to 2 pm Monday through Saturday and 11:30 am to 3 pm on Sunday for lunch. Dinner is served Thursday through Saturday from 5 pm to 9 pm.

Woodward

$ **Rib Ranch**, ☎ 580-256-6081, 2424 Williams Avenue, is a log-cabin-style restaurant that serves giant portions of barbecue in a family atmosphere. Lunch is served Tuesday through Friday from 11 am to 2 pm, Saturday from 11 am to 5 pm, and Sunday from 11 am to 5 pm. Dinner hours are Tuesday through Saturday from 5 pm to 9 pm and Sunday from 5 pm to 7 pm.

■ Where to Shop

Enid

 Robert Bartunek Winery, ☎ 580-233-6337, 1920 South Cleveland off US-412, gives tours on Friday and Saturday from 1 to 5 pm. A small shop that sells its own wine and other Oklahoma-made products is open during touring hours or "whenever the yellow flag is flying." If you're in the area at another time, call to ask about a private tour and tasting. The soil in this area that produces excellent wheat also grows a fine vine.

Okeene

Lorenz Seeds, ☎ 580-822-3491, next to the only stoplight in town, is famous for Oklahoma wildflower seeds. Workers go into the local fields and pastures to gather Indian blanket, Indian grass, and Indian paintbrush seeds, which are sold at the shop. Hours are 8 am to 5 pm, Monday through Saturday, closed for lunch from noon to 1pm.

Kenton

Kenton Mercantile, ☎ 580-261-7447, is near Black Mesa on SH-325. Part general store, part museum, Mercantile has been the center of life in Kenton since 1898. Stop in for information about local sites and a cold drink or snack. Check out the unusual stuff sitting around the store – and fill your gas tank for the long trip back east.

Kingfisher

Antique Mall, ☎ 580-375-3288, on US-81 north of El Reno, is an old house filled with antiques, gifts, and collectibles. Shoppers and browsers are welcome from 10 am to 5:30 pm, Tuesday through Saturday, and Sunday from 1 to 5:30 pm.

Watonga

The Place To Be, ☎ 580-623-2451, 110 North Noble, is a day spa featuring massages, facials, manicures, and pedicures. For a real treat, try reflexology – it's more than a foot rub, and the ultimate relaxation. Services are provided Tuesday through Friday from 10 am to 5 pm and Monday from 10 am to 2 pm.

Woodward

Trego's Westwear Outlet, ☎ 580-254-2379, 2215 South Oklahoma Street, has bargains on Western-style suits and rodeo shirts. Over the years, Trego's Factory has made clothes for Roy Rogers and Vince Gill. Call ahead for outlet hours.

■ Powwows, Festivals, Arts & Crafts Fairs

February

 Watonga/Roman Nose Resort Park Bitter Creek Frontier Daze, ☎ 580-623-7281, usually held the end of February. Historical re-enactors become cowboys, outlaws, soldiers, and lawmen to depict lifestyles and events in Oklahoma between 1830 and 1890. Characters set up Indian and buffalo hunters' camps, moonshiner stills, and outlaw hideouts in the woods so visitors can wander through history. This event includes an indoor arts and crafts sale.

April

Cimarron Territory Celebration, ☎ 580-625-4726, brings international attention to the Panhandle town of Beaver about the third week of April each year. This week-long event has been taking place since 1969 and includes bike races, a chili cookoff, and a concert. But the real attention-getter is the **World Championship Cow Chip Throwing Contest**. Yes, regular folks who act pretty normal most of the year get together and toss cow poop. The person who slings the stuff the farthest is named the World Champion Cow Chip Thrower – a coveted honor. Contestants follow strict guidelines, and the competition's nasty.

May

Okeene's Rattlesnake Hunt, ☎ 580-822-3005, is held the first weekend in May to coincide with the rattlesnakes' annual emergence from hibernation. Teams of hunters prowl around snaky spots with long, hook-end poles looking for sleep-happy rattlers. Anyone who is bitten, and lives to brag about it, is inducted into the prestigious White Fang Club. The team or person who captures the most or longest rattlesnakes is, of course, the Snake Hunt Champion. If you dare show up in Okeene on the first weekend in May, stop by The Den of Death to see live snakes, and try a batter-fried snake-meat treat from one of the street vendors. It does *not* taste "just like chicken."

Guymon Pioneer Days, ☎ 580-338-3376, is held the first weekend in May to honor early settlers and celebrate the Organic Act of 1890, which made the Panhandle part of Oklahoma. There are 5K runs, cookouts, a Professional Rodeo Cowboys Association competition, and an arts and crafts fair. Don't miss the Cowboy Breakfast.

July

Woodward Elks Rodeo, ☎ 800-364-5352, is one of the oldest rodeos in the state, and some of its winners move on to the National Finals Rodeo held by the Professional Rodeo Cowboys Association. This is a great place to see soon-to-be-nationally-famous performers. A parade and Western art show are part of the early-July activities.

August

Freedom Old Cowhand Reunion, ☎ 580-621-3276, is an annual tribute to cowboys past and present. Festivities begin with a no-charge Western dinner in the park. Later, the small town's residents re-enact (almost accurately) the historical "Great Freedom Bank Robbery and Shootout." The reunion winds up with a rodeo at sunset, followed by Country-Western dancing.

October

Watonga Cheese Festival, ☎ 580-623-5452. Usually held the first week in October, this fair includes food contests, frontier re-enactments and, of course, lots of cheese tasting.

Watonga/Roman Nose Resort Park Mountain Bike Festival and Races, ☎ 580-528-3101. This event includes trail rides, downhill races, and other sports contests. Call for exact dates – usually late in the month – and registration information.

November

Fairview Mennonite Relief Sale, ☎ 580-227-2701, at the Major County Fairgrounds, 200 East Bellman, features an auction on the Saturday morning after Thanksgiving. Sale items include handmade quilts, furniture, and toys. The event begins Friday evening with a dinner, live music, and a craft fair. All proceeds from the two-day event go to the worldwide hunger relief programs sponsored by the Mennonite Central Committee.

Northwest Oklahoma

Index

Accommodations: *Edmond, 54*; *Guthrie, 56*; *Jenks, 70*; *Norman, 48-49*; *Northeast Oklahoma, 111-16*; *Oklahoma City, 39-41*; *prices, 5*; *Sapulpa, 70*; *Shawnee, 52*; *Southeast Oklahoma, 177-82*; *Southwest Oklahoma, 189, 223-25*; *Tulsa, 67-68*
Ada, *183*
Adventures: *Northeast Oklahoma, 89-111*; *Northwest Oklahoma, 238-55*; *Oklahoma, 11-18*; *Oklahoma City, 37-39*; *Southeast Oklahoma, 141-76*; *Southwest Oklahoma, 203-23*; *top adventures, 9*; *Tulsa, 64-66*
Afton/Monkey Island, *111, 117*
Air travel. *See* Transportation
Alabaster Caverns, *233, 240, 244-46*
Alabaster Caverns State Park, *235, 250*
Altus, *202*; *accommodations, 223-24*; *golf, 212-13*; *shopping, 229*
Amber, *226*
Anadarko, *194-96, 213, 229*
Antique cars, *51, 63-64, 194*
Antlers, *139-40*
Apache (town), *229*
Arbuckle Mountains, *127, 134-35*
Arcadia, *52-54*
Ardmore, *135, 177, 183*
Artists, *29, 46*
Ataloa Art Lodge, *89*

Barnsdall, *73*
Bartlesville, *73*; *accommodations, 111-12*; *golf, 94*; *restaurants, 118*; *shopping, 120-21*
Bats, *245, 246-47*
Beard Cabin, *50*
Beaver River, *243*
Beaver State Park, *253*
Beavers Bend, *127*; *accommodations, 177-79*; *restaurants, 183-84*
Beavers Bend State Park, *145-46, 159*

Bessie, *230*
Biking: *Northeast Oklahoma, 95-100*; *Northwest Oklahoma, 249-52*; *Oklahoma, 11-12*; *Southeast Oklahoma, 157-61*; *Southwest Oklahoma, 214-18*
Billings, *112*
Bivin Garden, *79*
Black Kettle National Grasslands, *242-43*
Black Mesa, *233, 235-36, 244, 250*
Black Mesa Nature Preserve, *235-36*
Boating, *15-16, 37*
Bob Townsend's Antique and Classic Cars, *51*
Boiling Springs State Park, *233, 239-40, 250*
Boise City, *235*
Bricktown, *31-32*
Broken Bow, *177-79, 184*
Broken Bow Lake, *17, 166-69*
Buffalo, *78, 205*

Campgrounds: *Edmond and Arcadia, 53-54*; *Norman, 47-48*; *Northeast Oklahoma, 117*; *Southeast Oklahoma, 182-83*; *Southwest Oklahoma, 201, 226*
Canadian River Valley, *196*
Canoeing, *16, 86*
Canton Lake, *254-55*
Canute, *193*
Capitol Complex, *27-28*
Car rentals, *7*
Carnegie, *229*
Cathedral of the Osage, *79*
Cave exploring, *209, 211, 244-46*
Chandler, *112*
Charons Garden Wilderness, *201, 203*
Checotah, *112*
Cherokee Heritage Center, *84*
Cherokee National Museum/Adams Corner, *84*
Cherokee Queen (paddlewheel), *85*
Chickasaw National Recreation Area, *135, 151-53*

Chickasha, 194
Chickasha Antique Auto Museum of Transportation, 194
Chief's Knoll, 197
Cimarron Valley Winery, 127, 140
Circus City USA, 132
Civic Center Music Hall, 30
Claremore, 86-87; accommodations, 112-13; restaurants, 118; shopping, 121
Clayton, 179
Clear Creek Lake, 223
Cleveland County Historical House, 47
Climate, 18-19
Clinton, 192-93; accommodations, 224; golf, 213; restaurants, 227; shopping, 229-30
Coleman Theatre, 86
Cookson Hills, 83, 96
Cordell, 224, 227
Crystal-digging, 247-48

Daisey, Nanita, 53
Davis, 135, 136, 179-80
Dewey, 77
Dewey Hotel, 77
Dog Iron Ranch, 73
Duncan, 225, 230
Durant, 133, 180, 184

Eagle Fork Creek, 170-71
Eagle's Nest Trail, 93
Edmond, 52-54
El Reno, 225, 227
Elk City, 193, 214, 225, 227
Elk Mountain, 201, 207
Elsing Museum, 63
Erick, 193-94, 227, 230
Eufaula, 186

Fairland, 113
Fenster Museum of Jewish Art, 63
Festivals and events, 9; Native American festivals, 9, 35, 123, 124-25, 195, 232; Northeast Oklahoma, 123-25; Northwest Oklahoma, 237; Oklahoma City, 33, 34; Sand Springs, 70-71; Southeast Oklahoma, 132, 138-39, 187-88; Southwest Oklahoma, 231-32
Fishing, 17, 21
Five Civilized Tribes Museum, 88-89

Floyd, Charles "Pretty Boy", 83
On Foot, adventures: Northeast Oklahoma, 89-95; Northwest Oklahoma, 238-49; Oklahoma, 13-15; Southeast Oklahoma, 141, 143-57; Southwest Oklahoma, 203, 205, 207-14
Fort Cobb, 213
Fort Cobb Lake, 221
Fort Gibson, 94-95
Fort Gibson Lake, 97, 108-9
Fort Sill, 189, 197, 216-17
Fort Towson, 132
Fort Washita, 133-34
45th Infantry Division Museum, 36
Foss Lake, 255
Foss Lake State Park, 252, 254
Frank Phillips' home, 77
Frankoma Pottery, 70
Fred Jones Jr. Museum of Art, 46
Fuqua Lake, 223

Gardens, 30-31, 35, 79, 86, 137
Geronimo, 197, 198
Gerrer, Father Gregory, 51
Gilcrease Museum, 60-61
Glass Mountains, 241-42, 251
Glover River, 169-70
Golf, 14; Edmond, 54; Guthrie, 55-56; Jenks, 69; Norman, 48; Northeast Oklahoma, 94-95; Northwest Oklahoma, 248-49; Oklahoma, 14; Oklahoma City, 38-39; Sapulpa, 70; Shawnee, 51; Southeast Oklahoma, 154-57; Southwest Oklahoma, 212-14; Tulsa, 65-66
Gore, 113
Grand Lake, 95, 102
Grand Lake o' the Cherokees, 73, 85, 98, 107-8
Great Salt Plains, 233
Great Salt Plains Lake, 236
Great Salt Plains State Park, 221-22, 236-37, 241
Greenleaf Lake Trail, 91-93
Grove: accommodations, 113-14; restaurants, 119; shopping, 121
Guthrie, 54, 55-57
Guymon, 249

Har-Ber Village, 85
Harn Homestead, 28

Harrison, Benjamin, *26*
Henryetta, *114*
Hiking: *Northeast Oklahoma, 89-94; Northwest Oklahoma, 238-44; Oklahoma, 13-14; Southeast Oklahoma, 141, 143-54; Southwest Oklahoma, 203, 205, 207-9*
History: *Oklahoma, 10-11; Oklahoma City, 26-27*
Holy City, *200-201*
Honey Creek, *174*
Horseback riding: *Norman, 48; Northeast Oklahoma, 101-2; Northwest Oklahoma, 253-54; Oklahoma, 18; Southeast Oklahoma, 161-65; Southwest Oklahoma, 218-19*
Hugo, *132-33; accommodations, 180; restaurants, 184; shopping, 186-87*
Humphries Lake, *223*

I-44/Arkansas River Triangle, *96-98*
Ida Dennie Willis Museum, *61*
Idabel, *132, 184*
Illinois River, *73, 96, 103-5*
Indian City USA, *194*
International Photography Hall of Fame, *36*
International Professional Rodeo Association, *32*

J. M. Davis Historical Arms Museum, *87*
Jacobson House, *46*
Jay, *85*
Jean-Pierre Chouteau Trail, *89, 91, 98, 101-2*
Jenks, *69-70*
Jet, *236-37*
Jewish art museum, *63*

Kaw Lake, *99-100, 101, 109-10*
Kayaking, *16*
Kerr Beach, *81*
Keystone Lake, *101*
Kirkpatrick Center Museum Complex, *35*
Kirkpatrick Conservatory and Botanical Gardens, *35*
Krebs, *137, 185*

La Quinta (house), *77*
LaFortune Park, *65*

Lake Altus-Lugert, *219-20*
Lake of the Arbuckles, *153, 175-76*
Lake Arcadia, *53*
Lake Carl Etling, *235, 250*
Lake Ellsworth, *223*
Lake Eufaula, *137, 150, 176*
Lake Hefner, *37*
Lake Lawtonka, *222*
Lake Murray, *17, 134, 151, 165, 171-72*
Lake Overholser, *37-38*
Lake Tenkiller, *17-18, 83, 97, 105-6*
Lake Texoma, *150-51*
Lake Texoma State Resort Park, *132, 134, 172-74*
Lake Thunderbird, *47*
Lake Tom Steed, *221-22*
Lake Waurika, *208-9, 217, 220-21*
Lake Wister, *159*
Lawton, *196-97, 227, 231*
LenDonwood Gardens, *86*
Little River, *166-69*
Little River State Park, *47, 160*
Little River/Thunderbird State Park, *47, 154, 160*
Little Sahara State Park, *233, 252-53*
Locks, dams, and waterways, *111*
Lone Wolf, *202*

Mabee-Gerrer Museum and Gallery, *51*
McAlester, *137, 185*
McBirney Mansion, *68*
McGee Creek Natural Scenic Recreation Area, *159-60, 164*
McGee Creek Wildlife Management Area, *146-48*
Mac's Antique Car Museum, *63-64*
Mannford, *114*
Maps: *Northeast Oklahoma, 74, 90; Northwest Oklahoma, 234; Southeast Oklahoma, 128, 142; Southwest Oklahoma, 190, 204; Wichita Mountains Wildlife Refuge, 206*
Marietta, *184*
Marland Mansion, *80-81*
Marlow, *228*
Mattie Beal Mansion, *196-97*
Medicine Bluff, *198, 216*
Medicine Park, *198, 215, 228, 231*
Meers, *198, 228*
Miami, *86*

Mix, Tom, 77
Mohawk Park, 64
Monkey Island, 102, 111, 117
Moore-Lindsay House, 46-47
Motorcycles and off-road vehicles
(ORVs): Northeast Oklahoma,
100-101; Northwest Oklahoma,
252-53; Oklahoma, 12; Southeast
Oklahoma, 161; Southwest
Oklahoma, 218
Mount Olivet Cemetery, 132-33
Mount Scott, 200, 201
Mountain Fork River, 166-69
Murrell Home, 83-84
Muscle Car Ranch, 194
Museum of the Great Plains, 197
Museum of the Red River, 132
Music, 30, 36
Muskogee, 88-89; accommodations,
114; golf, 95; restaurants, 119-20;
shopping, 121-22
Myriad Convention Center, 30
Myriad Gardens, 30-31

National Cowboy Hall of Fame, 33-34
National Hall of Fame for Famous
American Indians, 195
Native Americans, 2, 35-36; Bureau of
Indian Affairs, 195; Cherokee history, 84; Choctaw Nation, 127, 129,
133; festivals, 9, 35, 123, 124-25,
195, 232; gaming, 133; Geronimo,
197, 198; Hall of Fame, 195; Kiowa
artists, 46; museums, 51, 80, 88-89,
195; Quanah Parker, 197; Satanta,
122; school, 195; Sequoyah, 81-83;
tribal trivia, 71; villages, 77-78, 194
Norman, 45-49
Northeast Oklahoma, 73; adventures,
89-111; camping, 117; Claremore,
86-87; festivals and events, 123-25;
hotels, resorts, and B&Bs, 111-16;
maps, 74, 90; Muskogee, 88-89;
Osage Hills to Ponca City, 78-81; restaurants, 117-20; Sallisaw to
Tahlequah, 81-85; shopping, 120-22;
Tahlequah to Miami, 85-86; Tulsa to
Bartlesville / Woolaroc, 73, 75-78
Northwest Oklahoma, 233; adventures, 238-55; Boise City to Black
Mesa, 235-36; festivals and events,
237; Jet to Great Salt Plains State

Park, 236-37; map, 234; Watonga to
Roman Nose State Park, 237-38;
Woodward to Alabaster Caverns,
233, 235

Oklahoma, 1-3; adventures, 11-18; climate, 18-19; facts and stats, 3; getting started, 8-10; history, 10-11;
how to use this book, 3-6; maps, 74,
90, 128, 142; money-saving programs, 20; questions and answers, 8;
services and information, 20-23;
state song, 25; top adventures, 9;
transportation, 6-7
Oklahoma Air and Space Museum, 35
Oklahoma City, 25; adventures,
37-39; bed and breakfasts / small
inns, 40-41; festivals and events, 33,
34; history, 26-27; hotels, 39-40;
nearby towns, 45-57; restaurants,
41-43; shopping, 43-45; touring,
27-36
Oklahoma City Zoological Park, 34-35
Omniplex Science Museum, 36
100th Meridian Museum, 193-94
Oologah, 118
Oologah Lake, 100, 107
Osage country, 73
Osage County Historical Museum, 79
Osage Hills, 78-79, 99-100
Osage Hills State Park, 78
Ouachita National Forest, 127, 129,
130-32; accommodations, 181; hik-
ing, 13, 141, 143-45; restaurants,
185
Overholser Mansion, 29
Oxley Nature Center, 64

Panhandle, 250
Parker, Quanah, 197
Paseo, the, 28-29
Pawhuska, 79, 114-15
Philbrook Museum of Art, 60, 62-63
Phillips, Frank, 75-76, 77
Pioneer Woman Museum, 80
Ponca City, 80-81, 115
Ponca City Cultural Center and In-
dian Museum, 80
Potawatomi Tribal Museum, 51
Prairie Song, I.T., 77-78
Price Tower, 76
Quartz Mountain, 189, 202, 212

Quartz Mountain State Park, *207-8*, *217*
Queen Wilhelmina State Park, *130*

Rafting, *16*
Red Earth Indian Center, *35-36*
Red River Valley, *132-34*
Red Rock Canyon, *189, 196, 217-18*
Redbud Valley Nature Preserve, *65*
Restaurants: *Edmond, 54*; *Guthrie, 56-57*; *Norman, 49*; *Northeast Oklahoma, 117-20*; *Oklahoma City, 32, 41-43*; *prices, 5-6*; *Shawnee, 52*; *Southeast Oklahoma, 137-38, 183-86*; *Southwest Oklahoma, 193, 226-28*; *Tulsa, 68-69*
River Parks, *65*
Riverside Indian School, *195*
Robbers Cave State Park, *148-49, 161*
Robber's Roost, *236*
Robert S. Kerr Lake, *81, 96*
Rock climbing and rappeling, *14-15, 209-12*
Rodeo, *32, 33*
Rogers, Will, *86-88, 100, 101*
Roman Nose, *233*
Roman Nose Canyon, *239*
Roman Nose State Park, *238, 251-52, 253*
Round Barn, *52*
Route 66, *189, 191-92*
Route 66 Museum, *192-93*
RS&K Railroad Museum, *193*

Sail and power boating, *15-16, 37*
St. Gregory's College, *50-51*
Saint Joseph's Cathedral, *29*
Saint Paul's Cathedral, *29*
Salina, *115*
Sallisaw, *81-82, 83, 96, 120*
Salt flat treasures, *247*
Sand Spings, *70-71*
Santa Fe Depot Museum (Shawnee), *50*
Santa Fe Depot (Norman), *45*
Santa Fe Trail, *235*
Sapulpa, *70*
Satanta, *122*
Satsuki Gardens, *86*

Scuba diving: *Northeast Oklahoma, 105-6*; *Oklahoma, 17-18*; *Southeast Oklahoma, 168*
Selman Bat Cave, *245, 246*
Sequoyah, *82-83*
Sequoyah National Wildlife Refuge, *83*
Sequoyah State Park, *97, 102*
Sequoyah's Cabin, *81-82, 96*
Services and information, *20-23*
Shawnee, *49-52*
Shidler, *79*
Shin'enKan, *76-77*
Shopping: *Norman, 47*; *Northeast Oklahoma, 120-22*; *Oklahoma City, 43-45*; *Southeast Oklahoma, 186-87*; *Southwest Oklahoma, 193, 229-31*; *Tulsa, 66-67*
Short Mountain Trail, *94, 96*
Showman's Rest area (Mount Olivet Cemetery), *132-33*
Skiatook, *73*
Southeast Oklahoma, *127-29*; *adventures, 141-76*; *B&Bs, lodges, and cabins, 177-82*; *camping, 182-83*; *festivals and events, 132, 138-39, 187-88*; *maps, 128, 142*; *Red River valley, 132-34*; *restaurants, 137-38, 183-86*; *shopping, 186-87*; *spas, 182*; *Talimena Scenic Byway and the Ouachita Forest, 129-32*; *Three Lakes and a Waterfall, 134-37*; *US-69 from Lake Eufaula to Krebs, 137-39*; *US-271 from Talihina to Antlers, 139-40*
Southern Plains Indian Museum, *195*
Southwest Oklahoma, *189*; *adventures, 203-23*; *Anadarko, 194-96*; *camping, 201, 226*; *festivals and events, 231-32*; *hotels and inns, 193, 223-25*; *Lawton, Fort Sill and Wichita Mountain Range, 196-202*; *maps, 190, 204*; *restaurants, 193, 226-28*; *Route 66 from Clinton to Erick, 189, 191-94*; *shopping, 193, 229-31*; *Wichita Mountains to Quartz Mountain, 202*
Spiro, *181*
Spring Creek Park, *53*
Spring River State Park, *86, 98-99*
State Capitol, *27-28*
State Museum of History, *28*

Index

State parks: *lodging, 21; Northeast Oklahoma, 78, 86, 97, 98, 102; Northwest Oklahoma, 233, 235, 237, 238, 239-40, 241, 251-52, 253, 254; Oklahoma City, 47; Southeast Oklahoma, 130, 131, 132, 137, 145-46, 148-49, 161, 172-74, 176; Southwest Oklahoma, 207, 217-18, 221-22*
Stillwater, *115*
Stockyards City, *32-33*
Stroud, *116*
Stuart, *181*
Sulphur, *135, 181, 185-86*

T. B. Ferguson Home, *238*
Tahlequah, *85-86, 96; accommodations, 116; restaurants, 120; shopping, 122*
Talihina, *129, 139*
Talimena Scenic Byway, *127, 129-30, 139*
Tallgrass Prairie Preserve, *73, 78-79*
Tatonka Cabin, *127*
Tenkiller Lake, *17-18, 83, 97, 105-6*
Thunderbird State Park, *47, 154, 160*
Tom Mix Museum, *77*
Trail of Tears Outdoor drama, *84*
Transportation: *airlines, 6; car rentals, 7; trains, 140, 161; travel centers, 6-7*
Treasure, legend of golden, *240-41*
Tsa-La-Gi Ancient Village, *84*
Tsain Saw Hay Valley, *195-96*
Tucker Tower, *134*
Tulsa, *59-60; adventures, 64-66; bed and breakfasts, 68; hotels, 67; nearby areas, 69-71; restaurants, 68-69; shopping, 66-67; touring, 60-64; tudor home, 68*
Tulsa Zoo, *64*
Tulsey Town, *60-64*
Turner Falls, *174*
Twin Bridges State Park, *86, 98-99*

Twin Rock Mountain, *201-2*

United Design Corporation, *47*
University of Oklahoma, *45-46*

Villa Philbrook, *62*

Wagoner, *116*
Washita River, *174-75*
On Water, adventures: *Northeast Oklahoma, 102-11; Northwest Oklahoma, 254-55; Oklahoma, 15-18; Southeast Oklahoma, 165-76; Southwest Oklahoma, 219-23*
Watonga, *237-38, 248-49*
Waurika, *228, 231*
Waurika Lake, *208-9, 217, 220-21*
On Wheels, adventures: *Northeast Oklahoma, 95-101; Northwest Oklahoma, 249-53; Oklahoma, 11-12; Southeast Oklahoma, 157-61; Southwest Oklahoma, 214-18*
Whispering Pines Trail, *93, 98*
Wichita Mountains, *189, 196, 202; biking, 214-16; lakes and rivers, 222-23*
Wichita Mountains Wildlife Refuge, *199-200, 203, 205, 206, 210-11*
Wilburton, *181-82, 186*
Will Rogers Country Centennial Trail, *100, 101*
Will Rogers Memorial, *87*
Winding Stair Mountains, *139, 158-59*
Wister State Park, *148*
Woodward, *233, 249*
Woodward Park, *65*
Woolaroc, *73, 75-76*
Woolaroc Wildlife Preserve, Mansion, and Museum, *73, 76*
Wright, Frank Lloyd, *76*

Zoos, *34-35, 64*

Adventure Guides
from Hunter Publishing

ALASKA HIGHWAY

2nd Edition, Ed & Lynn Readicker-Henderson

"A comprehensive guide.... Plenty of background
history and extensive bibliography."
Travel Reference Library on-line

The fascinating highway that passes settlements of the
Tlingit and the Haida Indians, with stops at Anchor-
age, Tok, Skagway, Valdez, Denali National Park and
more. Sidetrips and attractions en route, plus details
on all other approaches – the Alaska Marine Hwy,
Klondike Hwy, Top-of-the-World Hwy. Color photos.

400 pp, $16.95, 1-55650-824-7

BAHAMAS

2nd Edition, Blair Howard

Fully updated reports for Grand Bahama, Freeport,
Eleuthera, Bimini, Andros, the Exumas, Nassau, New
Providence Island, plus new sections on San Salvador,
Long Island, Cat Island, the Acklins, the Inaguas and
the Berry Islands. Mailboat schedules, package vaca-
tions and snorkeling trips by John Michel Cousteau.

280 pp, $14.95, 1-55650-852-2

EXPLORE BELIZE

4th Edition, Harry S. Pariser

"Down-to-earth advice.... An excellent travel guide."
Library Journal

Extensive coverage of the country's political, social and
economic history, along with the plant and animal life.
Encouraging you to mingle with the locals, Pariser en-
tices you with descriptions of local dishes and festivals.
Maps, color photos.

400 pp, $16.95, 1-55650-785-2

CANADA'S ATLANTIC PROVINCES

Barbara Radcliffe Rogers & Stillman Rogers

Pristine waters, rugged slopes, breathtaking sea-scapes, remote wilderness, sophisticated cities, and quaint, historic towns. Year-round adventures on the Fundy Coast, Acadian Peninsula, fjords of Gros Morne, Viking Trail & Vineland, Saint John River, Lord Balti-more's lost colony. Photos.

672 pp, $19.95, 1-55650-819-0

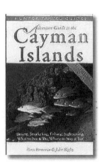

CAYMAN ISLANDS

Paris Permenter & John Bigley

The only comprehensive guidebook to Grand Cayman, Cayman Brac and Little Cayman. Encyclopedic listings of dive/snorkel operators, along with the best sites. En-joy nighttime pony rides on a glorious beach, visit the turtle farms, prepare to get wet at staggering blow-holes or just laze on a white sand beach. Color photos.

224 pp, $16.95, 1-55650-786-0

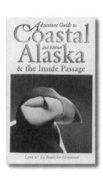

COASTAL ALASKA & THE INSIDE PASSAGE

3rd Edition, Lynn & Ed Readicker-Henderson

"A highly useful book." Travel Books Review

Using the Alaska Marine Highway to visit Ketchikan, Bellingham, the Aleutians, Kodiak, Seldovia, Valdez, Seward, Homer, Cordova, Prince of Wales Island, Ju-neau, Gustavas, Sitka, Haines, Skagway. Glacier Bay, Tenakee. US and Canadian gateway cities profiled.

400 pp, $16.95, 1-55650-859-X

COSTA RICA

3rd Edition, Harry S. Pariser

"... most comprehensive... Excellent sections on na-tional parks, flora, fauna & history." CompuServe

Incredible detail on culture, plants, animals, where to stay & eat, as well as practicalities of travel. E-mail and Website directory.

560 pp, $16.95, 1-55650-722-4

HAWAII

John Penisten

Maui, Molokai, Lanai, Hawaii, Kauai and Oahu are explored in detail, along with many of the smaller, less-visited islands. Full coverage of the best diving, trekking, cruising, kayaking, shopping and more from a Hawaii resident.

420 pp, $16.95, 1-55650-841-7

EXPLORE THE DOMINICAN REPUBLIC

3rd Edition, Harry S. Pariser

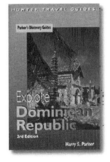

Virgin beaches, 16th-century Spanish ruins, the Caribbean's highest mountain, exotic wildlife, vast forests. Visit Santa Domingo, revel in Sosúa's European sophistication or explore the Samaná Peninsula's jungle. Color.

340 pp, $15.95, 1-55650-814-X

FLORIDA KEYS & EVERGLADES

2nd Edition, Joyce & Jon Huber

"... vastly informative, absolutely user-friendly, chock full of information..." Dr. Susan Cropper

"... practical & easy to use." *Wilderness Southeast*

Canoe trails, airboat rides, nature hikes, Key West, diving, sailing, fishing. Color.

224 pp, $14.95, 1-55650-745-3

FLORIDA'S WEST COAST

Chelle Koster Walton

A guide to all the cities, towns, nature preserves, wilderness areas and sandy beaches that grace the Sunshine State's western shore. From Tampa Bay to Naples and Everglades National Park to Sanibel Island.

224 pp, $14.95, 1-55650-787-9

GEORGIA

Blair Howard

"Packed full of information on everything there is to see and do." *Chattanooga Free Press*

From Atlanta to Savannah to Cumberland Island, this book walks you through antique-filled stores, around a five-story science museum and leads you on tours of old Southern plantations.

296 pp, $15.95, 1-55650-782-8

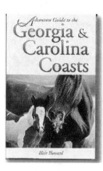

GEORGIA & CAROLINA COASTS

Blair Howard

"Provides details often omitted... geared to exploring the wild dunes, the historic districts, the joys... " *Amazon.com Travel Expert*

Beaufort, Myrtle Beach, New Bern, Savannah, the Sea Islands, Hilton Head and Charleston.

288 pp, $15.95, 1-55650-747-X

GREAT SMOKY MOUNTAINS

Blair Howard

"The take-along guide." *Bookwatch*

Includes overlapping Tennessee, Georgia, Virginia and N. Carolina, the Cherokee and Pisgah National Forests, Chattanooga and Knoxville. Scenic fall drives on the Blue Ridge Parkway.

288 pp, $15.95, 1-55650-720-8

HIGH SOUTHWEST

2nd Edition, Steve Cohen

"Exhaustive detail... [A] hefty, extremely thorough & very informative book." *QuickTrips Newsletter*

"Plenty of maps/detail – an excellent guide." *Bookwatch*

Four Corners of NW New Mexico, SW Colorado, S Utah, N Arizona. Encyclopedic coverage.

376 pp, $15.95, 1-55650-723-2

IDAHO

Genevieve Rowles

Snake River Plain, the Owyhee Mountains, Sawtooth National Recreation Area, the Lost River Range and the Salmon River Mountains. Comprehensive coverage of ski areas, as well as gold-panning excursions and activities for kids, all written by an author with a passion for Idaho.

352 pp, $16.95, 1-55650-789-5

THE LEEWARD ISLANDS

Antigua, St. Martin, St. Barts, St. Kitts, Nevis, Antigua, Barbuda

Paris Permenter & John Bigley

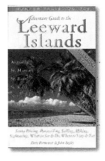

Far outdistances other guides. Recommended operators for day sails, island-hopping excursions, scuba dives, unique rainforest treks on verdant mountain slopes, and rugged four-wheel-drive trails.

248 pp, $14.95, 1-55650-788-7

NEW HAMPSHIRE

Elizabeth L. Dugger

The Great North Woods, White Mountains, the Lakes Region, Dartmouth & Lake Sunapee, the Monadnock region, Merrimack Valley and the Seacoast Region. Beth Dugger finds the roads less traveled.

360 pp, $15.95, 1-55650-822-0

NORTHERN FLORIDA & THE PANHANDLE

Jim & Cynthia Tunstall

From the Georgia border south to Ocala National Forest and through the Panhandle. Swimming with dolphins and spelunking, plus Rails to Trails, a 47-mile hiking/biking path made of recycled rubber.

320 pp, $15.95, 1-55650-769-0

Adventure Guides

ORLANDO & CENTRAL FLORIDA

including Disney World, the Space Coast, Tampa & Daytona

Jim & Cynthia Tunstall

Takes you to parts of Central Florida you never knew existed. Tips about becoming an astronaut (the real way and the smart way) and the hazards of taking a nude vacation. Photos.

300 pp, $15.95, 1-55650-825-5

MICHIGAN

Kevin & Laurie Hillstrom

Year-round activities, all detailed here by resident authors. Port Huron-to-Mackinac Island Sailboat Race, Isle Royale National Park, Tour de Michigan cycling marathon. Also: canoeing, dogsledding and urban adventures.

360 pp, $16.95, 1-55650-820-4

NEVADA

Matt Purdue

Adventures throughout the state, from Winnemucca to Great Basin National Park, Ruby Mountain Wilderness to Angel Lake, from Cathedral Gorge State Park to the Las Vegas strip. Take your pick!

6 x 9 pbk, 256 pp, $15.95, 1-55650-842-

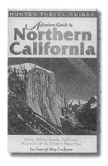

NORTHERN CALIFORNIA

Lee Foster & Mary Lou Janson

Waves lure surfers to Santa Cruz; heavy snowfall attracts skiers to Lake Tahoe; scuba divers relish Monterey Bay; horseback riders explore trails at Mammoth Lake. Travel the Big Sur and Monterey coasts, enjoy views of Yosemite and savor Wine Country. Resident authors.

360 pp, $15.95, 1-55650-821-2

PACIFIC NORTHWEST

Don & Marjorie Young

Oregon, Washington, Victoria and Vancouver in British Columbia, and California north of Eureka. This region offers unlimited opportunities for the adventure traveler. And this book tells you where to find the best of them.

360 pp, $16.95, 1-55650-844-1

PUERTO RICO

3rd Edition, Harry S. Pariser

"A quality book that covers all aspects... it's all here & well done." *The San Diego Tribune*

"... well researched. They include helpful facts... filled with insightful tips." *The Shoestring Traveler*

Crumbling watchtowers and fascinating folklore enchant visitors. Color photos.

344 pp, $15.95, 1-55650-749-6

SIERRA NEVADA

Wilbur H. Morrison & Matt Purdue

California's magnificent Sierra Nevada mountain range. The Pacific Crest Trail, Yosemite, Lake Tahoe, Mount Whitney, Mammoth Lakes, the John Muir Trail, King's Canyon and Sequoia – all are explored. Plus, excellent historical sections. An adventurer's playground awaits!

300 pp, $15.95, 1-55650-845-X

SOUTHEAST FLORIDA

Sharon Spence

Get soaked by crashing waves at twilight; canoe through mangroves; reel in a six-foot sailfish; or watch as a yellow-bellied turtle snuggles up to a gator. Interviews with the experts – scuba divers, sky divers, pilots, fishermen, bikers, balloonists, and park rangers. Color photos.

256 pp, $15.95, 1-55650-811-5

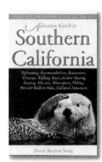

SOUTHERN CALIFORNIA

Don & Marge Young

Browse an art festival, peoplewatch at the beach, sportfish near offshore islands and see world-class performances by street entertainers. The Sierras offer a different adventure, with cable cars ready to whisk you to their peaks. A special section covers daytrips to Mexico.

400 pp, $16.95, 1-55650-791-7

TEXAS

Kimberly Young

Explore Austin, Houston, Dallas/Ft. Worth, San Antonio, Waco and all the places in-between, from Dripping Springs to Marble Falls. Angle for "the big one" at Highland Lakes, or try some offshore fishing. Tramp through the Big Thicket or paddle on Lake Texoma. Photos throughout.

380 pp, $15.95, 1-55650-812-3

VIRGIN ISLANDS

4th Edition, Harry S. Pariser

"Plenty of outdoor options.... All budgets are considered in a fine coverage that appeals to readers." *Reviewer's Bookwatch*

Every island in the Virgins. Valuable, candid opinions. St. Croix, St. John, St. Thomas, Tortola, Virgin Gorda, Anegada. Color.

368 pp, $16.95, 1-55650-746-1

VIRGINIA

Leonard Adkins

The Appalachian Trail winds over the state's eastern mountains. The Great Dismal Swamp offers biking, hiking and canoeing trails, and spectacular wildlife. Skyline Drive and the Blue Ridge Parkway – popular drives in spring and summer. Photos.

420 pp, $16.95, 1-55650-816-6

THE YUCATAN including Cancún & Cozumel

Bruce & June Conord

"... Honest evaluations. This book is the one not to leave home without." *Time Off Magazine*

"... opens the doors to our enchanted Yucatán." Mexico Ministry of Tourism

Maya ruins, Spanish splendor. Deserted beaches, festivals, culinary delights.

376 pp, $15.95, 1-55650-792-5

Send for our complete catalog. All Hunter titles are available at bookstores nationwide or direct from the publisher.

Adventure Guides

VISIT US ON THE WORLD WIDE WEB

http://www.hunterpublishing.com

You'll find our full range of travel guides to all corners of the globe, with descriptions, reviews, author profiles and pictures. Our **Alive Guide** series includes guides to *Aruba, Bonaire & Curacao, St. Martin & St. Barts, Cancun & Cozumel* and other Caribbean destinations. **Romantic Weekends** guides explore destinations from *New England* to *Virginia, New York* to *Texas*. **Charming Small Hotel Guides** cover Italy, Venice, Tuscany, Spain, France, Britain, Paris, Germany, Switzerland, Southern France, New England, Austria and Florida – all in full color. Hundreds of other books are described, ranging from *Best Dives of the Caribbean* to *Battlefields of the Civil War* and the *African-American Travel Guide*. Books may be purchased on-line through our secure credit card transaction system or by check.